Resisting Dispossession

The Odisha Story

"It is a truism that scholarship devoid of passion for the working people will make even good research bereft of gripping minds and hearts. It is this which sets apart Resisting Dispossession: The Odisha Story in which the authors have combined research with empathy and passion for those who suffered, survived and struggled. Beginning with Hirakud Dam in the fifties, the Missile Test Range in Baliapal in the eighties, Tatas' plan to take over prawn cultivation in Chilika Lake in the early nineties to POSCO and Vedanta in the 2000s, the book provides individual accounts of each struggle informed by historical insight and a thread which holds the book together and compels readers to think and engage. Two much admired activists offer us readers not just analysis but also remind us of the power of knowledge-based resistance."

—Gautam Navlakha, Democratic Rights Activist and Writer
Author of *Days and Nights in the Heartland of Rebellion* and *War and Politics*

"Resisting Dispossession: The Odisha Story is a hopeful book. It shows us what it means to make history in the circumstances given to you and yet retain a wistful sense of a better and more just world. The book also points to the importance of remembering past struggles in and through the voices of a resistant people."

—V. Geetha, Feminist Activist, Writer and Translator
Author of *Undoing Impunity: Speech after Sexual Violence*

"Dispossession is at the very root of India's postcolonial development trajectory, and its burdens have been disproportionately shouldered by subaltern groups. It is also subaltern groups—chief among them the nation's Adivasis—who have been at the forefront of struggles to challenge dispossession. This illuminating and beautifully crafted book tells this story from the vantage point of Odisha in Eastern India, and will be of interest to the activist, the scholar, and the public citizen."

—Alf Gunvald Nilsen, Professor of Sociology, University of Pretoria
Author of *Politics from Below: Essays on Subalternity and Resistance in India* and *Dispossession and Resistance in India: The River and the Rage*

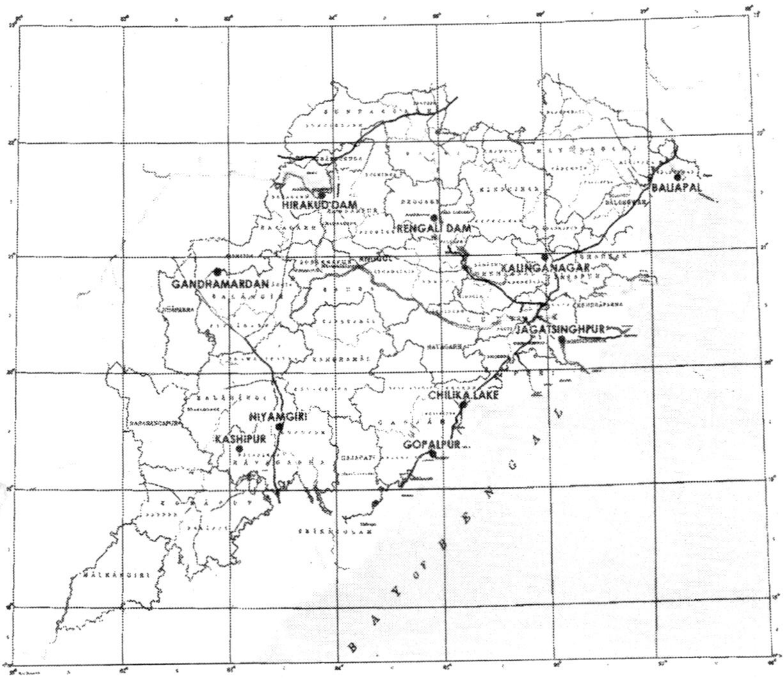

Map of Odisha highlighting locations covered in the book

Resisting Dispossession

The Odisha Story

Ranjana Padhi
Nigamananda Sadangi

AAKAR

Resisting Dispossession: The Odisha Story
Ranjana Padhi and Nigamananda Sadangi

First Aakar Edition 2020
Reprinted 2022

ISBN978-93-5002-649-6

The print edition is for sale only in India.
Customers outside India please order the print book from:
Palgrave Macmillan [978-981-15-0716-8].

Published by
AAKAR BOOKS
28 E Pocket IV, Mayur Vihar Phase I
Delhi 110 091, India
www.aakarbooks.com

Printed at
Sapra Brothers, Noida.

Dedicated to

Those who resisted the dispossession of lands, lives, livelihoods and natural resources in the past;
Those who struggle with immense courage and tenacity against all odds today; and
Those who will carry on protecting the planet and its people tomorrow.

A Note of Thanks

To all those who have shared their precious memories and current predicament—triumphs and tribulations—of resisting displacement and dispossession. These interactions have been marked by courage and honesty in sharing experiences and views, sparkling wit and humour in a bid to survive, and festering sorrows or pain that dare to ask profound questions of the regimes of power and human society. We have been humbled by their sense of rootedness and wisdom. All this contributed significantly in widening the overall canvas of this book.

To friends who made critical and constructive inputs during the various stages of the manuscript as it evolved into a book: Rajender Negi (Guddoo), V. Geetha, Nandita Roy, Pramodini Pradhan, Rajesh Gupta and Arunesh Maiyar.

To those who helped arrange field visits and often accompanied us too: Gopinath Majhi and Saroj Mohanty (Sambalpur district); Ranjan Sahu and Prabeen Acharya (Deogarh district); Lingaraj Pradhan, Sushant Samal, Amitabh Patro, Babrubahan Sahu and Rahasa Behari Sahu (Bargarh district); Arun Jena, Kushadhwaj Jena, Pradeep Jena and Dharmapada Jena (Balasore district); Tuni Behera, Bhagaban Behera, Debi Prasanna Rath, Srikant Mohanty and Pratap Cinara (Puri and Khurda districts); Gurudeb Behera and Jharana Patra (Ganjam district); Bhagaban Majhi, Mukundi Saunta, Biswanath Sahu and Sumitra Majhi (Raygada district); Lingaraj Azad (Kalahandi district); Sini Soi and Biswanath Sahu (Jajpur district); and Sujata Sahni (Jagatsinghpur district). Connecting with people, making frequent trips and spending time in their surroundings became the most vibrant and valuable experience in this long exercise.

To those who supported research and scripting with ideas, materials and other resources: Jai Prasad, Sailen Routray, Debaranjan, Satyajeet Puhan, Sujata Gothoskar, Smriti Nevatia, Sandhya Gokhale, Bharat Majhi, Satyabrata Mitra, Lenin Kumar, Bijay Upadhyaya, Surya Dash, Golak Behari Nath, Biswapriya Kanungo, Srimanta Mohanty, Jyoti Nanda, Sudhir Patnaik, Pabitra Mohan Das, Prafulla Samantara, Prashant Paikrai, Narendra Mohanty, Rumita Kundu, Kedar Misra, Ananya Mishra, Romila Padhi, Sanjeev Routray, Nirupama Singh, D. Manjit, Muktikantha Pradhan, Biswajit Apat, Gurudatt Khuntia, Bharadwaj Panda, Swapna Chakravarty, Sujata Chakravarty, Amiya Das, Pranab Jena, Rabi Pradhan and (Late) Sidharth Mohapatra.

And to our own long friendship and shared politics that made the experience of co-authoring deeply engaging and fulfilling.

Contents

CHAPTER 1

Introduction

Lying on the eastern coast of India, Odisha shares its borders with Andhra Pradesh in the south, Chhattisgarh in the west, Jharkhand in the north and West Bengal in the northeast. Its alluvial coastal plains run from the Subarnarekha River in the north to the Rushikulya River in the south. Three other major rivers—Mahanadi, Brahmani and Baitarani—that originate from the plateaus of Central India run eastward and empty into the Bay of Bengal. The state's mountainous and forested regions—from Mayurbhanj district in the northeast to Koraput district in the south—form part of the Eastern Ghats and almost run parallel to the coastal belt. This region abounds in mineral wealth, and it is also home to many adivasi communities. Odisha possesses almost 60 per cent of the country's bauxite reserves, 98.4 per cent chromite, 91.8 per cent nickel, 32.9 per cent iron ore, 24.8 per cent coal and 67.8 per cent manganese. This abundance of mineral wealth, along with its mountains and forests, coastline and rivers, land and cheap labour, makes Odisha the most coveted land. Always, the most ordinary people have risen up leading extraordinary struggles against big dams, mega steel projects and massive mining operations. It is their sacrifice that is called upon whether for building the temples of modern India at the dawn of independence or to keep step today with the march of the global economy. It would be no exaggeration to call the history of post-colonial Odisha the history of forced dispossession, state repression and resistance against it.

R. Padhi, N. Sadangi, *Resisting Dispossession*,
https://doi.org/10.1007/978-981-15-0717-5_1

Resisting Dispossession: The Odisha Story attempts to demystify the prevailing development paradigm in the state and dwell on people's indomitable spirit and unrelenting resistance. In chronicling these long drawn-out struggles, it lifts the veil of anonymity from those ordinary, unknown people who are its protagonists. The book brings to the reader many stories and testimonies; it also attempts to be a witness to their sorrows and sufferings, their triumphs and tribulations. In doing so, it yearns to fill up a significant gap in the resistance history of the state and its people.

We travelled across the coastal plains as well as the hilly and forested areas of south and southwest Odisha. Our familiarity with these areas and resistance movements since the late 1980s and early 1990s made the long winding journey easy and most fulfilling. We were fortunate to meet some great characters who have given shape and in turn been shaped by these struggles and who have been generous in sharing their abiding love for the land and the community, for the mountains, forests and streams. Their stories and ruminations began to slowly unfold a wide canvas. We got a peep into their deep sorrows and festering wounds caused by this affinity to and dependence on the land. All these made us painfully aware of our little knowledge about these struggles. For example, before writing this book, we did not know much about the resistance movement around the Rengali Dam. Even though the Hirakud movement is occasionally discussed in academic seminars and symposia, we were meeting oustees the first time ever. In Gandhamardan, Baliapal, Gopalpur or Chilika, we reconnected with many people, some after twenty or twenty-five years. The interactions in Kashipur, Niyamgiri, Kalinganagar and Jagatsinghpur had begun after the 2000s. Meeting familiar faces in dharnas and rallies or in solidarity meetings from these places kept us connected.

However, in this journey we were keen to learn how they see their own participation. We were keen to listen in order to connect the past with the present. We thus shared with those we met our own aspiration to collect similar stories and accounts from other parts in Odisha, from others like them who have resisted. Engaging with an open mind meant that people's narrations and accounts needed little time to be absorbed by us. In contrast, the sense of responsibility we felt was enormous, if not daunting. This book is not about the movements and the people only; neither is it our own indulgence to reflect through writing. As it began to take shape, there was another character that began to make its presence felt. Yes, the reader too quietly crept in from the beginning. So often we wondered whether the reader will make sense of these multi-layered interactions.

Images, memories, notions and assumptions from the long journey never left us while writing. Now as we aspire to become the conduit to bring this reality to a large audience, we make one active choice. We want to dwell on the characters we met and their worldviews. And let them speak to you. One of the richest experiences of this long exercise is that of accosting and absorbing the varied dialects across districts along with local idioms, metaphors and colloquialisms. What they narrate is so inextricably tied up to the language they speak. So the only misgiving we carry is the translation of these testimonies into English, which, at its best, is a mere faithful rendering of voices and accounts. Perhaps, the Odia version of the book will be a step closer to the accounts.

Our conversations with people always gave us a sense of the past and the uniqueness of each place. The local histories of each site of *andolan* were revealed through oral testimonies as well as through legends and myths of the habitat. To connect these stories of resistance to the past, we were inspired to look up recorded history in our own small way.

I

The Thirteenth Rock Edict of Ashoka, one of the earliest historical references to Odisha, then known as Kalinga, tells us a story of conquests, massacres, deaths and transportation of lakhs of inhabitants who resisted the invading imperial army of the powerful emperor. It tells us about his remorse for conquering the unconquered and the resultant all-round bloodbath. But who were those people? It is no surprise that resisters find no mention in the history of victors. On the other hand, the vanquished have also not erected 'hero-stones' commemorating the valour and sacrifices of those who fought for the land and its people.

People of Odisha have remained by and large anonymous throughout histories. At best, they are known to the outside world for 'lofty temples of stone' and religiosity. But to the mundane eyes of colonial administrator-ethnographers, people of Odisha 'rank the lowest, in the scale of moral and intellectual excellence, of any people on this side of India' (Stirling 1822).[1] They are so ordinary to be subject of any scholarly pursuit.

While sketching the history of Odisha, W.W. Hunter is at pains to point out anything redeeming about its people (Hunter 1872).[2] Even while launching the non-cooperation movement, an avowed nationalist like Mohandas Karamchand Gandhi laments the anonymity of the people:

> Most of us perhaps do not even know where Orissa[3] is... Orissa is part of one of the poorest regions in India. We do not hear much about the suffering there because the people are backward in every way. For most of us, it is a mere geographical expression... Nobody knows whether the people of Orissa are happy or unhappy. (Quoted in Sengupta 2015)

And in the post-colonial period, Odisha begins to draw occasional national visibility for all the 'wrong reasons' like starvation deaths and super cyclones; poverty and backwardness; or for the killing of a missionary. It is accused of being 'far too quiet to command scholarly or media attention.... And its political quiescence leads scholars to conclude that its politics is—and has always been—dull and uneventful' (Sengupta 2015). It is only by taking a view of history from below that we can put to rest any notions of anonymity or of quiescence of the people. Here are some glimpses.

II

With the fall of Barabati Fort at Cuttack on 14 October 1803, the East India Company wrested the *mugalbandi*[4] area (largely the undivided districts of Balasore, Cuttack and Puri) of Odisha from the Marathas and placed it under the Calcutta Presidency with direct financial and administrative control. Subsequently, the Company subjugated the chiefs of the hill tracts, known as *garhjats*. These are the land largely inhabited by the adivasis. The Company made these chiefs pay annual tributes and allowed them to enjoy relative autonomy in internal administration. And the colonial military force was ever ready to steady their regimes in case of any exigency. The Sambalpur region was tagged to the Central Province and later amalgamated with Odisha in 1905. Since 1765, the region to the south of Chilika had been under the Madras Presidency. This peculiarity had a bearing on the shape of political development of Odisha in times to come.

Soon after the occupation of the *mugalbandi* area, the Company brought about far-reaching changes in the revenue policy. The service tenure of erstwhile peasant militias, called *paikas*, was brought into rent-roll. Monopoly over manufacture and trade of salt was imposed. *Cowree* as currency was demonetized and silver was introduced in its place. All these developments led to a popular rebellion in the year 1817 known as *paika* rebellion. Though Khurda was the epicentre of the rebellion, a large part of the *mugalbandi* area came under its sway. The rebellion was brutally crushed in 1824. After that, the population of *mugalbandi*, especially peasantry, could not rise up for almost a century and silently suffered both feudal and colonial exploitation.

On the other hand, waves of revolts swept over the *garhjats* of Odisha from the mid-1830s till the last decade of the nineteenth century centred on issues of cultural practices and access to land and forest (Mishra 1983).[5] There was hardly any decade when the colonial and feudal power did not face resistance from adivasis, dalits, peasants and small and marginal farmers. Interestingly, when these parts went into silence, a new kind of political vocabulary developed in the Presidency area spawned by the Odia-language controversy.

In 1870, Kantichandra Bhattacharya, a Bengali school teacher of Balasore, wrote a pamphlet, *Udiya Swatantra Bhasa Nahe* (Odia is not an independent language), suggesting that it is a dialect of Bengali. The educated middle class vehemently protested against this perceived Bengali conspiracy to erase the language from the face of the earth and so the Odia people. Not only did it lead to the efflorescence of modern Odia literature, the identity of Odias as a people was projected so as to invoke its glorious historical and cultural past. Thus, the movement to protect the language prepared the ground to imagine an Odia nationality on the basis of linguistic and cultural affinity and to demand political unification of all Odia-speaking tracts under one separate province. In 1903, the 'Odia national aspiration' took an organized shape with the formation of Utkal Sammilani (Utkal Union Conference). Intellectuals, middle-class *babus* and some feudal chiefs took the lead. Like moderates in National Congress, the Sammilani remained shy from mass agitation politics and kept itself limited to passing resolutions, writing petitions and submitting memoranda. In fact, it believed in the goodwill of the British administration and prohibited 'criticisms of the actions of Government and Government Officials' in its forum (Dash 2005).

Gradually, the futility of the politics of petition-writing crept in. A section of the Sammilani leadership began to realize that unification of Odisha could be achieved through national independence. The novelist Gopabandhu Das articulated it thus: 'The sole objective of the Utkal Sammilani so far had been to unify Orissa. For the last seventeen years all the resolutions had been passed for achieving this goal. As a result, the Sammilani had little relevance to the common man. Orissa could aspire to achieve unification only through national independence' (Quoted in Pati 1993). With the launch of the non-cooperation movement by the Indian

National Congress (INC), the era of mass politics began in Odisha and Utkal Sammilani got relegated to the background. In the mid-1930s, radical peasant politics under the banner of Kishan Sangha backed by the Congress Socialists developed in the *mugalbandi* areas on the immediate issues of rent, *bethi* (corvee) and *Magana* (extra illegal cesses levied by rulers on ceremonial occasions). And the peasantry arose from their century-long slumber, shedding their quiescence and submissiveness. Fakir Mohan Senapati in his classic novel *Six Acres and a Fourth*, while depicting the silent suffering of the *mugalbandi* peasantry, had almost anticipated its arising.[6] His novel ends with the protagonist zamindar meeting his fate:

> He drifted back to sleep and saw looming on the horizon the horrifying skeleton of a human with its jaws wide open, watching him intently, waiting silently to devour him.... He also saw thousands of lunatics like Bhagia ... come rushing out of black clouds in the sky, holding swords and iron clubs. He felt as if all these clubs were raining down on his head. Mangaraj wanted to scream and run away; but he could not utter a word, and he felt too weak to move. (Senapati 2006)

The Congress Socialists and the Communists also took the initiative to mobilize masses in *garhjat* regions under the banner of Prajamandal against the feudal and colonial oppression. As the politics of Kisan Sangha and Prajamandal grew, the adivasis, dalits, peasants and small and marginal farmers occupied the centre stage of politics. The air of Odisha was rent with cries of the end of exploitation and the beginning of a new society:

> Dispelling dark night,
> We will bring about a red morning.
> Let the earth, the sky and the exploiters tremble.
> Let the strength of equality be established on earth. (Mishra 1936)

Soon, Odisha became a separate province on 1 April 1936 with the merger of the Odia-speaking tract of Madras Presidency; the *garhjat* areas were merged after independence. As per provisions of the 1935 India Act, election for provincial legislatures was held in 1937 and the INC formed the ministry. But it resigned with the outbreak of the Second World War and plunged into mass agitation that culminated in the Quit India Movement. With the massive participation of the adivasis, dalits, peasants and small and marginal farmers, the anti-colonial and anti-feudal struggles reached a new height; the end of the British Raj seemed imminent. In the undivided Koraput district, people felt that their slavery under the old feudal and colonial rule ended and Gandhi raj began (Nanda 2008). The euphoria lived short when in the mid-1940s people learnt that they would be uprooted from their soil for the Machkund Dam and Hydro-electric Project. They were entering yet another kind of enslavement—enslavement for development (Stanley 1996). And this process intensified post Independence.

III

This theme of 'progress' and 'development' has animated the political scene of Odisha since colonial times. The colonial ethnographers and historians saw Odisha as a 'backward,' 'deficit' land in terms of revenue generation:

> Orissa contributes scarcely anything to the general expense of government. It does not pay its share of interest on the public debt; it contributes nothing to the cost of defending the Empire; and hardly does more than support the charges of the local administration. (Hunter 1872)

The Odia nationalists too shared this perception. Year after year, the presidential addresses of the Sammilani parroted 'the Oriyas are much backward compared to other nationalities of India' and bemoaned its pitiable condition of agriculture and industry. In its very first meeting, the Sammilani formed a Central Committee 'for the purpose of improving agricultural and industrial condition of the Oriya speaking tracts.' It is also interesting to note that these presidential addresses emphasized exploration of minerals lying in the *garhjat* areas for the development of Odisha (Dash 2005). The king of Mayurbhanj, the first president of the Utkal Sammilani, invited Pramath Nath Bose to explore iron ore in his state and Tata began to source iron ore from Mayurbhanj in 1910–1911 for its Jamshedpur plant (Senapati and Sahu 1967). Even before the formation of Utkal Sammilani, its chief architect Madhusudan Das had formed a forum called Utkal Silponnati Sabha (Forum for Industrial Development of Utkal) in the year 1902 and set up Utkal Tannery and Odisha Art Wares to set an example. His biographer Surendra Mohanty writes: 'Coming back from London, Madhusudan Das set up Odisha Art Wares. It was the result of stirrings that the industrial revolution had generated in his mind. But there was no end to his effort and planning for the wider and larger industrialisation of Odisha. To integrate the effort for formation of a separate Odisha Province with that of industrialisation had become central to his political thinking' (Mohanty 1970).[7]

Though the Odia nationalists shared the colonial perception of Odisha's backwardness, they skilfully hinged it to the issue of Odisha's political dismemberment (Sengupta 2015). For them, 'the main reason of Odisha's backwardness and a hindrance to its progress' was its political disunity. They argued that Odisha could develop only when all Odia-speaking tracts were amalgamated under one administrative unity. As Sashibhushan Rath reflected:

> The Oriyas have come to realise that their educational starvation, economic helplessness and the resulting national decadence is due to the dissection and destruction of their living body as a nation under different territorial Governments, and that the sovereign remedy for all their woes lies in the administrative reunion of the Orissan tracts. (Quoted in Panda 1915)

Despite Utkal Sammilani's political irrelevance after the beginning of mass politics in Odisha, its messages about development, industrialization and exploration of minerals had found a chord in the large section of middle-class and upper-caste Odia elites. The novelist Gopinath Mohanty wrote, as early as 1937, in a geography textbook: 'The world of today is the world of factory and industry; the age of agriculture has gone. Where there are factories and industries, there is wealth and prosperity' (Mohanty 2018).[8] After independence when the Odia elites came to power, the urgency to industrialize Odisha by utilizing its mineral wealth became paramount.

IV

> When I read Mr Ramesh Dutt's *Economic History of India*, I wept; and as I think of it again my heart sickens. It is machinery that has impoverished India. It is difficult to measure the harm that Manchester has done to us. It is due to Manchester that Indian handicraft has all but disappeared. (*Hind Swaraj* 1958)

As written by Gandhi in *Hind Swaraj*, it meant that the industrial revolution in England and the rise of large-scale industry were at the root of India's poverty and economic ruination under British colonialism. The Indian nationalists under the umbrella of INC fought the anti-colonial political battle on this plank, rallying the peasantry and all other sections of toilers. But as the INC began to assume power, the economic question became a subject of 'rational planning' to be decided by 'experts' and was made free from political 'squabbles and conflicts' (Chatterjee 2010). The first experience in this regard was the setting up of the National Planning Committee in the year 1938.

After the formation of INC ministries in various provinces, the Congress Working Committee sat at Wardha in August 1937 to discuss economic planning, especially the policy of INC towards industry. A resolution was adopted to form a committee of experts to collect necessary data and to undertake surveys to chalk out a plan. While the Gandhians wanted to restrict the growth of modern industry, Jawaharlal Nehru and Subhas Chandra Bose sought to resolve this question within the framework of an 'all-India industrial plan' that would be drawn by the expert committee. In October 1938, following the Haripura Congress in February that year, the President of Congress, Bose, called all the industry ministers of provincial ministries formed by the Congress to a conference and declared the formation of the National Planning Committee. The committee comprised industrialists, scientists, technocrats, economists and political leaders. Nehru was made the chairman of the committee. There was a large consensus among the members for promotion of large-scale industry, although J.C. Kumarappa, the Gandhian, led a lone battle in favour of cottage industries. Nehru justified the position of the majority on the ground that large-scale industry should be promoted so long as it did not 'come into conflict with the cottage industries.' Secondly, according to Nehru, the political context for INC had changed: 'Now that the Congress is, to some extent, identifying itself with the State it cannot ignore the question of establishing and encouraging large-scale industries. There can be no planning if such planning does not include big industries ... [and] it is not only within the scope of the Committee to consider large-scale industries, but it is incumbent upon it to consider them' (Chatterjee 2010).

As the Second World War broke out and Congress ministries resigned, the Planning Committee stopped functioning. The debate over large-scale industrialization of India as a model of development continued for some time, especially between Gandhi and Nehru. The overall climate was in favour of industrialization. After India's independence and Gandhi's assassination, his followers, like Mira Behn and Kumarappa, were critical of Nehru's industrial policy. But they were not in a position to throw up any political challenge. Meanwhile, Nehru had become painfully aware of the havoc industrial development would create:

> The transition from pre-industrialized economy to an economy of capitalist industrialism involves great hardship and heavy cost in human suffering borne by masses of people... There was this hardship in England during the period of transition but, taken as whole, it was not great as the changeover was rapid and the unemployment caused was soon absorbed by the new industries. But that did not mean that the cost in human suffering was not paid. It was indeed paid in full by others, particularly by the people of India... It may be said that a great part of the cost of transition to industrialism in Western Europe were paid for by India, China and other colonial countries. (Quoted in Sanyal 2007)

Here, Nehru almost echoes what Karl Marx had said about the primitive accumulation of capital that became a precondition for capitalism to emerge, causing chaos and destruction galore. However, in Nehru's understanding it was the colonial situation that had caused such suffering, in the absence of which the benefits would have accrued to the masses. He believed that if it were socialized, the profit motive could be exorcised from the process and benefits of industrialization would reach the victims (masses) as well. Hence, free India could take the path of industrialization that the West did long back, as he said: 'We are trying to catch up as far as we can, with the industrial revolution that occurred long ago in western countries' (Quoted in Chatterjee 2010). After independence, the process of 'catching up' began in the framework of a mixed economy: the state would have monopoly over the core sector of the economy (heavy industry, mines, transport and communication) and the consumer sector would be left for the private sector. The Planning Commission, a body of experts, was entrusted with the task of drawing the national roadmap for development on the basis of 'scientific and rational calculations' and was insulated from the messy world of politics. It was also touted that the state at the command of the economy would make India inch towards 'socialistic pattern of society.' This arrangement was also largely suitable to the Indian capitalist class of that time, as their economic muscles were not strong enough to carry forward gigantic industrial and infrastructural projects on their own (Sanyal 2010). Politically, they did not have the necessary hegemonic control over the state and society to push their agenda; rather, they were only one of the constituents of the 'dominant coalition' (Bardhan 1998).

It would be interesting to note how the Communists responded to the political and economic reality of post-independent India. The undivided Communist Party of India (CPI) that had accepted India's independence initially changed its stance by December 1947 and declared India's independence to be a sham (*ye azadi jhuti hai*) and called Nehru 'a stooge of imperialism.' However, in the first general elections held in 1952, the party revised its thinking and participated in the 'bourgeoisie' parliamentary democracy. By 1956, it came around to acknowledging India's independence and actually began to see the possibility of 'peaceful transition to socialism' in 1958 (Chandra et al. 2008). When the second Five-Year Plan drew an ambitious industrial development plan of India, the party endorsed it: 'By linking the development of heavy industries with economic independence Prof. Mahalanobis has stressed an important aspect of national planning' (Mahalnabois 1955). Soviet Russia's collaboration in the industrial development of India (e.g. the Bhilai steel plant was set up with its collaboration) had a positive effect on the Communists. Hence, the Communists were 'notably uncritical' of Nehru's 'advocacy of a specific kind of "developmentalism" or "idea of progress" based on large-scale projects' (Bidwai 2015). Put differently, they were indifferent to the politics embedded in this developmentalism and the kind of dispossession that alienated people from their means of production.

This idea of development was projected as nation building, where mega projects were for the greater common good. By this, the politics of development—the dispossession of the masses on the one hand and the accumulation on the other—was throughout underplayed. These mega projects, especially big dams, also symbolized 'the progress of humanity from a life ruled by nature and superstition to one where nature is ruled by science, and superstition vanquished by rationality' (McCully 2001). And when science speaks, ideologies remain silent. Dr K.L. Rao, then civil engineer, who later became union minister of power and irrigation, reminisces in his autobiography about an anecdote while working for the Nagarjunasagar project in the early 1950s in Andhra Pradesh. At that time, the area was experiencing a peasant uprising led by the undivided CPI:

> Later, I got a letter from the leader of the Communist Party who was underground, that there was no necessity for me to have a police escort and that they would not have harmed me and the other engineers unless we were engaged in building roads to their hide-outs. Engineers dealing with dams and irrigation projects were most welcome. This was similar to what the Communists told Dr Savage when he went to the river Yangtze in China to see a storage dam site. The Communists sent word to him that he could freely move about without escort as they would not harm engineers engaged in the development of rivers. (Quoted in D'Souza 2008)

This heady mixture of development, nation building, science and rationality and, above all, the credibility of new leadership basking in the glory of anti-imperial struggle carried the day. And the process of building temples of modern India rolled on. Odisha was not spared.

Odisha is home to 62 tribes, officially referred to as Scheduled Tribes (STs), having distinct languages, customs and practices. They constitute 22.8 per cent of the population and form a major social group in a number of districts, especially in mineral-rich districts like Rayagada (55.9 per cent), Koraput (50.56 per cent), Kalahandi (28.50 per cent) and Balangir (23.05 per cent). As per the *Socio-Economic Survey*, out of the total 2,073,079 ST households, 1,836,190 (88.57 per cent) households are considered to be deprived. Though agriculturist par excellence, they do not have adequate arable land; neither is the land so fertile like the coastal plains. *Dangar chaas* (cultivation on the slopes of the hills) is the main means of survival for most adivasis. As ploughshare is not needed in *dangar chaas*, women carry the entire burden of the production process along with their assumed domestic roles. Theirs is a subsistence economy, where the main purpose of production is to consume. They grow *alsi* as cash crop to buy a few essentials like clothing and kerosene, or, at most, a warm blanket or a bicycle.

Given this socio-economic profile, the struggles against dispossession that the book has covered are waged by these landless dalits, fisherfolk, adivasis and small and marginal peasants to protect their means of subsistence. Though meagre and small, these means have been safe and secure to be bequeathed to the next generation. But the process of development poses permanent threat to their means of subsistence with no hope of gaining it back ever.

Gangadhar Majhi, a landless adivasi of Kashipur, sums it up most succinctly:

> I am landless. But as a member of the community, I have a share in the *dangar*. By cultivating it, I can secure food, at least for six months. Who will give me this in an unknown land? Where shall I go leaving this land? As we inherited this *dangar* from our grandfathers and fathers, so can it be bestowed to our children and grandchildren? That is why I am part of the movement.

In earlier years, when public infrastructural projects like dams, highways, airports or railway stations were made, people had to sacrifice for 'national progress' and 'the greater common good.' In more recent years, the same processes have been given a mask called 'development' that is once again being done at the cost of people. However, the similarity ends there. The world has changed and so has the entire economy. The march of extractive capitalism across the globe, hoarding minerals and other resources for value creation, is pauperizing vast sections of the people. Since the time when the Narmada Bachao Andolan called a halt to big dams that destructively displaced large communities, we have been witnessing the emergence of resistance across the country against Special Economic Zones (SEZs), mining projects and big industries. Though there has to be manufacturing of consent for semblance of democracy, these processes are more often than not backed by coercion. What is at work is systemic dispossession; it is not merely displacement. These are processes of accumulation that are far removed from mere destitution caused by displacement.

V

'Babu, I am going. Will Swaraj really come? Will the people live happily and peacefully?' These were the last words of the legendary freedom fighter Laxman Naik, who was an adivasi from Koraput. He asked this of the Congress leader Sadasiv Tripathy just before he was hanged from the gallows for his activity in the Quit India Movement (Quoted in Rabi 2011).

After independence, the juggernaut of development rolled on, crushing on its way the sinewy chests of hills, the leaf-green heart of jungles, the melodious soul of streams, the life-full habitats and sacred places of the people of Koraput. The temples of modern India were built: Machkund (1940s–1950s), Balimela (1960s), Hindustan Aeronautics Limited (1964) and Kolab (1976–1990s). Those who had been living on these lands for centuries were carted around and dumped like municipal garbage. Not once, sometimes even thrice. The collective sighs and cries coming out of the ruins of development went unheard by the politicians and government officials, who did not pause for a minute to listen in their zeal for nation building. They could not look back at the devastation they themselves caused.

The people of Koraput got the first real taste of swaraj right after Independence when they were forced to evacuate their villages for the Machkund Dam and Hydro-electric Project made in the early 1940s. Villagers who still resisted had to flee to the jungles when the water of the reservoir flooded their villages. Many of them went on their own to other places. They did not find place even in official statistics. Some of them who cleared the jungle and settled down in nearby areas were yet again displaced when the Balimela Project was implemented in the 1970s. They had to leave their land twice in two decades (Goud 2018).

And Laxman Naik was not there to see whether his people lived happily or not.

In 1948, Nehru re-laid the foundation stone for the Mahanadi River Valley Development Project and exhorted people: 'If you are to suffer, you should suffer in the interest of the country.' It was a prophecy of sorts. People did suffer and have been suffering till today. The quiet indignation borne by the stigma of *budianchalia* (people of submerged area) after being uprooted from their own land haunts their memory forever. It has happened within their life time. Such deep memories of being forced to forsake their land have thus become part of a collective ethos in western Odisha. The Orissa Military Police was used to evacuate people from the submerged villages of Hirakud. In fact, the Publicity Department played out a song those days that the dam would 'feed the hungry bellies' and usher in 'an era when every person in the state would reap the benefits of development' (Padel and Das 2010).

Let alone such rhetoric, the dam could not even meet its stated objectives of flood control, irrigation and generation of electricity (Viegas 1992). But INDAL (Indian Aluminium Company) built its aluminium smelter plant keeping in view the availability of cheap electricity and water from the reservoir (see Chap. 2).[9] Thus began the trend of the reservoir-industrial complex in Odisha. This experiment intensified in the years to follow and was projected as the panacea of all ills of Odisha. Dr A.N. Khosla prepared a master plan to write:

> Orissa mirrors the paradox of all backward areas—poverty amidst potential plenty. Orissa has untold wealth of natural resources—land, forests, water, minerals, a long sea coast... Yet it is the poorest and most backward state of India. Any plan for the development of these vast natural resources, which will help transform poverty into plenty in the state of Orissa, may well serve as a model for other similarly situated areas in India and elsewhere in the world. (Khosla 1963)[10]

Khosla not only proposed to build dams for hydel electricity but also prescribed to develop thermal power plants utilizing the huge coal reserves. As a result, the Government of Odisha went on a dam-building spree: the Rengali Dam on the Brahmani River (1970s) (see Chap. 3). The Odisha Military Police was again used to suppress the emerging people's movement in the Rengali region, which also coincided with the declaration of the National Emergency in June 1975. In 1976–1978, the Geological

Survey of India undertook the East Coast Bauxite Project survey and found huge reserves of bauxite in the *malis* (hills) located in Koraput, Kalahandi and Balangir. Besides, Odisha had proven reserves of coal, iron and chromium. The reservoir water, hydro-electricity and minerals became a magic recipe that did its work. In 1981, the public sector company National Aluminium Company Limited (NALCO) set up an alumina refinery plant at Damanjodi, extracting bauxite from Panchpatmali of Koraput district and using water and electricity of Upper Kolab. Bharat Aluminium Company (BALCO) followed suit by targeting the bauxite reserves of the Gandhamardan mountain (see Chap. 4). It was not only minerals, the coastline of Odisha too seemed strategic for the central government to set up a National Test Range in the year 1984 (see Chap. 5). When people's barricades against entry of police and administration became a marked feature from the 1980s in both Gandhamardan and Baliapal, the government began to use economic blockade to break the morale of people. In Baliapal, the supply of kerosene and public distribution system (PDS) services were blocked and people were not allowed to sell paddy or vegetables outside their villages.

Since the early years of Independence, leaders had been spouting the rhetoric of 'national interest' and appealing for people's sacrifice. Therefore, many believed that the Bhakra Nangal Dam was in national interest. The intelligentsia, urban middle class and the media were, by and large, of the opinion that these projects were for the greater common good. Many critical voices got lost in this cacophony. The experience around the Hirakud Dam has been the same as narrated by Bharat Nayak (Nayak 2004).[11] The intoxication of development had become too heady for politicians, planners and technocrats to see the ruins and devastations they had wrought on the lives of local people. Obviously, that would have been sentimental. In the arithmetic of development, somewhere some people had to pay the price. It is in this manner that the convenient logic had begun to draw currency from those early years. In short, there was a kind of consensus on the economic model being followed.

Despite decades of development, horrendous stories of hunger, starvation death, child selling and seasonal migration, especially from undivided Koraput, Kalahandi and Balangir districts, hit the national headlines in the 1980s. Food for work and employment guarantee schemes were introduced as firefighting measures. But structural reasons like inequitable land distribution or people's lack of access to forests and common property resources were not given any thought (Deo 2009, Mohanty and Bahidar 1993).[12] On the other hand, industrial development was sought to be the answer as the then Chief Minister Janaki Ballabh Patnaik gave a clarion call for 'one thousand industries in one thousand days with an investment of one thousand crore' (Mohanty and Bahidar 1993).

The 1990s marked a watershed in the Indian economy. Privatization, globalization and liberalization became the new mantra. Even the lip-service paid to creating a society along socialist lines died a quiet death; the promise of a self-reliant economy through state-driven economic development was given a hasty burial. The public sector that was created in the last three decades by enormous sacrifice of the people began to be de-regulated. The most notable feature was the opening up of the mining sector for private corporate houses, both national and international. This had ominous implications for the people of the mineral-rich areas of Odisha, Chhattisgarh and Jharkhand. The governments of these states signed hundreds of Memorandums of Understanding (MoUs) with corporate houses to dig out mines and to set up mineral-based plants. Even water bodies were handed out to corporations. In 1991, some 1,400 hectares of the Chilika Lake was signed off for the Tatas to carry out prawn cultivation (see Chap. 6). In 1994, approximately 7,000 acres of fertile coastal land, famous for *kewda* flower, was forcefully acquired for Tata's steel plant at Gopalpur in Ganjam district (see Chap. 7). In 1991–1992, the Industrial and Infrastructural Development Corporation of Government of Odisha began a process to acquire 11,000 acres of land to set up an industrial complex, which was soon named the Kalinganagar Industrial Complex, utilizing the iron ore reserves of the Sukinda-Keojhar iron belt and water of River Brahmani (see Chap. 10). Bauxite hills of Koraput and Kalahandi were leased to Hindalco, Tata, Norsk Hydro, L&T and Sterlite-Vedanta (see Chaps. 8 and 9). The icing on the cake was the MoU with POSCO to set up a steel plant in the coastal strip of Jagatsinghpur district. It was hailed as the biggest foreign direct investment (FDI)—a tantalizing dream of Rs 50,000 crore (see Chap. 11). Odisha became the cherished pilgrimage for industrial houses from all over. The plans are aplenty still. To export those minerals and to import materials for those industries, as many as 13 new ports were proposed to be constructed along the 480 km coastline of Odisha from Bahuda mouth in Ganjam district to the mouth of the Subarnarekha River in Balasore district (Business Standard 2012).[13]

For the policy makers and the mainstream media, the euphoria was infectious. The long-benighted land would regain its past glory in which the proverbial honey and milk would flow again. It was a moment of reckoning for the Odia middle class that had been dreaming of an industrially prosperous Odisha since colonial times. And their children sent off to private IT or engineering institutes with their hard earnings would get the coveted high-salary jobs in these corporate houses. The regional press and private TV channels hyped the signing of each MoU as a moment of glorious celebration. Private agents of companies (goons or henchmen) began to lure the youth of Kashipur, Lanjigarh, Kalinganagar and Jagatsinghpur with the readymade, hyped-up promise of employment through development.

For each dam, for each industry, for each mining operation and for each port, land has to be acquired, people who have been living off and on these lands for centuries have to be evacuated, and their sacred places, mountains, hills and rivers have to be destroyed and polluted. But these people nourished different dreams and different perspectives of a different tune altogether from the cacophony created by the development mongers. So, what followed in each region were protests and contestations, resistance and revolt. Resistance to dispossession that had been going on in Odisha since the eve of independence became even more intensified in the neo-liberal era.

VI

Gaan chhadiba nahin, jami chhadiba nahin[14] is the war cry that runs through the banks of Mahanadi and Brahmani to the mouth of the Subarnarekha River and hills of Gandhamardan, from the lake of Chilika to the *kia* bushes of Gopalpur, from Baphlimali to Niyamgiri, from the betel vines of coastal Jagatsinghpur to the Kiajhar hillock of Kalinganagar. This is the song of dalits, adivasis, peasants and fisherfolk of Odisha when confronted with the threat of dispossession. Just have a look at some of the socio-economic features of their lives to make sense of their struggles.

Even if rich in mineral resources, Odisha is a predominantly poor and agrarian society. Here are the demographics: Over 70 per cent of the population depends on agriculture, and the bulk of the peasantry comprises marginal and small farmers. According to the Agricultural Census of 2011, the marginal holdings (below 1.0 ha) constitute 72.17 per cent and small holdings (1.0 to 1.99 ha) 19.68 per cent of the total land holdings.

According to the 2011 census, the dalits, officially designated as Scheduled Castes (SCs), constitute 17.1 per cent of the total population. In some districts like Kalahandi and Balangir in south and southwestern Odisha and Balasore and Jagatsinghpur in the coastal region, their percentage is higher than that of the all-Odisha figure: Kalahandi (18.17 per cent), Balangir (18.12 per cent), Balasore (20.62 per cent) and Jagatsinghpur

(21.82 per cent). They are one of the poorest sections of Odisha. The *Socio-Economic Survey* shows that out of a total of 1,564,447 SC households, 1,358,584 (86.84 per cent) are considered deprived.

Though the majority of dalit workers eke out their living through manual labour, there is a marked variation between the dalits of the coastal region and those in the south and southwestern parts in their livelihood patterns. During our field visits to Kashipur, we often came across dalit women carrying a basket on their hips or heads moving from village to village bartering salt, dry fish or puffed corn (*lia*) with *ragi* or *alsi* and dalit men sitting in their tiny shops at the village corner vending groceries.

The picture in the coastal strip is quite different. In the Baliapal-Bhograi region of Balasore or the POSCO plant area of Jagatsinghpur, the majority of the dalits are into fishing. Some of them grow betel vines or cashew plants on a tiny patch with family labour to supplement the family income. The entire dalit population of Chilika belongs to the fishing community, albeit with graded inequalities within the hierarchy. While menfolk are in the waters to catch fish, women clean and carry them to the nearby market to sell. The waters, the coasts and the dwellings all become one, with entire families absorbed in work.

The land is as much a means of survival as a marker of one's identity, one's belongingness. It has been expressed in many ways in different struggles: *Gaan Maati*, *Ma-Maati*, *Bheetamati*, *Janam-Maati*. *Maati* or the Earth becomes the fulcrum and assumes a mother figure always—one who nourishes, gives emotional succour and is the provider. The emotion invested with that figure goes beyond economic logic and quantification, as Bhagaban Patra, a landless fisherman of Baliapal says:

> Forget about large chunks of land, I do not even have record of rights over this small patch on which my house is built. Still, I am born here. My umbilical cord is buried here. It is my *Bheetamati*. How can I leave this?

Eighty-three-year-old Lakhpati Pradhan, a Hirakud Dam oustee who has spent almost sixty years in Mura Camp, still dreams of going back to his old village if the dam somehow disappears miraculously! As Mourid Barghoti had said:

> The fish,
> Even in the fisherman's net,
> Still carries,
> The smell of the sea.

This intimacy with nature—be it a mountain or a lake or a land or a forest—has evolved over centuries into an entire way of life, which makes nature both divine and sacred. Gandhamardan and Niyamgiri are not merely mountains. They are the Gods for the local community. Similarly, it is the goddess Kalijai who presides over and protects the dalit fisherfolk and the entire Chilika Lake. At times, a religious myth gets resurrected to give an aura of sanctity to a place, or to foster a sense of community subsuming all social differences like caste, class or gender. In the Baliapal movement, the land became Lord Shiva's chosen destination to teach cultivation to people on earth. In a musical drama enacted by people, Lord Shiva appears on the stage and castigates the then chief minister for handing over the land to a missile-testing range project. Thus, the fight to protect the land becomes a spiritual and moral act. Similarly, in the anti-BALCO movement, people's faith in the local deities is galvanized to protect two temples—Nrusinghnath, a Vishnu temple, and Harishankar, a Shiva temple—on either side of the Gandhamardan mountain. In fact, the Gandhamardan itself is *Dangar Mahapuru* (mountain god), who has been their protector and therefore must be saved from bauxite mining. It is this abiding faith that has practices of conservation inbuilt into their worldview. The issues of conserving the biodiversity of the mountain and the livelihood of people dependent on it are part of this holistic tie with nature and environment.

The religious sentiment attached to the temples in western Odisha was counter-posed with that of the Jagannath temple at Puri in the coastal part. As someone asked: 'Will the coastal people allow the Jagannath temple to be destroyed if a gold mine is discovered under its soil?' It is yet another matter that the dominant Hindu ethos also leads to the brahmanization of an adivasi god. By projecting homogeneity based on faith, these movements did not take note of the place of dalits in the religion and, most importantly, the social inequality thrust on them.

While the struggles rest on the valour and sacrifices of poor adivasis, dalits, peasants and small and marginal farmers, the leadership, more often than not, remains in the hands of the rich and affluent sections. For example, the lawyers and ex-bureaucrats living in Sambalpur town, possessing huge properties in villages, took the lead in the anti-dam movement of Hirakud. Similarly, the *gountias* (village headman having huge amount of land) were at the forefront of the Rengali Dam movement, the *paan* traders held the leadership of the movement in Baliapal and the school teachers and government employees did so in the tribal region of Kashipur. This apparent contradiction can partly be explained by the defensive nature of the struggle to simply protect the available livelihood resources. Therefore, people who own more resources or perceive more loss naturally take the lead in these movements. As Sarada Giri of Baliapal said:

> The rich people got most but we poor had the solace that our small huts or tiny piece of land survived.

It is indeed an ironical reflection that the participation of the same set of social groups in the anti-feudal and anti-colonial struggles of the 1930s and 1940s had dreamt of building a *chasi-mulia sarkar*. All these anti-displacement struggles are localized and project specific. Each movement primarily seeks to halt the project and simply hold on to existing means of production. The localized nature of the struggle inhibits the process of forging a broader vision of social transformation. Put differently, the movement fails to see the economic and class interest of those who bring development to their doorsteps.

This allowed the space for the apologists of development in the early decades of the post-independent period to prescribe 'proper rehabilitation.' And when that did not happen, the facile question of alternative was posed to the movements. If you only delve into the literature of any movement, you will see that people have proposed alternatives throughout. For example, when there was hardly any debate in India on the merits or demerits of big dams, the anti-dam movements of Hirakud and Rengali had questioned their proposed benefits of flood control and irrigation. They had suggested bunds and check dams as an alternative in the 1950s, a demand that gained more currency in recent years. The movements had predicted that the dams would only benefit industrialists and turn ordinary people into coolies. Remember, the 'who-pays-and-who-reaps-the-benefit' discourse in the wake of the Narmada Bachao Andolan. Alternatives have been put forth by all these movements in Kashipur, Niyamgiri, Kalinganagar and Jagatsinghpur. But voices articulating feasible alternatives are simply not heard. Isn't the widespread sweep of such struggles across the country by itself the most assertive of alternatives to the dominant development paradigm?

The slogan *Maati laagi, party naahin* in the Baliapal movement caught the imagination of all these struggles since then. It simply means that there can be no party interests or party differences in the struggle to save one's land. People have seen the chameleon's changing colours too closely, with a heavy price each time. For years on end, parliamentary parties unabashedly made electoral gains out of these movements and continue to do so. Parties in power have safeguarded the interest of corporate houses as they benefited in open or in clandestine manner right from the earliest elections (Patnaik 2013).[15] Also, wherever people stood up to resist displacement, those in the opposition rushed to put in their stakes for accruing quick electoral benefits. They would not lose an opportunity to cry foul in projecting the ruling party as anti-people. After independence, when the first general elections were held on the basis of adult franchise, the INC was thoroughly defeated in Sambalpur for thrusting the Hirakud Dam on people. The same happened in Rengali. Once those in opposition win the elections, they have been notorious in reneging on the promise of cancelling the project. When Biju Patnaik of the Janata Party became the chief minister in 1990, he proposed to mine bauxite from Gandhamardan from the side of Harishankar. Patnaik did the same in Chilika. Movements used to influence electoral politics at the local level with people venting anger on the party under whose government a project had been initiated. Thus, the Congress met the same fate in Baliapal and Gandhamardan.

However, this old familiar trend took a big somersault towards the end of the 1990s with the rolling out of the package of neo-liberal economic reforms. All political parties had arrived at an unwritten consensus about corporate-driven development. They had become subservient to the mantra, or by then, the tyranny of development. Its horror was first felt in Kashipur when an All-Party Committee was constituted comprising the Biju Janata Dal (BJD), the Congress and the Bhartiya Janata Party (BJP) to build consensus for the project. Together they led physical attacks on the movement, which became the precursor to the Maikanch killings of 2,000. The complexities grew. What was earlier being done behind the scene and with a bit of shame became brazen and open. In Kalinganagar, the ruling BJD mobilized its own local party machinery to intimidate and sabotage the movement. The pro-POSCO lobby in Jagatsinghpur did the same with the active support of the local MLA. Since the 2000s, there has been an unwritten consensus among mainstream political parties on the neo-liberal agenda. In any case, they have never had any principled position critiquing the overall development paradigm.

Two broad joint platforms that played a dynamic role for a brief period in rousing public opinion against the ruling regime were the *Deshpremi Jana Samukhya* (Patriotic People's Front) and the *Daman Virodhi Manch* (Forum Against Repression). Both had attempted to bring together these struggles and highlight the dispossession of the struggling people. While their own turf wars came in the way of galvanizing resistance across the state and consolidating any unity, the state too throttled the process by declaring the DVM a Maoist front. This ban on the Manch is being legally challenged. In 2017, the Niyamgiri Suraksha Samiti and the Visthapan Virodhi Jan Vikas Andolan were declared Maoist fronts by the home ministry. The witch hunt continues.

Against all odds, these movements have marched on. The most unique aspect of these movements is the participation of entire communities: children, elderly and women. Women activists have deliberated on the nature and importance of their participation in anti-displacement movements (Nayak et al. 1998). The overwhelming participation of women in both Gandhamardan and Baliapal became legendary.[16]

VII

Women in struggle are the eyes of the movement whose voices in interviews and testimonies bring insights that deepen the canvas of resistance. These are marginalized voices from even within the community. Their stories and ruminations become the lens to see the resistance more closely, especially when they express what informs the impetus underlying their involvement, or when they reflect on the movement in retrospect.

Women's relationship to land is precious as it is their only means of production. Any threat of alienation from their productive asset deepens the resolve to protect it, which, in itself, adds more compelling dimensions to collective resistance. And this relationship to land is the same in subsistence economies across the world. In the words of Rigoberta Menchu:

> There is something important about women in Guatemala, especially Indian women, and that something is the relationship with the earth—between the earth and the mother. The earth gives food and the woman gives life. Because of this closeness the woman must keep this respect for the earth as a secret of her own... There is constant dialogue between the earth and the woman. This feeling is born in woman because of the responsibilities they have, which men do not have. (Burgos Debray 1984)

Societies dependent on subsistence are still found in Asian, African and Latin American countries. They have contact with the moneyed economy and market dynamics in varying degrees, depending on their physical proximity with the outside world. Yet their production and sale (however little) of agricultural, forest or fishery products is for their own consumption.

As the chapters of this book will reveal, those in Baliapal and Jagatsinghpur are betel leaf growers, or those opposing the steel plant in Ganjam district grow *kewda* flowers; in Chilika, it is the fisherfolk resisting Tata and the prawn mafia, or those in the mountains, sell forest produce. They even cultivate paddy, vegetables and tubers and are able to work hard for their own sustenance and meet their monetary needs. The basis of the subsistence economy is land, whether in mountains or plains and water bodies. It is no wonder that subsistence producers form the backbone of these movements. And it is women largely who are directly involved in subsistence production.

In the continuing conflict between capital and subsistence, women defend their present and future sustenance. They have a direct link to the production process—whether it is agriculture, fishing, collecting forest produce or even doing sporadic wage labour. They resist dispossession, however hard their lives may be otherwise. Their lives accommodate their subsistence, its protection for future generation and the fight to hold on to the land. They are ordinary women, otherwise largely invisible, trying to hold on to their livelihood to protect it for their children and their children from the rapaciousness of state and capital. That is their dream in all its 'ordinariness.'

Within the family and community, women are subject to a division of labour that leaves them with a disproportionately large range of activities, including sustaining dependents with scarce resources. They are dependent on land for subsistence in order to meet all these demands made on their labour and on each and every waking hour of their lives. Therefore, once the land is under threat, they get subsumed in resistance with an altogether rare commitment. Ambai Majhi, who had whole heartedly participated in the movement against bauxite mining in Kashipur, evokes the collective spirit:

> Our community is dependent on each other. Any gain is for everyone. I was part of the movement because I did not want mining for all of us—not one village or one community—but for the entire of Kashipur. The struggle was not for me alone or for my family. I think of my children and their children. I think of her children and her grandchildren (pointing at the other women present). Women think of one thing and see it through. Men cannot do that.

And once they question, women do not spare the lens on the contradictions within family and community. In contrast to seeing the enormity of the cause, men tend to evoke the patrilineal descent in situations of conflict. This happens in adivasi society as well as in other marginalized communities. Ambai Majhi continues:

> If you plead with men not to sell the land, they say: 'I am selling my father's and grandfather's land. It is not your land. Is the *patta* in your name?'

Even while opining thus, she is quick to attribute the acrimony and discord within the four walls to a larger world where their vulnerabilities are manipulated:

> So how can I say my people are bad? These are the same people who stood against the company and were ready to die for their land. The way the company wants to do mining by using lies, force, coercion, deceit, arrests, murder is bad. It is not only the land that they have destroyed. They have destroyed much more than that.

These movements bring you close to thousands of women who are saying NO to 'development' even as they live on the edge of life. Their own self-perception of being in resistance is an extension of their hard labour from morning to night. That alone made Jemma Katakia in Dhinkia panchayat show her outstretched palms and predict with pride and confidence:

> These are not ordinary hands, they do magic. Where nothing could ever grow, we grew paddy and vegetables. Anything that we touch bears fruit. Our hard work will pay. You wait and see. POSCO will have to go from here one day.

They are the subjects of resistance as subsistence peasants; women acquire a moral legitimacy from the labour accorded to them in peasant society (and outside). It is not only that they have been able to feed and nurture dependents but also, more significantly, they have been able to fend off deprivations and destitution.

Survival is fraught with a tenacity that makes them aware about the immediate conditions they are mired in. It is the same social and economic placement in subsistence societies that endows them with grit and courage, setting them apart over other members of the same community. On the one hand, this tenacity endures all attempts by pro-company lobbies created within the same ranks to dilute or mislead the movement; on the other, they become more vigilant and articulate about any lapses made by those in the leadership. The singular difference that informs such participation is that these women are waging a battle on behalf of the community, its immediate sustenance and its future too. This very dynamic distinguishes the nature of resistance potential from women's resistance in other contexts.

By including women just to add to the numbers or do door-to-door mobilizing or be in the forefront of rallies and marches and, at the same time, by systematically excluding them from decision-making processes, male leadership has seldom been able to channelize the politics of a rich and diverse worldview that emanates from women's lived realities.

VIII

There is one common refrain across all these movements: 'Where shall we go leaving our land?'

Subsistence refers to the act of living at the minimal or supporting oneself at the minimal level, including the minimal need of income. Subsistence agriculture implies farming for the basic needs of family and community; it refers to the non-monetary economy such communities live in. Basically, the community clears and cultivates its own land, produces food grains, fruits and vegetables for consumption and has minimal need of cash. They work hard to guard against the uncertainties of future, mainly food scarcity. If there is surplus, it is usually consumed within the community or sold. With market dynamics leaving no corner of the globe untouched, the need for money has gone beyond the purchase of oil, sugar and clothes. There is a mix of engaging in monetary activities like sale of forest produce or fish. We can safely assume that subsistence societies depend on small incomes for basic needs. The precarious balance of life and survival can be easily upset by a small debt that grows each day as we see in the life of the protagonist Sukru Jani in the novel Paraja (Mohanty 1987).[17] Or it can mean ruination in the event of a drought or flood. Despite that, they continue to live within the subsistence economy along with all the hardship such a fragile existence denotes. It is only when their land or living assets are under direct threat that they rise in unison. They reject modern-day 'development' because they are too wary of the fact that they will be dispossessed of the precious little they ever had for themselves and the future generations. Getting severed from all roots that they have in the past and being hurtled into uncertainty propels them to resist. And as capital coercively makes inroads into these areas, the people are recasting political geographies for the world to see. How many people knew of the Hos of Jajpur or the Dongria Kondhs of Niyamgiri before they rose up in rebellion?

Subsistence peasants can rebel when market and state make intrusion into their economy. This has been well studied in countries of Southeast Asia. James Scott introduced the concept of 'subsistence ethic' that is born out of the acute fear of food shortages in pre-capitalist peasant societies:

> There are districts in which the position of the rural population is that of a man standing permanently up to the neck in water, so that even a ripple is sufficient to drown him. (Quoted in Scott 1976)

Subsistence risks can be tolerated up to a certain degree. The point when the peasantry can rise in rebellion is when traditional forms of social norms, functions and obligations are threatened by the intrusion of state and capital (Scott 1985).[18]

Indeed, the water has risen up to the neck of the adivasis, dalits, peasants and small and marginal farmers in India. It is easy to mouth a cursory enquiry into relief and rehabilitation, as if that evens out the plunder, and it is easier still to dismiss these struggles as being defensive in saying NO to development. And you might even be filled with disbelief when the wretched of the earth so often land up amplifying their self-sufficiency. But the stark reality is that they (and they alone!) know that development is a lie, a farce; therefore, they become ready to physically confront the militarized state apparatus that hand-holds the companies to their doorstep. It is subsistence at war with capital.

IX

> Force is itself an economic power. (Marx in Capital, Volume 1, 1988)[19]

In India, the alienation of adivasi land and the loot of minerals could happen only with the invoking of the principle of eminent domain that has remained in the statute books since the colonial period. The word eminent domain connotes expropriation or appropriation of resources like land for public use by virtue of superior power. When this plunder of natural resources is met with stiff resistance, it becomes the biggest obstacle on the way of the masters, whether it was for construction of dams in early years, public sector enterprises in the 1970s and 1980s or accumulation of capital in later years. No wonder that dispossession has to always rely on the police and paramilitary aided by the state government and local administration.

The coercion of capitalism to churn up the seas, twist the rivers, dig up the earth, raze down the forests, poison water bodies and pollute the air became the bloodiest of wars in contemporary times. Police firing on resistance movements became endemic to the process of territorial conquest. The guns were triggered on fisherfolk in Chilika in 1999. The state's belligerence became manifest in deploying battalions at both Chilika and Gopalpur. Instead of opening dialogue with the villagers opposing Tata, the administration built a police station right opposite the CPI office in Chamakhandi. The siege of Sindhigaon by the police to break down the will of those resisting, along with the huge number of criminal cases on leaders, which have not been closed till today, sought to dissipate the anti-Tata movement. In later years in Kashipur, police stations were constructed in Doraguda and Maikanch.

In the 2000s, repression only intensified as corporations coveted for land and mountains rich in minerals, largely inhabited by adivasis.

On 2 January 2006, the police opened fire on a gathering in Kalinganagar. The shock and horror of the Maikanch police firing that had still lingered in our minds or that of the paramilitary doing flag marches in Kashipur in December 2004 receded for a while. It was a moment of reckoning as the funeral pyres of 12 adivasis in Kalinganagar were telecast on all TV channels. The state had finally caught up with the race of capitalism, drawing the same weapons from its arsenals that have been used the world over.[20]

To hasten the process of accumulation, the ruse to use repression in 'law-and-order' situations found greater legitimacy in policies of repression mandated by the centre. There are two classic statements of our times. On 24 May 2010, at the end of the one-year rule of the United Progressive Alliance (UPA)-II in power, Prime Minister Manmohan Singh categorically stated that Naxalism was the biggest threat to national security. Being the finance minister in the early 1990s, as the harbinger of economic reforms, he was now saying that controlling left-wing extremism (LWE) was crucial, else it could affect economic growth. It became an open war cry, justifying the central government's step of boosting up the police and paramilitary forces and replenishing arms and ammunitions. It is the civil war of modern times. LWE was the all-encompassing target area that included all struggling people standing up against coercive land grab, armed or unarmed, communist or socialist. Odisha was one among several states that was already covered under the Security-Related Expenditure (SRE) scheme, where the centre would reimburse expenditure incurred by the state governments in combating LWE. A doddering economy with corporate aid carries out the war on behalf of capital spending crores of rupees. What came to be known as Operation Green Hunt had the centre holding the strings of the macabre set of events across more than hundred districts in ten states:

Andhra Pradesh, Telangana, Odisha, Chhattisgarh, Madhya Pradesh, Bihar, Jharkhand, West Bengal, Maharashtra and Uttar Pradesh.

Odisha, which had already seen the brutal face of the state, saw more intense repression now. Yet another statement that marks our times is that of Chief Minister Naveen Patnaik: 'Our government believes in peaceful industrialization.' The month of May 2010 remains ingrained in our minds for the barbaric violence unleashed by Odisha police and paramilitary at both Chandia and Baligotho in Kalinganagar and on anti-POSCO demonstrators at Balitutha in Jagatsinghpur. Laxman Jamuda was killed in Chandia on 12 May 2010 while the village was held under siege. Many more died as you will see in the chapter on Kalinganagar. Around 100 kilometres away, the protest against land acquisition for POSCO was at its height as people came out in hundreds and gathered at the Balitutha site, which is the entry to the area. On 15 May, the day the chief minister had expressed his belief in peaceful industrialization, the police carried out one of the most brutal and bloody assaults ever on an unarmed protest demonstration. The double-speak of the centre and the state was so clear in the events of May 2010.

While anti-POSCO protestors were fighting a life-and-death battle in January 2010, President Lee Myung Bak of South Korea was regally felicitated as the nation's Guest of Honour on 26 January, Republic Day in New Delhi. The agenda of accumulation of the neo-liberal state has its own rituals and ceremonies. The guest is always the head of a country or state chosen after much deliberation for India's economic and strategic interests.

The cold planning is expressed in the 2010 White Paper of the state government, which stated that the ultra-left had provoked the affected people of mega projects to take up the arms against setting up of such projects and that these agitations have been confronted for the greater interest of the state.[21] On 23 November 2009, Kendruka Singana and Andru Nachika were killed in police firing outside the Narayanpatna police station. They had gone to the police station to complain against the harassment and violence of combing squads. The Chasi Mulia Adivasi Sangathan (CMAS) had become a grave threat to local moneylenders, liquor traders, forest mafia and the district administration. The fight was for the redistribution of land among agricultural workers. On 27 January 2010, Gananath Patra, 70, was picked up by plain-clothes police in Bhubaneswar while returning from a meeting with members of a proposed fact-finding team to Narayanpatna. In barely five minutes, the electronic media splashed it as a major feat of the Odisha police, thereby criminalizing the leader of a mass movement of agricultural labourers. They had just begun emerging from the oppressive bonded labour system (*goti*) in feudal Odisha after generations. Indeed, the greater interest of the state had made the White Paper happen. The year 2010 proved to be eventful in the turn the war on people had taken. The hunt for Maoists swept across districts in Odisha; the brunt was borne by all anti-displacement movements, irrespective of their political ideologies or affiliations.

The stories became more and more bizarre each day. On 28 December 2010, Madhav Singh Thakur and Ramesh Sahu were killed by the Special Operations Group (SOG) and the Central Reserve Police Force (CRPF) as they were returning home on a motorbike in Paikmal in Bargarh district. The police claimed that they were cadres of the CPI ML (Maoist) and were killed in an encounter. The state unit of the BJP tore their story to bits, claiming both of them as active BJP members. On 14 November 2012, five villagers were gunned down by security forces in Bhaliaguda, which is on the border between Gajapati and Kandhamal districts. They were walking down the hill slope after a meeting to settle a dispute regarding pilferage of PDS rice. On 26 July 2015, a couple was killed by CRPF forces in Pangalpadar village of Kotagada block in Kandhamal. They were speaking on the mobile with their son in Kerala. It was the usual practice for their three children to receive calls from the parents who would climb atop an adjoining hill to get proper mobile connectivity. On 8 July 2016, six people were killed by security personnel while travelling in an auto rickshaw in Gumudumaha village in Kandhmal district. Two women and a child were among those killed. In this case, the police admitted they were civilians. To justify the funds pouring in from the centre, statistics were revved up as murders took place in cold calculation. Countering LWE and the hysteria orchestrated by the media made one reality possible: villages across Odisha have become aware of an entity named Naxalites that fight for the poor!

Security forces march across villages for months and years on end, enjoying complete impunity. On the night of 13 February 2010, a twenty-year-old woman was picked up from her house in Gajapati district by the SOG and the CRPF and was sexually assaulted by four security personnel on the way to the police station. It took a few months for her father to simply trace her. This was part of the combing operations when they had come looking for her brother. In the Niyamgiri region, the police picked up a young woman activist from her house around midnight on 1 May 2017 in typical zamindari style of olden times. In a prolonged drama in the Raygada police station, the police first declared her and seven others, including Dodi Pusika, a leader, to be Maoists. Yet the police had to give up eventually. A school girl from Kunduli village in Koraput, who was allegedly gang-raped by the paramilitary living in camps in the area, committed suicide on 22 January 2018. In the absence of any proper investigation and heightened media publicity, her act of suicide left behind a palpable disquiet among us all.

Women, along with children, continue to be strategically positioned as shields in the front of a rally or a march by the leadership. While the assumption that the police will target the men and brutally wreak violence is correct, these women take on the proxy violence. The notion that women will be less severely dealt with has outlived its time. They are subject to degrading verbal abuse and molestation like grabbing of breasts, torn blouses and being hit on private parts. For months on end they nurse fractures, ligament ruptures, blood clots and skin tears as they carry on with the daily grind. The pain and anger such trauma causes is refuelled each time they narrate these experiences. The coercive measures used by trained police personnel do not discriminate between genders in the march of capitalism.

To pick up people from weekly haats or on the way to hospital becomes a regular ploy in Kashipur, Kalinganagar, Jagatsinghpur and Niyamgiri. People are unable to buy or sell produce, repair a bicycle or see a relative or a friend in need in an adjoining area. When the gram sabhas that were held in 2013, as ordered by the Supreme Court, gave a unanimous verdict against mining in the Niyamgiri region, nothing changed. In fact, surveillance became more intense each year with daily harassment and random arrests that continue unabated. Demanding the implementation of the gram sabha verdict is met with foisting of criminal charges and random arrests. In the anti-POSCO movement where much of the area is also protected forest land, the Forest Rights Act virtually went into coma with brutal state repression. Even after the company quits, people find themselves mired in criminal cases, paying litigation fees for their remaining lives. Incarcerations continue even as we write. The reader can well imagine why villagers in many places ask: Who does the government belong to? Who will punish those in the government who break democratic processes? What can you do when the government does not follow the due process of law?

X

> Capital is faced with difficulties because vast tracts of the globe's surface are in the possession of social organizations that have no desire for commodity exchange or cannot, because of the entire social structure and the forms of ownership, offer for sale the productive forces in which capital is primarily

> interested. The most important of these production forces is of course the land, its hidden mineral treasure, and its meadows, woods and water. (Luxemburg 2003)

Dispossession is akin to an ideological warfare where the thin line between consent and coercion collapses. An orchestra is at work 24 × 7 drumming in the common sense around 'development.' This propaganda cloaks dispossession as benign or as a panacea. Educational and health services suddenly appear at the doorsteps; scholarships for students get announced and promises of jobs are made to the youth. Cyberspace is abuzz with dreams of modernity within the easy grasp of the marginalized sections. And seductive advertisements dot the urban landscape whether it is Tata's proclaiming 'We Also Make Tomorrow' or Vedanta's 'Mining Happiness.' The promise of employment for young engineers is conjured as imagined benefits are splashed on the media. It effectively masks how the process of land acquisition is deeply flawed.

Most projects are marked by a lack of transparency from the time of announcing of MoUs that have already been signed to conducting surveys for land acquisition. Those possessing or inhabiting the land only get to know when they are served a notice or read about it in the newspapers. Even the rituals of consent (or persuasion) are twisted and manipulated. Gram sabha resolutions opposing land acquisitions are ignored or the district administration manipulates the outcome as seen in the anti-POSCO struggle or in Niyamgiri. When the affected people exercise the right to say NO to land acquisition, it is immediately turned into a law-and-order situation where the local administration swings into action on behalf of the company. A wide range of repressive measures are used, such as intimidating individuals, slandering the emerging leadership and foisting false cases. Random arrests take into fold entire panchayats and women and elderly as seen in Kashipur, Kalinganagar and Jagatsinghpur. Repression of movements, which is endemic to the agenda of dispossession, intensified after the banning of the CPI (Maoist) in 2009. The criminalization of all democratic movements has become routine by branding any resistance to dispossession as Maoist. The persecution of Maoists to purge adivasi areas is but a ploy for the processes of accumulation to continue unhindered.

The emergence of the militarized state along with its laws and institutions, arms and ammunition, media and judiciary calls the shots. The laws of the land are punctured lifeless by the law makers. The Samatha judgement of the Supreme Court in 1997 that assured safeguards to the adivasis and the Panchayats (Extension to Scheduled Areas) Act, 1996, have been left unimplemented in most areas. The Fifth Schedule of the Indian Constitution that guarantees protection of land belonging to adivasis has also been routinely bypassed as in Kashipur. In both Niyamgiri and Jagatsinghpur, it is collective resistance that demanded the implementation of the Forest Rights Act that came into force in 2006 as a result of prolonged struggle by forest dwellers' campaigns and organizations. These hard-won rights are always under attack. On 13 February 2019, the Supreme Court passed an order directing twenty-one states to evict 11.8 lakh forest dwellers whose claims to forest land had been rejected.

Dispossession necessitates collaboration with the neo-liberal project. The beneficiaries of the steel and mining industries are aplenty; the profits trickle down in descending order from metropolitan cities and state capitals to the henchmen and agents in village lanes. The neo-liberal paradigm relies on the manipulation and manufacturing of consent through a range of non-state actors that propagate the same ideology: the media, development and funding agencies, big NGOs, corporate social responsibility (CSR) of corporate houses and sections of the corporatized academia and intelligentsia. Just as the upper-caste *babu*-dominated early Odia nationalists found more meaning in their association with the rajas and zamindars in their demand for a separate province than with the suffering peasantry, the privileged classes collaborate with corporates in our times. This total disconnect with the struggling masses is what Arundhati Roy calls the biggest secessionist movement in India.

In the years between 2006 and 2008 in Kalinganagar, the exodus of people to rehabilitation colonies was done by soliciting and hiring the services of big NGOs that the administration relied upon to smoothen the edge of coercion. There is a wide range of non-state actors that take the agenda of dispossession ahead as they reap the grand harvest. The ground is shifting so rapidly that a large section of the urban middle class is—wittingly or unwittingly—part of the dream project. The ideological war necessitates the creation of common sense; the spinning of dreams and desires leaves no one untouched, privileged or not.

At the local level too, the non-state actors are brought into play to caricature democratic processes like the creation of a pro-company lobby. A trust deficit is engineered within the community along with other devious means to divide people. There is hiring of agents and henchmen to go door to door and 'motivate' people to sell their land or move out. There is an emergence of small-time contractors, agents and brokers at the village level who aid company plans and objectives. These divisive tactics often strain the social fabric of the community, giving rise to mistrust and mutual suspicion for long periods. Money is used by the non-state actors to foment divisions among people using lies, bribes, the promise of compensation and instigation. Bribes range from mobile phones, rucksacks and sports shoes to motorbikes and Boleros. The game does not last too long. Pro-company lobbies fizzle out too soon when the company acquires the land.

After TISCO began its operations in Kalinganagar, the residents of the rehabilitated colonies, who once filled the ranks of the pro-Tata legion attacking those in the *andolan*, were at the gates of the company, sometimes demanding the promised jobs or protesting against the termination of water and electricity supply to their new colonies. The landless dalit labourers continue to appeal to the administration for granting of homestead land as assured under the rehabilitation policy. Earlier still, when the people of Kashipur were taken by the company to see the rehabilitation colony of NALCO in Damanjodi, those in the colony cautioned them with folded hands not to leave their villages and listed their woes for having agreed to rehabilitation. Members of the United Action Committee, a pro-POSCO lobby set up by the ruling party, was left bewildered when POSCO finally quit. They had drummed up support aggressively one day; today, they are also mired in criminal cases.

Indeed, the nefarious ways of capital have become an open book in Odisha. Teenagers of the late 2000s today are at the gates of Tata, Jindal and Aditya Birla for the promised employment. On 18 March 2019, villagers of Rengapalli, Chatrapur and Bandhaguda in the Niyamgiri region were protesting outside the gates of the Lanjigarh plant to demand permanent status, enrolment of their children in a nearby school and more jobs to those in the community. Vedanta had acquired the land from these villagers more than ten years ago through coercion and false promises. Promises included education for children, jobs in the plant and a hospital.[22] Dani Batra, a contract worker who was going to report to work was bludgeoned to death in a lathi charge carried out by the Odisha Industrial Security Force (OISF) on the protestors. An OISF personnel, Sujit Minz, also lost his life.

A young man in a meeting shared how he regrets today for having been lured by *moddo aau mansho* (alcohol and chicken) while his parents were opposing the company. So, pro-company agents simply give a feast to buy acquiescence. *Moddo aau mansho* was the refrain wherever we heard about villagers being diverted to the pro-company lobby.

As Ambai Majhi says:

> When a man drinks, he stops thinking. It is only him who matters. Leave alone wife and children—even God ceases to exist when they are drunk. And then they fight. Some cry like children. They become beasts and begin hit-

> ting their wives. If we were in the forefront of the struggle, this would not have happened. The compensation came in because it is the men who became weak. They fail to understand that compensation is bribery.

The company continues with its dirty tricks by throwing some in prison and luring others with money. Sini Soi in Kalinganagar evokes a moral high when she says:

> After a certain point, we felt that male folks could be bought by money, meat and liquor. So we formed Bisthapan Birodhi Mahila Sangha.

A tummy full of rice goes a long way in some economies. No wonder that officially rice is made available at Re 1 per kilo for the disenfranchised while the plunder lasts. Or else, the entire edifice would collapse.

In fact, the state and private entities rope in thousands of women through institutionalized means by leading them to believe that they can self-help themselves out of poverty. Jambabati Bijira of the Gandhamardan region holds the self-help groups (SHGs) responsible for weakening the bonds among women who had once led the movement against the public sector company BALCO:

> Now every woman is trapped inside this SHG or that and I think these are being funded by companies who have their eyes on the bauxite of Gandhamardan. How will we fight together when we receive money from them? Women actually think the government is helping them earn. I told them it is only in the interest of the companies and the government that they give us loans. That also divides us. The SHGs have tied down everybody and broken our unity. Nobody comes for meetings anymore.

Neither have they become thriving entrepreneurs nor have managed to reduce their poverty. Poverty alleviation schemes become the most formidable barrier to rural women's ability to make unity with peasant and working-class movements. The agenda of dispossession keeps marginalized sections as discrete and disparate as it alienates them further from their natural resources.

Through the usurpation and appropriation of natural resources and commons, capitalism ushers in continuous changes in ownership of the means of production. No wonder that machinations of capital involve the state itself acquiring and selling land, reaping manifold profits. The state is the biggest zamindar of our times. In the late 1990s, the land acquired by the Odisha government from the people in Kalinganagar at a lower rate was sold at an exponentially higher rate to the companies. In fact, the Kalinganagar firing happened on a day when a delegation of villagers was waiting to discuss a second round of compensation before the company began construction work. Again, simply getting rid of POSCO or TATA did not result in people being able to retain their own land. In the Gopalpur area, Tata had already acquired 3,585 acres, of which almost 800 acres was government land. Tata converted this land to a multi-product SEZ when it failed to set up a mega steel plant with Nippon Steel Corporation of Japan because of local resistance. The Gopalpur Industrial Park SEZ was inaugurated by the chief minister on 24 August 2010 without any of the earlier resistance. As soon as POSCO quit officially, the Odisha government acted upon the revision it had made in the land acquisition policy in February 2015 and fenced off the acquired area as part of its land bank policy.[23] It is being handed over to Jindal Steel Works negating the 12-year-old long struggle of the local inhabitants. Land is no more for the landless or the peasantry or forest dwellers but for corporate houses. And the state is the custodian. Since it is not private property that chief ministers of mineral-rich states can dole out like gift vouchers to corporations, these transactions become the land wars of our times.

XI

It is the optimism of the will that kept us going to simply make lucid to a larger audience how and why people still resist the development plans of the state. Each movement is a saga; each *andolan* is replete with people's own accounts that get narrated many times over. Their stories, conversations, highs and lows, nostalgic ruminations, sparkling wisdom and even the residues of bitterness had to see the light of day. These stories have always been with us, manifest in myriad ways. They run through our more sonorous fact-finding reports and appeals and memoranda; they remain hidden in discarded writing pads in our shelves, or roll in slow motion as crushed pamphlets on the road after a rally. They stretch to become the invisible spine of a public interest litigation or even jazz up the simple scrawl of a placard. But there comes a time when these stories and narratives fester more, knock more to create a clamour. And they have to be narrated. This repertoire—palpable and cumulative—goaded us to look for a method or the means to give it form. Therefore, reconnecting with people and places for the explicit purpose of chronicling or documenting seemed a privilege; revisiting sites of struggles brought in its wake even more narrations and more insights. As we made our way through this labyrinthine process, the method in the madness began to reveal itself. Connecting to the reader through the time-tested method of narratives and stories began to appeal to us.

These political narratives took shape from our written notes and audio recordings as well as from old fact-finding reports, newspaper cuttings, personal correspondence, leaflets and many conversations. These are the narratives of our times where voices and testimonies of each person speak of collective resistance.[24] At times, some people would narrate events from much earlier times as if they themselves have been through it. The stolen idols from the Nrusinghnath temple and the Kapiladhara stream spewing blood are collective memory for the people of Gandhamardan. Often, as in Baliapal or Rengali village, there was no single narrator. Nudging each other with bits and pieces of memory, an entire story would take shape in no time as group expression. To establish time or sequence of events, we corraborated people's accounts with a minimal use of other available publications. These accounts are precious; they are part of the historical struggle that is etched in people's memory and subjectivity.

These oral accounts are not merely interviews to weave a narrative. For those who speak, there is pride in recall and some pain too. The horrors that tumble out from the development narrative are hard to stomach. The threshold of sharing would at times give way when narrators would abreact experiences. Betrayals by leadership or by one's own people till today seem more incomprehensible to our narrators than the cunning of company agents. Perhaps, engaging with as much openness as we could muster helped us glimpse the many scars left by time along with the dreams that keep them alive. Indeed, it is people's testimonies and voices that tell us how wide the canvas of resistance can be. It is history, and it is history in the making too.

The tremendous significance we believe these struggles hold for those living outside such an economic and social arrangement inspired us to seek the form. Narratives become a powerful means of evoking the empathy of a society that might seem silent witnessing the events of its times. The silence might be ambiguous not knowing what to absorb of the reportage from mainstream media or it might even be vexed with disbelief. Narratives bridge the yawning gap; what exists between the reader and the narrative is the truth underlying these stories. The stories would cease to exist otherwise; they would cease to connect us with you too. They are based on the lived reality of flesh-and-blood people, with emotions of rage and anger, with emotions of love and longing and with dreams of a future. There is yet another compelling truth. These stories are about a world different from yours or mine or anyone who has been able to buy or borrow this book or even get to read it. As a form, narratives alone can absorb such a multitude of contending realities. These narratives convey a worldview of a vast peasantry and fisherfolk that asserts to say 'NO.' And we too have been infused by the dreams their resistance made possible. We find in their worldview a voice of sanity against the madness of development. The aim of this collection of narratives is simple; their wisdoms are affirmed.

No doubt, writing holds up a mirror to see society. But it is equally true that it helps face the deep disquiet within ourselves. As the writing comes to an end, we see the spaces we inhabit a bit clearer. The sense of inadequacy that activist work can fill you with can be tormenting; firefighting at times and at times applying band aid is the schizophrenia that characterizes our lives and times. The rapid pace of changes and the havoc created by the aggression of state and capital keep all on their toes but seldom with any space for critical reflection. Events not only in Odisha but across the country and the continual state repression (that got named Operation Green Hunt for a few years only) sent all sanity for a toss. How could we look for answers when sometimes even the framing of questions eluded us? These were times when any deep discussion or reflective articulation on the ongoing movements or its direction or trajectory would be in vain; solidarity became patronizing all too often, while critical engagement seemed antithetical to loyalty. Writing about our times brings us a step closer in naming the deepening sense of alienation within as political and social beings. It is our belief that these struggles raise fundamental questions of the times we live in and the direction in which the future of humanity is perilously poised. The advancement of capitalism is turning the entire earth, land, forests, jungles, hills and streams, water bodies and beaches into commodities. Not only that, it is fast eroding human relations too. In the face of processes that are inherently so destructive, these struggles in Odisha have been able to put a few spokes in the wheels of the juggernaut. It has been halted at Gandhamardan, Baliapal, Gopalpur, Chilika and Jagatsinghpur. The Niyamgiri stands mighty till today. POSCO quit exhausted to its last bone after waiting for twelve long years.

These narratives are clearly in the context of larger resistance sweeping across the globe in search of the brave new world. Put simply, the fight against capitalism has to see decisive victories against the rapacious greed of corporations, ostensibly 'mining happiness' as the Vedanta advertisement brazenly proclaims. And against the audacity of elected governments that stand guard to the grand loot to dispossess multitudes of the poorest of the poor. This book is perhaps a journey and a search where we simply ask of all of us: will we allow this great derangement to continue? Putting these stories together is but a small, humble endeavour to bring Odisha on the map of resistance politics and social movements in India and elsewhere.

> *Ho gayi hai peer parvat si, pighalni chaahiye,*
> *Is Himalaya se koi Ganga nikalni chaahiye*
>
> *Har gali mein, har shehar mein, har nagar, har gaon mein,*
> *haath lehraatee hue, har laash chalni chahiye*
>
> *Aaj ye deewar pardon ki tarah hilney lagi,*
> *shart lekin thi, ki yeh buniyaad hilni chahiye.* (Kumar 1988)
>
> [Let it melt now, this mountain of sorrow,
> That from its Himalaya, a river may flow
>
> Through each town and city, each village and lane,
> Let every corpse walk, waving hands, once again
>
> These walls tremble today, and flutter like curtains,
> But we had set out to rock the foundations]

NOTES

1. Andrew Stirling writes how while invading Odisha in the year 1580, Sawai Sai Singh, who was the General of Akbar, exclaimed: 'This country is not a fit subject for conquest, and schemes of human ambition. It belongs wholly to the Gods, and is one entire Tirth.'
2. In the words of W.W. Hunter: 'To the world's call-roll of heroes, it will add not one name. The people of whom it treats have fought no great battle for human liberty, nor have they succeeded even in more primary task of subduing the forces of nature to the control of man. To them the world stands indebted for not a single discovery which augments the comforts or mitigates the calamities of life. Even in literature—the peculiar glory of the India race—they have won no conspicuous triumph. They have written no famous epic; they have struck out no separate school of philosophy; they have elaborated no new system of law.'
3. In 2011, the name of the state was changed from Orissa to Odisha, and the name of its language from Oriya to Odia.
4. Most non-English words have been italicized barring those found in dictionaries as Indian English entries. A glossary of Odia words used in this book is provided in Annexure B.

5. See *Political Unrest in Orissa in the 19th Century* written by Prasanna Kumar Mishra. The Kandhas and Savaras of Ghumsur, Surada, Chinakimedi, Parlakhemundi, Boudh, Daspalla, Nayagarh, Kalahandi and Patna (present Balangir) revolted against the colonialists from 1837 to 1856; Binjhals and Gonds actively participated in the Sambalpur region from 1857 to 1864; the Bhuyans, Juangs and Kols and the peasantry rose in revolt against British imperialism and the feudal king in Keonjhar and its adjoining region in 1867–1868 and in 1891–1993. See also *Roots of Poverty, A Social History* by Fanindam Deo, where he describes how the Kondhs of Kandhan, the kandha land, rose in rebellion in 1881–1882.
6. Fakir Mohan Senapati's novel *Chha Mana Aatha Guntha* was first published in Odia in 1902. The novel depicts the misery of the Odia peasantry under the zamindari system in the early colonial system. The novel was serialized in the journal *Utkal Sahitya* beginning in 1897 and continued till its publication as a book in 1902. Its realistic depiction made people think that events narrated in the novel were real. When the story reached the court trial, hundreds of people from nearby villages gathered at the court in Cuttack in anticipation to actually see Mangaraj—a zamindar—on trial!
7. The biography of Madhusudan Das has been written in fictional style.
8. It was written by Shri Mohanty during 1930s as a school textbook but remained unpublished. Gopinath Mohanty Foundation Trust & Centre for Human Sciences published this in e-book format in 2018.
9. See Annexure C for a project profile of each project covered in the chapters that follow.
10. It was a master plan for the integrated development of the river basins of Odisha and presented as the sixth Sir M. Visvesvaraya lecture delivered at the 43rd Annual Convention of the Institution of Engineers (India). Khosla was then the Governor of Odisha.
11. Bharat Chandra Nayak has recounted his experience in his autobiography how in a meeting at Cuttack, nobody approved his idea of scrapping Hirakud project but rather wanted that people should be properly rehabilitated.
12. *Roots of Poverty* by Fanindam Deo is a study on Kalahandi. Manoranjan Mohanty and Bijay Bahidar, in their book *Odisha Daridra Kahinki* (Why Odisha Is Poor), have also shown how the socio-economic structures are responsible for the poverty of Odisha, which no amount of industrialization can remove.
13. *Business Standard* (Orissa to notify Talasara as 14th port site—18 April 2012).
14. Song composed and set to tune by Bhagaban Majhi, a leading activist of Prakrutika Sampad Surakshya Parishad (PSSP) in Kucheipadar, Kashipur. It became popular across all anti-displacement movements in India.

15. An interesting anecdote from the biography of Sarangdhar Das, the pioneer of the *garhjat praja* movement, reveals how before the finalization of list of candidates for the Odisha Assembly in 1946, a registered letter from Sardar Vallabhbhai Patel, the President of Congress Parliamentary Board, reached the Odisha Congress Office in the name of Harekrushna Mahatab. The letter contained a cheque of Rs. 10,000/- and a letter from Patel. It was written that this was a donation by the Birlas for the Odisha Congress. It was also suggested to elect G.D. Thirani from the Industry and Commerce seat of Odisha.
16. Vikalpa Sandhani Manch was an alternative forum in Bhubaneswar that was started in the year 1994. It was devoted to understand Odisha and its people, to explore some unexplored aspects of much publicized happenings in Odisha and to identify people ignored by the mainstream media in order to listen to them and to their viewpoints. The Manch used to organize discussions around people's issues every year on Utkal Divas, which is April 1, and publish the discussions in *Sameekshya*. It was edited by Birendra Nayak, Pradumna Bal and Debiprasad Dash. The theme of *Sameekshya* '96 was on 'People's Movements in Post-independent Odisha' and *Sameekshya* '98 was on 'People's Movement in Post-independent Odisha and Participation of Women.'
17. The novel Paraja by Gopinath Mohanty was published in 1945. The protagonist is an adivasi peasant who gets trapped in a debt from the local sahukar that ultimately leads to the tragic destruction of his small family. Written on an epic scale, it reflects the fragility of lives dependent on subsistence production in the forested mountains of undivided Koraput district. The book has been translated into several languages, including English.
18. James Scott begins the book *The Moral Economy of the Peasant: Rebellion and Subsistence in Southeast Asia* with a graphic description of a man standing permanently in water with water up to his neck, which was used by Tawney in writing about China in 1931. Scott outlines the economic and political tensions in peasant communities of Burma and Vietnam during the 1930s. Influenced by E.P. Thompson's understanding of the moral economy, he elucidates how the moral economy becomes an important variable that can impact social movements. Nine years later, in *Weapons of the Weak,* James Scott examines everyday forms of resistance depicted in a village in Malaysia taking into account the Gramscian notion and concept of hegemony and peasant resistance to it.
19. Karl Marx had explained how different methods of accumulation depend in part on brute force, but they all employ the power of the state. Force is instrumental to shorten the transition of any old society that holds within it a new one because force is itself an economic power.

20. Books like Howard Zinn's *A People's History of the United States* and Eduardo Galeano's *Open Veins of Latin America* provide rich accounts of hundreds of years of pillage, destruction and exploitation of the most ordinary people.
21. The White Paper (2010) published by Govt. of Orissa, Department of Home testifies (p. 2).
22. In Tuticorin in Tamil Nadu, thirteen people were killed in police firing on 22 May 2018. The state government had acquired land from many of these villages in the early nineties with the promise of jobs and compensation that never came. The people were protesting against the contamination of the entire area and its villages by Sterlite Copper company, which is owned by the same Vedanta Limited.
23. In February 2015, the Odisha government issued a notification on the basis of a revision made in its revised land acquisition policy that such land can be kept in a Land Bank by the state government. However, after the Supreme Court on 31 August 2016 ordered the West Bengal government to return the 997 acres it had acquired for the small-car Nano plant of Tata Motors in 2008, there are demands from many other communities in Odisha and elsewhere to implement the same and return the acquired land.
24. A list of names and dates of interviews with people is provided at the end of the book as Annexure A. All names used in the interviews are real with their permission. Interviews or interactions in the past have been mentioned in Notes.

References

Bardhan, Pranab. 1998. *The Political Economy of Development in India*. New Delhi: Oxford India Paperbacks.

Barghouti, Mourid. https://www.goodreads.com/quotes/375886-the-fish-even-in-the-fisherman-s-net-still-carries-the.

Bidwai, Prafulla. 2015. *The Phoenix Moment*. New Delhi: Harper Collins Publishers.

Burgos Debray, Elizabeth. 1984. *I, Rigoberta Menchu*. Translated by Ann Wright. London: Verso.

Business Standard. 2012. *Orissa to notify Talasara as 14th Port Site*. 18 April.

Chandra, Bipin, et al. 2008. *India Since Independence*. New Delhi: Penguin Books India.

Chatterjee, Partha. 2010. *Empire and Nation (Development, Planning and the Indian State)*. Ranikhet: Permanent Black.

D'Souza, Rohan. 2008. Framing India's Hydraulic Crisis: The Politics of the Modern Large Dam. *Monthly Review Press* 60 (3): 112–124.

Dash, Debendra Kumar, ed. 2005. *Utkal Sammilani (1903–1936)*. Rourkela: Pragati Utkal Sangha.

Deo, Fanindam. 2009. *Roots of Poverty, a Social History*. Bhubaneswar: Amadeus Press.

Goud, Bideshi. 2018. *Machhkund O Balimela Prakalpa: Bikaaso ro Karala Drushya (Machhkund and Balimela Project: the horrible picture of Development)*. Bhubaneswar: Ganavitti, Vol. II, No. 6, May–June 2018.

Hind Swaraj. 1958. *The Collected Works of Mahatma Gandhi*. Vol. 10. New Delhi: Publications Division.

Hunter, W.W. 1872. *Orissa, or the Vicissitudes of an Indian Province under Native and British Rule*. London: Smith, Elder & Co.

Khosla, A.N. 1963. *Orissa's Decade of Destiny (1963–1973)*. 43rd Annual Convention of the Institution of Engineers (India).

Kumar, Dushyant. 1988. *Jawaab Dar Sawaal – Jan Geeton ka Sankalan*. Hoshangabad: Eklavya.

Luxemburg, Rosa. 2003. *The Accumulation of Capital*. London and New York: Routledge.

Mahalnabois, Prasanta Chandra. 1955. Not a People's Plan. *Mumbai: Economic Weekly*, June 18.

Marx, Karl. 1988. *Capital*. Vol. 1. London: Penguin.

McCully, Patrick. 2001. *Silenced Rivers: The Ecology and Politics of Large Dams*. London: Zed Books.

Mishra, Gangadhar. 1936. *Chasabhai* (Odia Pustika), Puri.

Mishra, Prasanna Kumar. 1983. *Political Unrest in Orissa in the 19th Century*. Calcutta: Punthi Pustak.

Mohanty, Surendra. 1970. *The Sun of the Century*. Calcutta: Lark Books, Cuttack.

Mohanty, Gopinath. 1987. *Paraja*. Delhi: Oxford University Press.

———. 2018. *Bhougalika Kahani*. Bhubaneswar: E-Book Gopinath Mohanty Foundation Trust & Centre for Human Sciences.

Mohanty, Manoranjan, and Bijay Kumar Bahidar. 1993. *Odisha Daridra Kahinki*. Cuttack: Odisha Book Store.

Nanda, Chandi Prasad. 2008. *Vocalizing Silence*. New Delhi: Sage Publication.

Nayak, Bharat Chandra. 2004. *Mora Purbasmruti Katha*. Cuttack: Agraduta.

Nayak, Birendra, et al., eds. 1998. *Odia O Odisha: Sameekshya '98*. Bhubaneswar: Vikalpa Sandhani Manch.

Padel, Felix, and Samarendra Das. 2010. *Out of this Earth*. New Delhi: Orient Blackswan.

Panda, Harihar (Shashibhushan Rath ed). 1915. *United Orissa: A Plea*. Berhampur: Utkal Union Series.

Patnaik, Bibhuti. 2013. *Viplabi Sarangadhar Das*. Cuttack: Prachi Sahitya Prakashan.

Rabi, Sailaj, ed. 2011. *Collected Works of Manmohan Choudhury*. Part 4. Cuttack: KABIR.

Sanyal, Kalyan. 2007. *Rethinking Capitalist Development*. New Delhi: Routledge India.

Sanyal, Amal. 2010. *The Curious Case of Bombay Plan*. Contemporary Issues and Ideas in Social Sciences (CIISS). http://journal.ciiss.net/index.php/ciiss/article/viewFile/78/75/. Accessed 30 June 2019.

Scott, James. 1976. *The Moral Economy of the Peasant and Subsistence in Southeast Asia*. New Haven and London: Yale University Press.

———. 1985. *1985. Weapons of the Weak: Everyday Forms of Peasant Resistance*. New Haven and London: Yale University Press.

Senapati, Fakir Mohan. 2006. *Six Acres and a Third*. New Delhi: Penguin.

Senapati, Nilamani, and Nabin Kumar Sahu, eds. 1967. *Mayurbhanj Gazetteer*.

Sengupta, Jayanta. 2015. *At the Margins, Discourses of Development, Democracy, and Regionalism in Orissa*, 12. New Delhi: Oxford University Press.

Stanley, William. 1996. Machkund, Upper Kolab and NALCO Projects in Koraput District, Orissa. *Economic and Political Weekly*, June 15.

Stirling, Andrew. 1822. *An Account: Geographical, Statistical and Historical of Orissa Proper or Cuttack*. Calcutta: Asiatic Society of Bengal.

The Samaj, 29-01-1921 quoted in Biswamoy Pati's Resisting Domination, Peasants, Tribals and the National Movement in Orissa 1920–50, Manohar, 1993.

Viegas, Philip. 1992. The Hirakud Dam Oustees: Thirty Years After in Rivers of sorrow Rivers of change. In *Big Dams, Displaced People: Rivers of Sorrow, Rivers of Change*, ed. E. Ganguly Thukral. New Delhi: Sage Publications.

White Paper. 2010. Bhubaneswar: Govt. of Orissa.

CHAPTER 2

The Disease of Gigantism

Until the lions have their own historians, the history of the hunt will always glorify the hunter.
—Chinua Achebe, 1994

Jawaharlal Nehru was flying to the venue of the inaugural ceremony of the Hirakud Dam on the Mahanadi River on 13 January 1957. With him on board was the Italian filmmaker Roberto Rossellini, who was invited by Nehru to accompany him. He recalls:

> As the plane approached the dyke, Nehru stepped out from his private cabin and asked the pilot to fly low around the entire area. There were still 35,000 men working, sometimes in 113-degrees [45 degrees Celsius] heat. So it was like building of the pyramids. Of course the pilot immediately turned the plane. The site was on Nehru's side and I, sitting on the other side, could not see anything at all. After a while, Nehru gestured to me to sit beside him in the same row of seats. Now I was seeing Nehru's profile as he looked at this immense work, and through him, was seeing it too. I was suddenly very moved as I watched Nehru. He wasn't staring at the sight below with joy or exaltation but with a deep sadness. (Quoted in Padgaonkar 2008)

Indeed, Roberto Rossellini captured the most telling moment of this country's nation-building project and its ambiguity that lasted decades. Nehru's sadness, which was both momentary and personal, evaporated in

R. Padhi, N. Sadangi, *Resisting Dispossession*,
https://doi.org/10.1007/978-981-15-0717-5_2

a jiffy. It was the architect of the new nation-state that emerged composed from the confines of the plane to face the huge gathering present for the inaugural ceremony. In his speech, Nehru evoked the need for people to sacrifice in building 'the modern Konark' of Odisha.

Nehru's dreams of a new nation became recorded history. But those who suffered the history of dispossession and fought back valiantly are not even a footnote in such accounts. The anti-dam movement in Sambalpur district known as the Bandha Virodhi Committee put up a spirited fight against the Hirakud Dam. Sixty years later, when we tried to meet some of them to record their voices and experiences, they had all grown old and fragile. Many who were active on the forefront of the movement had already passed away. Those we met hold on to fading memories. Sometimes only a slogan or a line of a song is all that they recall. Calling upon their memory or recall would reveal residues of bitterness that are intact till today. Memoirs and biographies of some pro and anti-dam leaders helped us piece together the account. And short stories and poetry continue to cherish the nostalgia and longing for submerged villages.

Tryst with Destiny

Lalmudia dekhle dariba nahin/Jamin badi chhadiba nahin
Hirakud bandh band karenge/Jami dakhal nahi chhodenge

[Shall not fear policeman/Shall not leave home and land
We will stop construction of dam/We will stop land acquisition]

The first notification for land acquisition was served on 13 September 1946 on 95 villages in Hirakud. In this notification, people were asked to express their grievances within a month. Immediately, *hartals*, meetings and processions began in Sambalpur town and many of the affected areas, in which women also participated in large numbers. On 30 September, almost 30,000 people began a procession at Samaleswari Temple that went around the city to culminate in a meeting on the Mahanadi riverbed.

As the protest gained momentum, the anti-dam movement got to know that Harekrushna Mahatab[1] had written a letter to Mahatma Gandhi seeking his blessings for the project. The Anti-Dam Committee immediately delegated two leaders, Sankar Prasad Mishra and Bodhram Dube, to meet Gandhi in Delhi to discuss the issue and persuade him to lend his voice for the scrapping of the project:

> Gandhi gave a surprising smile hearing about the news and said that he had received the letter from Mahtab. But as he was completely in the dark about the whole issue, he had not given any words of blessing to him. Gandhi gave them a patient hearing and told them to give their opinions in writing. Gandhi had also instructed Sarat Bose to invite Khosla to put forth his views on the proposal. (*Hirakhand Samachar* January 1947)

The movement sent yet another delegation to seek the opinion of M.G. Rangaiya, who was a member of the Flood Committee, 1937. The committee members, Laxminarayan Mishra and Chandra Prasad Mishra, went to Mysore to meet Rangaiya. On 2 November, he released a twenty-six-page note on the Hirakud project, pointing out 'the technical and financial defects of the scheme.' The note in its concluding paragraph said:

> If, however, they still think that the Hirakud project as at present contemplated should be proceeded with, the people affected would be justified in asking for a suspension of the operations, and for an enquiry by an impartial and competent committee presided over by a high judicial officer of the rank of a high court judge. (Rangaiya 1946)

The expert opinion of Rangaiya was like fresh oxygen for the movement. The Anti-Dam Committee sent the report to Mahatma Gandhi and subsequently women delegates were sent to discuss with him:

> Mahatma Gandhi, (the devotee of truth), read the opinions of Rangaiya with deep interest and realized the truthfulness of the demands of people of Sambalpur and promised to take the responsibility with pleasure and sympathy to write on behalf of the people of Sambalpur to the Government of India against the project. (*Hirakhand Samachar* January 1947)

After seeking the Mahatma's blessings and the opinion of an expert, the movement also sought divine blessings by organizing a *yagna* (sacred fire) in Samaleswari Temple. 'Though the mass movement to stop the dam and to form a separate province is strong and solid, it is still most essential to resort to divine help to make the movement most successful. Nothing is more powerful than the divine power,' read the appeal (*Hirakhand Samachar* January 1947).

Hawthorne Lewis left and Chandulal Trivedi became the Governor of Odisha. In response to his scheduled visit to Sambalpur from 10 to 20 November 1946, leaders of the anti-dam movement organized a massive rally to demonstrate that the movement was not that of a handful of *gountias* (the headman and landed gentry) as propagated by the Congress government.

The government imposed Section 144 of the Criminal Procedure Code in Sambalpur for three months. Meetings and processions were not allowed without prior permission. Section 144 was also served on leaders like Bodhram Dube, Achyutananda Purohit and others, preventing them from organizing meetings for two months. In protest, Purohit, an important leader, resigned from his role as Public Prosecutor. Even then, thousands of people gathered at daybreak:

> On 12 November, before daybreak, the area around the river was teeming with men and women. By sun break, everybody spilled onto the road. Nearly 200,000 people participated. One-third of them were women. Many of them were with their children. The disciplined crowd began to walk on Jail Road so that the Governor could see them from the circuit house nearby, atop the hillock. Women of Sambalpur town were at the front of the demonstration; all others from the villages were at the end. It was a heart-pleasing sight. They were shouting slogans like, 'Stop Hirakud dam, Odisha Government' and 'Leave Sambalpur.' They also sang a song (Nayak 2004).[2]
>
> *Chal re chal re chal/Hirakud ke chal,*
> *Sarkar jene bandha bandhuchhe/band karma chal*
>
> [March and march, march to Hirakud,
> Let us stop the dam, the government building there]

The Mahanadi fervently murmured prayers for its people. She had so long quietly absorbed their many moods and many secrets. She has seen them immersed in their daily chores near the riverbed; jubilant and happy during festive times and pensive and sad while bidding farewell to visiting relatives. This time she flowed on most bewildered.

In defiance of prohibitory orders, women of Sambalpur town held processions twice a day almost daily. Finally, a meeting of the Anti-Dam Committee on 20 April decided to serve an ultimatum to the government to scrap the project within one month and to declare that Sambalpur was free to merge either with provinces or with princely states of its choice. It declared that an indefinite satyagraha would start after a month. Bodhram Dube also resigned from the assembly. The government, in response, warned people to stay away from such an illegal activity and threatened to use force in order to maintain law and order. On 20 May, yet another meeting was organized on the riverbed and the decision was taken to start satyagraha before the court premises from the next day. Leaders took oath to court arrest disobeying the law.

On the first day, the procession went round the town and reached the court premises under the leadership of Janardan Pujari and Kamala Devi. They were arrested and sentenced to three months of imprisonment. Women satyagrahis were loaded into vans and were left 20 km away from Sambalpur town. Subsequently, leaders like Sradhakar Supakar,[3] Prasanna Panda[4] and many others were arrested and sent to prison. People were mercilessly lathi-charged. Cameras were snatched from press photographers. Satyagraha continued till 27 May. The entire country was nearing the end of the long fight for the nation's independence; the euphoria and militancy was at it its peak. But the repression of the anti-dam struggle left the people of Sambalpur with crushed dreams. Many leaders who were put into jail were released only after India gained independence. These incarcerations became the final blow to the growing militant anti-dam movement.

In the nation that became free of colonial rule, the planning that was afoot got blindly adopted by the new rulers in pursuit of self-glory. The taming of the Mahanadi had been planned to only maximize return from land revenue by the British. And that is the history that we put together here.

Taming of the Mahanadi

In 1803, the undivided districts of the coastal belt of Odisha—Balasore, Cuttack and Puri—came under the rule of the East India Company. This coastal tract is the floodplain area of three turbulent rivers: Mahanadi, Brahmani and Baitarini. The Mahanadi traverses a distance of 470 kilometres from Amarkantak in present-day Chhattisgarh. It enters Sambalpur in western Odisha and flows eastwards via Cuttack to empty into the Bay of Bengal.

While travelling across India in the mid-nineteenth century, W.W. Hunter gave a picturesque description of these rivers:

> Three great rivers collect the drainage of 57,000 square miles of central India and gradually converging towards the coast, dash down their accumulated waters within thirty miles of each other upon the Cuttack District. The velocity which they had obtained in descending from the inner table land finds itself suddenly checked upon the level delta and they break into a hundred distributaries like a pitcher of water thrown violently on the ground. These distributaries roam over the delta, struggling by a thousand contortions and convolutions towards the coast forming a network of rivers which after innumerable interlacings and bifurcations generally reunite with one of the three parent channels as they approach the sea. (Hunter 1872)

When the East India Company went on a drive to maximize revenue from this newly conquered land, recurrent floods in these rivers were impediments. This led them to see flood as a calamity. The administration then thought of devising ways and means to tame the river. As a first step, they undertook the building of river embankments. It continued for almost half a century. But neither could it control high floods, nor did the supposed beneficiaries—the peasants—accept it. Rather, they indulged in cutting or breaching embankments. Captain Young, one of the military engineers, engaged in embankment work of Odisha's delta area, records an interesting account:

> This practice is even systematized by the villagers, that is, they insert a hollow trunk of a tree in the embankments where they wish to obtain water, and carefully conceal it from the executive officers with earth and turfing. Through this at the desired time [when the flood currents are reasonably mild] they obtain the water they require, and take their chance of a breach occurring and of discovery. The water as they say is life to them; for without it, they could not rear their crops or pay their revenue and the *darogas* are paid to connive at the practice, while in the case of discovery, any one villager, whose family is during punishment and imprisonment supported by the rest, is voluntarily made the scapegoat. This, I am informed by the superintendent, is common, and that he has discovered many such hidden sluices at places where it appeared to him strange that breaches were constantly occurring at the same spot. (Quoted in Papers Relative to the Rivers of Cuttack 1860)

The technical staff engaged in embankment work for half a century realized the futility of the embankment policy and wanted to abandon the project. The revenue administration did not want to lose the revenue from the protected land. While the tug of war between the technical and revenue staff continued, the idea of controlling the flood water at the mouth of the river was mooted. Arthur Cotton, in his celebrated report on the Mahanadi River, proposed to impound flood water through barrages and divert it by a network of navigable canals. In other words, flood water could be harnessed for irrigation and navigation, which, in turn, would earn a huge profit. The novelty of his proposal was that private capital could be attracted for this enterprise.

In fact, the Orissa Irrigation and Canal Company was soon floated in 1863 with British private capital and canals were built. However, the Company kept on incurring losses as there was no such great demand for canal water. Peasants opposed it as the canals destroyed their traditional water structures and water from the canals lacked the 'rich red mud water' of the floods that fertilized their land. Finally, the Company chose to hand over the canals to the colonial administration by a deed of surrender. Construction of embankments and canals, motivated by financial considerations of the colonial administration, could not even achieve the stated objective of flood control. The Flood Committee Report of 1927 observed how the solution itself became the cause of the problem (Quoted in D'Souza 2006).[5]

This radical observation of the committee did not translate into any concrete action. The Mahanadi continued to flood large areas. Finally, the idea of building a reservoir on the river as a solution to the flood problem gained ground.

Dam as a Cure of All Maladies

The deltaic belt of Odisha experienced a devastating flood in the year 1937. The Congress ministry under Biswanath Das sought the help of Mahatma Gandhi. Gandhi advised him to invite M. Visvesvaraya, an eminent Indian engineer who had designed the Krishna Raja Sagara Dam in the region of Mysore, to enquire into the flood problem of Odisha. Visvesvaraya suggested the idea of a big reservoir on Mahanadi and advised the government to collect data to give a scientific basis to the project. To buttress his argument of a big reservoir, he mentioned the American experience of the river valley project, particularly, Tennessee

Valley Authority (TVA) established in 1933. It had set the trend of multipurpose river valley projects for many countries. As World War II broke out, the Mahanadi project was shelved. At that time, A. Khosla was working as an Indian engineer with the TVA, which had begun its work in the Damodar Valley Project in West Bengal. After the war, Khosla became the chairman of the newly constituted Water-ways, Irrigation and Navigation Commission. He took up the Mahanadi project and made a visit to Odisha in May 1945. He recommended the damming of rivers as a cure for all maladies of Odisha:

> As a result of local inspection and discussions I came to the definite conclusion that the only cure for the troubles of Orissa namely, floods, droughts, poverty and disease, lay in the control of its rivers by means of storage dams to provide flood control, irrigation, navigation coupled with anti-malarial measures. I felt that an immediate start should and could be made on investigations for the multi-purpose development of the Mahanadi which held promise of the greatest benefits to the people of Orissa and the neighbouring states. (Khosla 1947)

He proposed three big dams to be built in phases on the Mahanadi: Hirakud, Tikarapada and Naraj. The final decision on this was taken at a meeting at Cuttack, which was then the capital of Odisha. Without studying its financial and technical aspects in detail, Sir Hawthorne Lewis, the then Governor of Odisha, soon laid the foundation stone of the Hirakud Dam on 15 March 1946.

In this haste, who had the will and time for knowing people's views on it? Rulers always seem to know what is best for the ruled.

Disbelief, Hope and Despair

> I was then twenty-two-years-old and I had been married for two years, when I got to hear about the dam. We got to know of it when government officials began surveying and collecting information. One of our village elders from Kulta caste said that this was being done to raise the *malguzari* (land rent) and that it was a conspiracy of the Katkias (people from coastal Odisha) to settle down here by displacing us. He told us that water flows downwards, so how could you make it flow upward? And that too, the water of the ferocious Mahanadi! So for us, the news of the construction of dam on the Mahanadi was false propaganda.

Eighty-year-old Sukhdeb Kisan from Chhuipali village recalled some of the discussions the elders had. The news of the proposed dam took time to arrive from the centre to the periphery—from Cuttack, the then capital of Odisha, to Sambalpur. Towards the end of February 1946, Sambalpur was abuzz with speculation about the Hirakud Dam. People became restless and apprehensive. As Lewis reached Sambalpur a day before the laying of the foundation stone, a mass meeting organized at the Municipality Hall passed a resolution opposing the construction of the dam. It was sent to the Governor that very evening. People knew that many prosperous villages would be submerged if the dam was built and that it would be a curse for Sambalpur.

It was a historical moment. After the Congress party headed by Harekrushna Mahatab formed the interim government on 23 April 1946, people's hopes were raised assuming that now the elected government would at least reconsider the dam proposal imposed on them by alien rulers. Many wondered that only the feverish imagination of a bunch of madcaps could conceive such an ill-conceived idea of damming the Mahanadi. Many others viewed it as mere propaganda.

Was it naive of them to believe in the law of nature against the rationality of science?

The reality of the actual construction of the dam loomed large. The news of the proposed dam and impending displacement swiftly travelled across the villages situated on the banks of the Mahanadi and its tributary Ib. As the news spread, it struck terror in the hearts of the people. For them, the very thought of having to leave the village where they had been living for generations was akin to a living death (*than chhadle, paranchhadsi*). The village *gountias* quickly took the lead in organizing people. They drew resolutions against the dam and sent them to the government.

On 18 May 1946, Radhakrishna Biswasray, a minister in the government of Odisha, visited Sambalpur. Four thousand people gathered to demand the scrapping of the dam project. In response, he declared that the Hirakud Dam was mainly being designed to save the people of Cuttack and Puri from the menace of floods in the largest populated area of the province. He said that the disaster caused by floods each year brought poverty and misery to people. He reiterated that the Congress government was committed to addressing the problems of the people. He even said that, if the dam was constructed, the princely states of Sonepur, Bauda and Athamallik (Sonepur and Bauda are districts today while Athamallik is part of Angul district) along the course of the Mahanadi would also benefit. He showed dreams to the people saying that their dry, one-crop land would become fertile and honey and milk would flow!

People still hoped and carried on the dialogue with their *desi sarkar*. The Sambalpur District Peasant Union invited Chief Minister Harekrushna Mahatab, former CM Biswanath Dash and Minister Nabakrushna Choudhury for a dialogue on 21 July 1946. Janardan Pujari, a philanthropic doctor of Sambalpur town, presided over the conference. He was brought to the conference venue in a congregation of around 7,000 people. Mahatab, in his address said, 'If people did not want the dam, they could have written it in a six-paisa envelope. Why this widespread movement?'

While he had assured the dam would not be constructed against the wishes of the people, a few days later he announced in a meeting at Cuttack that he had convinced the people of Sambalpur about the benefits of the dam. This doublespeak opened the eyes of thousands of protestors. They realized that the dam was no more a rumour. What was left for them was to fight to save their land and home.

In August 1946, an eleven-member Bandha Virodhi Committee came into being in Sambalpur town, which soon became the epicentre of the anti-dam movement. The *Hirakhand Samachar* weekly was also launched to act as the mouthpiece of the movement. In addition to spreading the message of the movement, this weekly also carried out debates over flood control, development and regionalism.

Radhakrishna Biswasray's statement that the dam was being built to save the people of Cuttack and Puri gave an edge to the growing dissent. It seemed as if the *Sambalpuria* (people of Sambalpur) had to be drowned to save the *katakia* (people of coastal area). People asserted that if the people of Cuttack had to be saved from floods, they had to also bear its cost. Some demanded that the dam at Naraj, just 10–11 km from Cuttack, should be first built as proposed in Khosla's report. Some more argued for the implementation of the recommendation of Flood Committee Report of 1927 and for the renovation of canals and embankments already built. In response, the government played down the issue of flood control as one of the main benefits of the Hirakud Dam. Instead, benefits like irrigation, generation of electricity and industrialization were highlighted to give it the face of 'development.'

People vociferously questioned the idea of industrialization and irrigation from different perspectives:

> More than a hundred villages along the banks of the Mahanadi and Ib will be submerged for the Hirakud dam; around one lakh people will be rendered homeless and landless and ten lakh maund [one maund is approximately 37 kilos] of crops like rice, mung, wheat, etc. produced annually would be destroyed. (*Hirakhand Samachar* September 1946)

They argued that such industrialization was meant 'to create one millionaire by turning one lakh countrymen into faceless daily wagers.' Some more demanded 'we do not want machine-industry; we want cottage industry; we wouldn't allow the wealth of the country to be looted for the lure of machine-industry' (*Hirakhand Samachar* September 1946). They even questioned the alleged benefit of supplying irrigation facility to the dry, less fertile land by submerging the most fertile land of the region. Instead, they proposed the renovation of old water harvesting structures for irrigation. It was even said that once electricity was extracted from the water, the water would lose its vitality for agriculture.

When all suggestions of alternatives fell on deaf ears, a section of the Anti-Dam Committee floated the idea of separation from Odisha so as to escape the impending danger of the dam. Articles in *Hirakhand Samachar* discussed how the people of Sambalpur were different from Oriyas in terms of language and culture, practices and customs, history and geography:

> Just as water and oil cannot mix, Katkias and Sambalpurias cannot mix too. (*Hirakhand Samachar* October 1946)

In effect, the anti-dam movement questioned the foundation of Odia nationality along with its shared history, common language and cultural affinity of the Odia-speaking tract that had been assiduously built since the late nineteenth and early twentieth centuries (Dash 2005). The Congress government alleged the demand to secede from Odisha was primarily a machination of the princely states, especially that of Patna state (now Balangir district). However, the anti-dam movement and the demand for a separate state became enmeshed, giving way to the battle cry: 'Stop Hirakud Dam and Odisha, Hands off Sambalpur.'[6] This battle cry led to one of the most militant anti-dam protests. The events that followed the formation of the Bandha Virodhi Committee in August 1946 lasted a year.

The movement was weakened by some of its leaders. One of the leaders, Sradhakar Supakar, reflected in later years:

> Some senior lawyers, who had joined in the movement, refused to take part in satyagraha at the last moment because at that time a big civil suit was going on in Sambalpur court. Big lawyers like Achyutananda Purohit and Bodhram Dube were advocates for either of the parties. In such a situation, if they were arrested due to satyagraha, they would have lost huge fees, which was not acceptable to them. (Supakar 1982)

Pundit Laxminarayan Mishra was a member of the Odisha legislative assembly. On behalf of the movement, he went and met Mahatma Gandhi in East Bengal for his blessings for the movement. But, he took a somersault and became an opponent of the movement. He was even appointed by the government to propagate the benefits of the dam. It is still a mystery what exactly transpired. He went from Khariar to Baripada, Baripada to Paralakhemundi and Paralakhemundi to Balangir propagating benefits of the dam (Supakar 1982).

The president of the Anti-Dam Committee wrote to the Deputy Commissioner that the Committee was dissolved and he would not be held responsible for any satyagraha in future. In a shocking turn of events, Achyutananda Purohit assumed the office of the government lawyer and stood against the people of the submerged area in their legal battle for better compensation. Bodhram Dube too became the government advocate in the Odisha High Court towards the end of 1948.

As Nehru delivered the midnight speech about India's tryst with destiny, anti-dam protestors were languishing in Sambalpur jail. They awaited their destiny of being destitute in free India. It was not happening for the first time in India.

The Mulshi Satyagraha, which began in April 1921, was in protest against a dam proposed by the Tata Hydro-electric Power Supply Company Limited for generation of hydro-electricity in Pune district of Maharashtra. The dam was going to be constructed on the confluence of Mula and Nila Rivers to supply electricity to the textile mills, factories and railways in Bombay. In March 1919, the Bombay government approved the project and served notice for land acquisition in June. Soon, the fifty-two villages of Mulshi Peta that were going to be submerged began a satyagraha with a resolve not to leave the land but die. Although the Mulshi Satyagraha drew the attention of the INC and Gandhi expressed concern, neither did he visit the area nor oppose the Tata project. The satyagraha continued intermittently till 1924 but could not withstand the oppression of the colonial government and Tata's money and muscle power. Finally, the dam was built.

The fifty-two villages that were submerged were resettled near the dam without electricity. A primary school was all they had in the name of education. The villagers had to contend with severe scarcity of water in summer. With a reservoir of water before their eyes, the villagers had to go without drinking water. The hamlets which had been moved to make place for a project meant to generate electricity were themselves in darkness (Vora 2009).

The plight of the oustees of Hirakud became the same, if not worse. Let's see their journey into the wilderness.

Broken Promises

> The government had promised to give all facilities available in the original village. But the ME school was made only after we sat on a fast-unto-death and electricity reached us after 23 long years! Such was our fate that wherever we went, people called us *budianchalia* (people from submerged area) and viewed us with suspicion as if we were thieves. We were no longer human beings, we became *budianchalia* forever. It is a name and a stigma that we still bear. (Lakhpati Pradhan)

With the crushing down of the movement, the government machinery made loud proclamations about its offers of compensation and rehabilitation. A house and land for land for those displaced became official propaganda. A brochure with pictures of a model village, good houses, roads and hand pumps was widely distributed. The radio played a song sung by the famous singer Nimain Harichandan, urging people to step back and leave space for the deity of prosperity coming to reside at Hirakud. Broadcast by the department of publicity, the song assured the people that the Hirakud project would bring laurels to the country, would make stars shine and would feed the hungry and rebuild their homes.

While writing on the Hirakud Dam Project Report, Khosla had also drawn a rosy picture for those displaced:

> The policy of the government in respect of compensation should be to give, as far as possible, land in exchange for land and that too well ahead of actual submergence. The compensation, in kind or cash, should be on terms which are equitable and, if anything, generous. Government should assist the people in rehabilitation and strive to create conditions in the new colonies, which should be a definite improvement on the existing ones. This can be

> done by setting up model villages and providing them with essential amenities of life like drinking water, sanitation, public schools, community centres, electricity, etc. Any expenditure on such improvements, which is in excess of the compensation allowance in the project, should be met from general revenue as a contribution towards raising the standard of living of the people. (Khosla 1947)

The rhetoric and songs and false promises evaporated on 2 April 1948 when the first village was displaced. Twenty-four adivasi-dalit families of a small village called Jamada on the lap of the Mahanadi were forcibly evacuated without any talk of house or land for land. Ten days later, Nehru laid the foundation stone of the project for the second time with the same lies: displaced would be provided with land for land and house for house, and a generous compensation. Perhaps, the people of Jamada were cursing their fate under a banyan tree and piecing together their broken lives to make a new beginning:

> Our sufferings had no end. We came here by a truck and brought some rice and paddy with us. But it did not last long. There were times when we had nothing to cook and went to sleep on an empty stomach. To keep our thatched house warm, we used to keep a fire pot in the house. Our poverty was such that if my father-in-law brought paddy from the field in the evening, we immediately boiled and spread it on the veranda to dry. The next morning, it was husked by the *dhenki* and cooked. This situation continued at least for ten years. In those days, there was no motor vehicle to commute. We had to walk miles and miles even to buy rice, salt or oil. There were dense forests all around. We could not even go to the *katta* to take a bath alone. Elephants were on the prowl. (A woman at Mura camp)

The assembly proceeding of January 1950 mentions that the people of Jamada were given compensation of Rs 519 for twenty-seven acres and seventy-six decimals of land after one year, that is, on 14 April 1949. That means 18.12 *anna* per acre and 3 *anna* per decimal. All the stalwarts from Mahatab to Nabakrushna Choudhury and Sadasiv Tripathy believed this to be a generous compensation! Interestingly, Mahatab justified it by taking recourse to a special Act enacted for land acquisition of the Hirakud project. This Act stipulated that there would be an agreement between the government officials and the peasants on the rate of compensation and the aggrieved peasant could go to the court for redressal:

> As I have already said the compensation is paid with the agreement of the parties. If the parties did not agree, it was open to them to come to court. But as it appears, this compensation is at the rate of 300 times the deduced rent that is to say much more than the ordinary rates provided in the Land Acquisition Act. (Supakar 1988)

The Act not only wiped out even any semblance of uniformity in compensation, but also forced the most vulnerable peasants to make an 'agreement' with mighty government officials fed on a diet of imperial bread. People made an agreement and moved to a new colony as promised. Eighty-five-year-old Lakhpati Pradhan at the Mura Rehabilitation Camp relives the pain and trauma as he recalls:

> Police and government officials forced us to accept compensation arbitrarily decided by them. It was like: accept it or go to the dogs. What could we do? We had no other option but to accept and leave our village as soon as we could. We were ordered to go and see the place of our rehabilitation. We went all the way crying. The jungle was our rehabilitation camp. We built small huts thatched with date leaves and straws. You would not believe if we say that tigers and elephants were prowling near our huts. Tigers often pounced on our calves near our huts. After sunset, nobody moved out of the hut. We had no kerosene to even light a lantern. People would finish with their dinners before sunset. There were days when we lived on chewing tender bamboo stalks. Once I spent the whole day in the jungle chewing bamboo stalks and fainted from hunger. Men and women went into jungle to dig roots and collect leaves and bamboo stalks. We boiled it, cleared the water and had it with salt and chilly. The drinking water was mud red in colour. There was nothing else to do but drink it.

Where was the generous compensation proclaimed on radio? Mahatab, who was at the helm of affairs in Odisha from 1946 to 1950 and 1957 to 1961, wrote an editorial (*Gan Majlis*) in *Prajatantra* on 1 January 1964 in which he revealed that nearly 50,000 real peasants of Sambalpur did not get much compensation. More than two decades later, the government of Odisha admitted in the assembly on 26 March 1987 that 9,913 *rayats* (those possessing record of rights) had not yet been given compensation. The Committee on Government Assurances (1989–1990) visiting Sambalpur area noted that compensation for the lands and houses was paid at ridiculously low rates of Rs 100, Rs 50 and Rs 10 per acre. There is no record available as to how many people were left out of compensation. We met Durga Prasad Nayak, a retired Economics Professor in Sambalpur. He pointed out to us:

> The worst sufferers were the *jhankar* (worshippers of village goddess), *chowkidar*, *nariha* (belonging to milkman caste and their job was to look after government officials when touring the villages), *dhobi* (washermen) and *bhandari* (barbers). They were providing services to the villagers and were cultivating lands in lieu of that. The government decided not to give a single pie to them as they were only service tenure holders. After much protest, it decided to pay 50 per cent of the compensation as late as 6 January 1956. The implementation took its own time to pass through the serpentine route of bureaucracy. By then most of the villages had been forcibly evacuated and the government did not have any record of their whereabouts. The compensation amount kept lying in the government treasury. When the government decided to disburse it, a few people came forward to accept. The amount was so meagre that even their expenses on bus fares would not have been met by this.

To drive the last nail into the coffin, the government deducted 20 per cent of compensation money (5 per cent for *gountias* and 15 per cent towards welfare in the rehabilitation colony). Besides, the government decided the rate of compensation on the basis of the settlement of the year 1925. Thus, the hard labour of *rayats* of the following twenty-five years in making the land arable and fertile was overlooked. Secondly, any objection to the rate of compensation decided by the land acquisition officer had to be filed within seven days. But such interventions were kept pending for years without any arbitration.

It was yet another ingenuous expression of government generosity to deprive even more people of compensation.

All villages had been evicted by the summer of 1956. The reservoir was filling in that monsoon the first time. On 25 September 1956, the chief minister admitted in the assembly that 2,540 cases had not been referred to any arbitrator. Clearly, those with objections had also been evicted. Some big landowners went up to the Supreme Court and got compensation at market rates. Obviously, they had the means to continue prolonged legal battles over the years. This was unthinkable for the displaced majority.

Another tall promise of the government was to provide land for land for the displaced people who did not want monetary compensation. The department of publicity went hoarse announcing that 99,000 acres of lands had already been identified, of the total requirement of 120,000 acres, as on 13 March 1950. However, the reality was different. By the end of April 1956, the government announced that it had managed to evict 15,000 families and acquire 147,363 acres of fertile land. Only 1,410 families were allotted 3,790 acres of barren land (Quoted in Supakar 1982). The best quality of land was forcibly acquired at a rate less than Rs 100 per acre, whereas lower quality land near the rehabilitation centre was sold to the displaced people for more than Rs 1,000 per acre. Only those who could afford such rates with their compensation and hard earned savings could buy. As people say, 'The land was of such quality that it was fit for foxes to shit but not for cultivation.'

People became further pauperized making the land cultivable:

> We were promised five acres of cultivable land. But we got two-three acres after depositing Rs 1,000. That too, the land was not levelled. To make it cultivable, we became paupers. When we reached the camp, there was nothing but the forest all around. So, except the forest department, there was no sign of existence of any government department. It was the exact reverse of our original village where there was a primary health centre, a Middle English (ME) school, a veterinary centre, an excise department and many other offices. Many old people died within two to three years, pining for the old village. Here in the colony the government only cleared the jungle and allotted plots to families. Stumps of big trees were still standing and were thinly covered with soil to give the impression of cultivable land. Till date the stumps are there and water runs through the dead roots. It is not fit for cultivation. (Group Interview at Mura camp)

Khosla in his report had recommended a model village and housing facility. The government implemented it so sincerely that not a single soul came to live in it:

> Towards the end of December 1947, a notification was issued to acquire 200 acres of land near Larpanka. The land belonged to me. The idea was to build a model village for 60 villagers evacuated from Jamada and twenty gountias. Two designs of the house were prepared; one for the ordinary villagers and the other for gountias. The proposed model village was to be completed by March 1948. In the first phase, sixty houses were built. Each house was of 8 × 8 feet having three rooms; 3 × 4 feet width veranda, both on front and back of the house. It was impossible for a family of four to five members to live in such a small house along with domestic animals, agricultural implements and other household goods. When people of Jamada saw these houses they did not come to live here. The houses remained unused for years. They became a den of thieves and miscreants. Subsequently, they collapsed. It was the first and last model village. (Nayak 2004)

Local people did suffer 'for the country' as Nehru wanted them to. They had no opportunity to share the fruits of the project either as contractors or as daily labourers:

> Punjabi and Sindhi contractors were brought in from Delhi. Even daily wage-labourers were brought in from Punjab. Odisha was supplying Sal sleepers for railway lines all over India. But when railway lines were laid from Sambalpur Station to Burla and Hirakud, sleepers were supplied from Punjab. Even buffaloes were also fetched from Punjab to pull the rollers on the canal road. (Behera 2011)[7]

The Exodus

> There were 6,000 men, not counting women and children. A large number of other people and many sheep, goats and cattle also went with them. They baked unleavened bread from the dough that they had brought out of Egypt so suddenly that they did not have time to get their food ready or to prepare leavened dough. (Old Testament)

As the construction work progressed, the fear of leaving one's own land, the uncertainty of a new place and the resentment at the injustice done gripped the elders. Children had their own nightmares too. Karunakor Bhoi recalls:

> We as children could not understand much what was going on. But we had heard rumours that children were being stolen away and sacrificed at the dam site. So, when we saw any government vehicle coming to our village—whether we were playing or plucking mangoes or blackberries—we would run and run. Such vehicles were called *Churni* motor (a motor vehicle that stole away the children). We would shout '*churni motor aasilla churni aasilla*' and flee as fast as we could in sheer terror. We were told that the dam needed human heads and blood to stay put. At times, we had nightmares that our heads were being sliced and blood being offered to the dam.
>
> Finally, the day to leave arrived.
>
> It is beyond words to express the feelings of separation from our land, which is our mother, and from our near and dear ones. Even today after so many years, our eyes well up remembering those times. It was heart-breaking. The entire atmosphere was filled with sobs and cries. My paternal aunt's family went to Raigarh in Chhattisgarh, another family went to Brajaraj Nagar. We were separated and strewn all around. I cannot describe what it was like.

It was the months of April and May 1955. The first batch of villages was to be evacuated. By then, 149 villages had not been given compensation. Leaders like Prasanna Panda were mobilizing people around the demand of compensation before eviction. The administration prohibited them from entering villages by declaring Section 144 of Cr.P.C. The armed police also began flag marches in the villages to be submerged, striking fear and terror. The gentle murmurs of the river were rent by 'Leave the village, leave the village.' People began to dismantle their houses piece by piece by their own hands to salvage something from the impending deluge. Many took with them a handful of earth from the original village to keep with them till death. Some were overcome by emotion and were moving reluctantly or were a bit slow at the moment of parting from their village. They were slapped and kicked by the police before being thrown like gunny bags into the trucks.

Elderly women cursed the government and wished the dam would collapse by the weight of their tears. Mitrabhanu Khamari in his poem *Budi Anchala Durdasa* (Wretched condition of submerged area) in 1957 gives a graphic description of the police atrocity and the trauma of leaving villages.—

The process of evacuation continued in full swing through the summer months of 1956; the reservoir had to be filled up the following monsoon. People were not even given enough time to leave. Seventy-eight-year-old Kunjabihari Pradhan of Duanmunda remembers:

> Our village was given three days' notice to vacate. On the fourth day, armed police in two vehicles reached our village at around 11 am. We had not seen such a large force in the village before. It was terrifying. We began to pack simply out of fear. Our village *gountia* ran away crying with only rice pots, leaving behind all other belongings. He could barely save himself, what could he do for us?

On the one hand, there was no compensation money; on the other, people had to leave at gun point like war prisoners. They left with whatever belongings they could manage to carry. Domestic animals were let loose. Some of the well-off families settled in Sambalpur town; some went to their relatives. Those who could go nowhere walked miles and miles to the rehabilitation camps. Thousands and thousands of people moved to the offshore of the reservoir to settle down in what is known as periphery village in government records. The Assurance Committee opined:

> The site for rehabilitation of displaced persons was made wrongly as a result of which out of seventeen proposed colonies people only moved to seven. That too against their own desire. Had they been able to find out alternative source of rehabilitation, they would not have gone to these seven colonies constructed by the government without any planning. (Assurance Committee 1989)

The Story of Unending Misery

Barun Kumra (age 90) of Banharipali says:

> The Hirakud dam had swallowed up some of our land. But the village was saved. Our family had still twenty acres of land. The Ib thermal plant took away that too, along with the village. Once we were a landed family. Within thirty years, we lost everything. Two government projects made us landless, homeless and village-less. We became servants of the company from being free peasants on our own land.
>
> The Ib thermal plant gave Rs 30,000 per acre and one job to each family as compensation. I had a son, but he died. So I signed a will to give my job to someone from Jajpur district with the condition that he would take care of my maintenance. For that he has been giving me Rs 700 since 1995. At that time his salary was about Rs 7,000–8,000. It must have increased manifold by now, but still I am getting the same amount for my maintenance. We were shifted to this place. It was a transit camp just across the boundary of the Orissa Power Grid Corporation (OPGC) campus. But the company converted it into a rehabilitation colony by adding one more hut. Now we are living here. I think it was written in our destiny.

Villagers of Duanmunda say that though they have been living there since 1956, they do not have any record. As a result, they are deprived of the facilities available at the panchayat or block level. Since 1957, the villages have been demanding the revenue status. Kunja Bihari Pradhan sadly says, 'The fact is that the government did not consider us as human beings. It just played with us.'

Gopinath Majhi, the leader of Budi Anchal Sangram Samiti, Lakhanpur, narrating the ongoing problems of periphery villages, says:

> Though it was planned that the reservoir level would be 630 feet, land was acquired up to 632 feet. Periphery villages are those 46 villages that exist within this difference of two feet. The people of these villages moved to the offshore of the reservoir. Human settlements were there but not on revenue records—a village without a post office. Around 1964–65, there was a big

> movement when these lands were proposed to be handed over to a Russian farm company. The company had begun its work at Lacchipali. Sometimes, it is heard that the land would be transferred to some plantation company. This land is like an orphan. People have managed to hold on to it because of their organization and protest. The day people would sleep off, the land would go out of their hands simply because it did not exist on revenue records.

In the year 1985, when the government decided to establish a thermal power plant at Banharipali, it was like a bolt from the blue for the people living in the peripheral villages. Despite people's protest under the leadership of Prasanna Panda, the government displaced them once again.

Although irrigation facility was one of the objectives of the dam, none was provided. The peasantry of the Hirakud command area is now waging a struggle for access to water. Since 2005, the government of Odisha has been selling water to industrial houses. When water did not reach the lower end of the canal, people discovered that companies were directly drawing water from the reservoir through intake wells. On 26 October 2006, 20,000 peasants formed a human chain from one end to another end of the reservoir, demanding water for irrigation.

On 7 November 2007, 50,000 peasants participated in a programme, Occupy the Reservoir, to assert their rights over the water of Hirakud Dam for which their forefathers had shed tears and blood. With many barrages being constructed by the government of Chhattisgarh on the upper reaches of the Mahanadi, the fight for the reservoir water has intensified since the last two years.

The Supreme Sacrifice

In the well-known poem *Dharmapada*, Gopabandhu Das narrates the story of Konark by extolling the supreme sacrifice of the protagonist for the sake of the larger community. The story goes thus:

> King Langula Narasinha Dev wished to build a gigantic temple in honour of the Sun God for which 1,200 sculptors were engaged. They worked for twelve years without going home. One day, the king inspected the work and gave two days' time to complete the task. 'Else, all would be beheaded,' thundered the king. It struck terror among the sculptors. The final task was to fix a pitcher on the crest of the temple. The sculptors were unable to do this due to some technical flaw in the design of the temple.

At this juncture, Dharmapada, a twelve-year-old boy came to meet his father Bisu Maharana. He did not know his father by appearance because his mother was only four-months pregnant when his father had left home. Finally, he met his father and it was a moment of joy for both of them. But their happiness was short-lived as the king's diktat struck terror in their hearts. As Dharmapada listened to everything, he asked his father whether he too could participate in the meeting of the sculptors. Both son and father went to the meeting together. Dharmapada requested the assembly of the sculptors to allow him to see the work. After inspecting the site meticulously, he assured them that he would fix the problem. They agreed to the proposal, but they feared that if the king got to know that a twelve-year-old accomplished the task, all the sculptors would be beheaded. Dharmapada succeeded in his mission. Thus, the prestige of the clan of sculptors was redeemed. However, the question that haunted them was that if he remained alive, he would be felicitated by the king and the sculptors would have to pay for it with their lives. It was a moral dilemma: the life of an individual versus the entire community. Dharmapada finally took a call to save his clan. He went atop the temple and jumped into the sea. (Adapted from Das 1980)

Was Nehru familiar with *Dharmapada*?

Nehru had said at the inauguration: 'If you have to suffer, you have to suffer in the interest of the country.' Indeed, the supreme sacrifice of thousands of landless and small peasants who were uprooted from their home and hearth was called for the great Hirakud enterprise to be accomplished.

Years after the tryst with destiny, we went on moving from one end to the other of the reservoir that Nehru had flown over, meeting people of submerged villages and listening to their unmitigated tales of misery, deceit and betrayal. The reservoir seemed vast and unending. The crest of a submerged temple had risen above the water. The temple stood on the spot that once was Mura village. Some birds were twittering. A few were perched on the crest in meditative silence. It was a moment of epiphany. We were reminded of a poem by Saroj that asks a bird:

Do the souls of villages that drowned
Beckon you to the crest of the temple?
Do the trunks of those fallen trees call you
On whose dry branches your ancestors had once perched?
Had you ever asked them

What was the look on Nehru's face
When so many villages were buried in the reservoir-coffin?
What did Nabakrushna Choudhury do
When people were thrown into trucks
Like gunny bags at gun point? (Saroj 2014)

Notes

1. Harekrushna Mahatab was a freedom fighter and also a leader of the Indian National Congress. He was the Chief Minister of Odisha from 1946 to 1950 and from 1956 to 1961.
2. Nayak was a deputy magistrate under colonial administration. He became an active member of the Bandha Virodhi Committee after retirement. After one year of the movement, he initiated a legal battle for better compensation. His autobiography *Mora Purbasmruti Katha* devotes a full chapter to the anti-dam movement. The autobiography was serialized for five years in an Odia monthly magazine *Navjeevan*. It was first published in the year 1966.
3. Sradhakar Supakar was one of the popular leaders of the anti-dam movement. He won the election to the Odisha Assembly from Ganatantra Parishad and continued to fight for the rehabilitation of oustees. His autobiography *Madhyama Purusa* sheds much light on the various aspects of the movement.
4. Prasanna Panda (19.06.1922–26.12.1997) was a student of Fine Arts in Kolkata. He became one of the most prominent leaders of the anti-dam movement. He joined CPI in 1952 and was elected to the Odisha assembly six times from the Brajrajnagar constituency. He remained committed to the rehabilitation of Hirakud oustees till his death. He is remembered fondly till today; a statue and memorial have been made for him in his village Adhapara.
5. The Report stated: 'Orissa is a deltaic country and in such a country floods are inevitable; they are nature's method of creating new land and it is useless to attempt to thwart her in her working. The problem in Orissa is not how to prevent floods, but how to pass them as quickly as possible to the sea. And the solution lies in removing all obstacles which militate against this result.... To continue, as at present, is merely to pile up a debt which will have to be paid, in distress and calamity at the end.'
6. During 1895–1905, Sambalpur had successfully demanded to be part of Odisha. It was under the Central Province of the British administration. The Odia nationality project had already taken a concrete shape when Utkal Sammilani was formed in the year 1903 (see Introduction). In 1936, just a decade before the proposal of Hirakud Dam, Odisha finally became a separate province. However, seeing the turn of events where their lands and livelihoods were going for a toss in nation-building, the anti-dam movement

questioned both Odia nationalism and development and made a demand for a separate province. Till date, the demand continues to be made in response to the abject neglect of the region.

7. Bhubaneswar Behera began his professional life as a young hydraulic engineer in the construction of Hirakud Dam who had studied in USA. Written in a fictional style, the autobiography of Behera narrates interesting aspects of construction works and bemoans how Odias are being neglected.

References

Achebe, Chinua. 1994. *An Interview with Jerome Brooks*. The Paris Review. The Art of Fiction, No. 139. Issue 133. Winter.

Behera, Bhubaneswar. 2011. *Ganra Daka (Appeal of the village)*. Cuttack: Grantha Mandir.

Committee on Government Assurances. 1989–1990. Government of Odisha. September.

D'Souza, Rohan. 2006. *Damned and Drowned: Colonial Capitalism and Flood Control in Eastern India*. New Delhi: Oxford University Press.

———. 2008. Framing India's Hydraulic Crisis: the Politics of the Modern Large Dam. *Monthly Review* 60 (3): 112–124.

Dash, Debendra Kumar, ed. 2005. *Utkal Sammilani (1903–1936)*. Rourkela: Pragati Utkal Sangha.

Das, Gopabandhu. 1980. Dharmapada. In *Part One: Poetical Works*, ed. Radhamohan Gadnayak. Bhubaneswar: Odisha Sahitya Academy.

Hirakhand Samachar. 10 September 1946. Balangir.

Hirakhand Samachar. 17 September 1946. Balangir.

Hirakhand Samachar. 24 September 1946. Balangir.

Hirakhand Samachar. 15 October 1946. Balangir.

Hirakhand Samachar. 5 November 1946. Balangir.

Hirakhand Samachar. 7 January 1947. Balangir.

Hunter, W.W. 1872. *Orissa, or the Vicissitudes of an Indian Province under Native and British Rule*. London: Smith, Elder & Co.

Khamari, Mitrabhanu. 1957. *Budi Anchala Durdasa* (Wretched Condition of Submerged Area). Sambalpur.

Khosla, A.N. 1947. *Mahanadi Valley Development, Hirakud Dam Project*. CWINC, Simla Press.

Nayak, Bharat Chandra. 2004. *Mora Purbasmruti Katha*. Cuttack: Agraduta.

Orissa or the Vicissitudes of an Indian Province under Native and British Rule. 1872. Vol. II. London.

Padgaonkar, Dileep. 2008. *Under Her Spell: Roberto Rossellini in India*. New Delhi: Viking Penguin.

Rangaiya, M.G. 1946. *A Note on the Hirakud Project across the Mahanadi*. Sambalpur.

Saroj. 2014. *Tu Thibu Re Pakshi*. Bhubaneswar: Nisan.

Supakar, Sradhakar. 1982. *Madhyama Purusa*. Cuttack: Cuttack Writer's Co-operative Ltd.

———. 1988. Itihasara Parihas (Mockery of History).

Vora, Rajendra. 2009. *The World's First Anti-Dam Movement-The Mulshi Satyagraha (1920–1924)*. Permanent Black.

Young, Captain C.B. *Officiating Chief Engineer, Lower Provinces, to the Secretary to the Government of Bengal, Fort William, no. 5364, 1st December 1857*. Papers Relative to the Rivers of Cuttack, Part I, Calcutta, 1860, p. 159. Quoted in D'Souza.

CHAPTER 3

What the King Gave Happily

The struggle of man against power is the struggle of memory against forgetting.
—Milan Kundera, 1981

My mother was very fond of our ox named Nila. She was the one who used to feed him most times of the day. Nila had become so spoilt that he would not even touch food, however hungry he was, unless my mother caressed and pampered him. When we were leaving our village Bhatsingh, sometime in June 1984, we brought Nila along with us. The new place where we had moved in had neither enough space nor sufficient means for us to build a shed for him and he had to be tied to a stake in the open, exposed to the torrential rains. We were barely able to look after or protect ourselves from the vagaries of nature. All our precious little belongings were strewn around in the open. Our relatives had given us their verandah to live in. There was only one large makeshift shed on the verandah where we all used to huddle together. Everything else was in the open. Sometimes a stray dog would prowl in to sniff at the rice pot. With the monsoons arriving, the going got even tougher. There was no place where we could take Nila to protect him from the rains, which was sometimes accompanied with frightening thunder and lightning. Seeing him in these pitiable conditions, my mother would weep copiously, the tears making the corner of her saree dripping wet. Finding it difficult to take proper care of him, we decided to set him free. We feared that he might trespass into other people's houses and fields. He chose to disappear from our sight as soon as we untethered him. We searched for him everywhere and finally gave up the search. He was not to be found anywhere.

R. Padhi, N. Sadangi, *Resisting Dispossession*,
https://doi.org/10.1007/978-981-15-0717-5_3

Our sorrows deepened. But a few days later, we were told by someone that Nila was spotted in our old village, at least 30 kilometers away from our new settlement. He had travelled back to his old familiar abode. We were told he would graze in and around the village and come back in the evenings to sleep at the same spot where he always used to. The water had receded from the village but nothing of our old mud house had remained. Two months later, we got to know that he had died on the same spot where he used to sleep. Nila chose to embrace the eternal sleep exactly where he wanted to. The longing for that piece of earth had taken Nila there. Three years later my mother too died longing for Nila and that same piece of land. It's not just humans but also animals who suffer the trauma of displacement.

People lost everything they had and never managed to pick up the threads of life again. They could never overcome the trauma of being displaced from the space they had inhabited for generations. We were like cursed souls who forever came to bear the label of *budianchalia* on our foreheads. Yes, *budianchalia*, the displaced people from submerged area. That's what we were called ... that's what we were referred to as. Wherever we went the tag never left us. It never let us erase the memories of that traumatic experience that we had to go through in some distant past. There is no one who does not carry that pain even until today. They might pretend to have forgotten and not talk about it but they carry it deep within.

Those were the times when the figure of mother was the fulcrum of your life. There were two mothers. One who gave you birth; the other was the village-mother—the village where you were born, where you grew up playing in its soil, where you learnt to embrace sorrow and laughter, and love and dreams. We knew that the mother who gave you birth would one day die; but your village-mother was imperishable. These were the values we had imbibed from our elders and we cherished them and believed in them. So suddenly when we were forced to leave our village-mother, it came as a shock. The feeling was so overwhelming that it almost left us numb. We are at an utter loss for words when some say that we were compensated for the losses. Really? Is it something that can be tallied in a balance sheet and weighed in terms of loss here and gain there?

So different people opted for different coping mechanisms. Those who were more sentimental did not pursue the fight for enhanced compensation and so on. Perhaps letting go of some just demands helped them in keeping their pride and dignity intact. Perhaps, they also wanted to forget that suffering and did not want their children to relive it despite their economic hardships.

This was Ranjan Sahu, who is today a government advocate based in Deogarh. Some friends had said that he would help us get in touch with people from submerged villages for our interviews. Little had we realized then that Ranjan himself was a survivor of the calamity that had befallen the people of the region because of the Rengali Dam project. A couple of days later as we were leaving Deogarh by the night bus, Ranjan dropped in to bid goodbye to us. We could see the bus waiting from our hotel. And Ranjan recounted these poignant tales from more than 30 years ago. We sat and listened to him in benumbed quietude. He broke down several times while narrating, measuring his words every now and then to convey the emotional weight of his feelings.

> I still remember those days. I was a student then. I had just appeared for matriculation examination. I was young and at a juncture in life, where the worries of the world had not yet begun to weigh on my shoulders. I had no such worries as: how would I arrange my livelihood or manage my family. My father was still alive and working and was getting a monthly salary as a school teacher. All worries were his; not yet mine. Yet life was testing me in other ways. I remember feeling humiliated having to live on other people's verandas—the deep pain of being a refugee in your own land. We spent six months like that. I also had to undergo the pain of dismantling my own house with my own hands, loading the dismantled pieces of it, that was our home, onto a truck; a home where I was born, a home where my mother had prayed to the Goddess *Sathi* for my long life and wellbeing. When the truck was ready to depart, the rest of the families from the village gathered and cried together. Not just women, even men cried out aloud. It had become such a tragic scene that it is still etched in my memory. When finally, the time came to leave we all went and paid obeisance to our village goddess, whose abode was on the edge of the village boundary. It was like a living death.
>
> When we settled at Kulhada, our new settlement, one of the first problems that we faced was the problem of social assimilation. At the new place, we did not have the permission to cut big trees from the jungle for construction of houses. No one lent us bullock carts to carry back the wood from the jungle because we were not one of them. We had to make do with wooden materials we had brought with us from our old village to construct our houses. Some of that material is still lying unused out there. We never threw it away. Perhaps to feel the connect with the past. So many years have passed by, so many new memories have been formed and yet I don't feel as if I belong here; I feel as if I am a guest, a visitor. Ours was a big village, inhabiting 450 families. Now all those families have drifted, gone and settled in 84 separate places at varied distance from each other.

The time for the bus to leave had arrived and our hearts were heavy, listening to this heart rending story. Does the trauma of being uprooted from one's soil ever find a place in the science of building big dams? The rational balance sheet of cost-benefit analysis does not account for this. But people who are rooted to the earth know the cost. For them, it is a story of endless suffering.

And Quiet Flows the Brahmani

The Brahmani River originates from the confluence of the South Koel and the Sankha, at Vedavyasa, near the steel city of Rourkela. After traversing 540 kilometres across the State of Odisha, it empties itself into the Bay of Bengal at a place called Dhamra. Once the confluence was the prettiest spot in the Princely State of Gangpur (*The Imperial Gazetteer of India* 1908). So, it was natural that it would produce its own folklore: The sage Parashar fell in love with Matsyagandha, the daughter of a fisherman at this place. Vyasadev, the author of the sacred texts of the Hindus, *Vedas* and the Mahabharata, was born of their union. The famous Odia poet, Gangadhar Meher, celebrates this union of high and low caste in his poem, *Vedavyasa*. Interestingly, the poem notes the large presence of fisherfolk in Odisha, who are believed to be the descendants of Matsyagandha's father (Meher 2006). While religious mythology elevated Matsyagandha to Satyabati for her relationship with the Brahmin sage and she was regarded as the great matriarch of the Mahabharata, the fate of her descendants was different. Centuries later, her own people, the fisherfolk—the jharas, the koibortas and the dhibaras—were to be sacrificed at the altar of the temples of modern India.

As if cut off from their umbilical cord, they were scattered everywhere. As we went tracing the story of the Brahmani-Rengali Dam, we came face to face with them all too often. They can be found at the site of a satyagraha, protesting to claim their land; at the rehabilitation colonies deep inside the jungle; at the roadside *bastis* and at hotels and *dhabas* in Deogarh town, doing menial jobs. They came to be labelled as the people of *Budianchala* (submerged area)—victims of displacement of the Rengali project.

Taming the Turbulent Brahmani

After the Hirakud Dam came up on the Mahanadi, it was the turn of the Brahmani River to be tamed. The demand for dams was gaining popular and wider support since 1961 itself, when Utkal Banya Sammilani (Odisha Flood Conference) was floated to demand for construction of dams on the

Brahmani and Baitarani Rivers as the permanent solution to the state's recurring flood problems.

Banka Behari Das wrote in his memoirs how floods would come and go; relief would be disbursed and people would accept it as beggars. He went on to say that it was more essential to organize a movement for the permanent solution of the flood problem (Das 1998).[1] In this, he was not any different from many others who thought that dams were the only solution. However, what he probably failed to foresee was that the 'permanent solution' that he was advocating for was going to lead to permanent destitution of the same 'beggars.' Should it not have been obvious from the experience of Hirakud?

In June 1971, in a conference of irrigation ministers of all Indian states held at Srinagar, in the backdrop of the devastating deltaic flood that year, the demand for the Rengali project was resurrected with greater vigour. It was decided that two multipurpose dams in Odisha would be built—one at Rengali on Brahmani and another at Bhimkund on Baitarani. Dr K.L. Rao—the then union minister of state for irrigation and power—went on a tour of the flood-hit areas. In August 1971, he announced that both dams would be built at the earliest to save the people of Odisha from recurrent floods.

The Bhimkund project was also feasible. But as Nandini Satpathy was then the chief minister of Odisha, she prevailed upon the construction of the Rengali Dam. The land area to be benefited in the downstream was part of her assembly constituency and the submergence was to occur in Deogarh sub-division of undivided Sambalpur district (Sahu 2012).[2]

Thus, the second multipurpose dam on another deltaic river became a reality, especially with the then Prime Minister Indira Gandhi laying the foundation stone on 23 December 1973. The construction work that started in 1975 continued till 1985. Located in Rengali village of Dhenkanal district, official statistics claim that 302 villages were submerged and 12,000 families were displaced due to the construction of the dam.

Before we listen to the stories of those whose lives were affected, let's attempt to trace some of the events of the resistance movement.

Threading the Rengali Resistance

Little is known to the rest of the world that the imposition of the National Emergency in June 1975 made it possible for the government to push the construction work despite growing local resistance. It is intriguing that the struggle against the Rengali Dam is not widely known even within Odisha and does not figure in any discussions and deliberations on mass movements. It is this nearly complete lack of information that makes the little documentation done by a few local scholars so valuable. After reading up those documents and talking to people several years later, the picture that emerges here reveals how fierce the resistance to the dam was at one point of time and how ruthless the repression thereof. In our interviews, many stories and accounts came to the fore through people's memories and recall. They supplemented the documentation we read and left us with even more questions.

From early 1971, the news about the Rengali Dam had begun to appear in local dailies. Despite this, no one knew about the height of the dam or the area to be submerged or the number of people to be affected. This created a breeding ground for rumours and confusions, as people had no idea what it held in store for them. Golak Nath, who wrote on the anti-Rengali Dam movement, shared people's perception of the dam:

> One such rumour was that it is impossible to construct a dam on the proposed site because the depth of the water in the river at this spot was immeasurable and that several sea-elephants (sic!) lived there. Another rumour, of course, with a hidden political interest, was that since people of Garhjat area did not render support to the Congress government, formed and dominated by the people from coastal belt of Odisha, the government would drown this area in water. (Nath 2013)

Caught in the whirlpool of rumours and confusion, people seemed immobilized to take any initiative. Some leaders did not hesitate to galvanize the moment for electoral gains. It was mainly the Swatantra Party and the INC, which formed an organization called Rengali Bandha Pratikriya Samiti to oppose the dam. The Samiti was largely dominated by the *gountias*, the big land-owning people of the area. Initially, it confined its activity to sending delegates to meet ministers, submitting memoranda to various authorities, issuing press statements and organizing a few meetings in important villages.

In February 1972, preliminary survey work at the proposed dam site started and the reality of the dam began to seep into people's minds. It became clearer still when Prahallad Mallick, the then state finance minister, declared that a big dam was going to be built at Rengali. The Samiti organized huge protest meetings and got leaders like P.K. Deo, the former king of Kalahandi, and the then president of Swatantra Party from outside the area. Gogua, the largest village of the affected area, became the centre of the resistance movement. A mass meeting of over 15,000 people took place in Gogua on 8 February 1972. The Samiti also tried to extend its activity to the affected part of the Pallahara sub-division by organizing meetings at Gurusulei.

P.K. Deo warned:

> If the government forgets reality and remains adamant on constructing the dam, I will not hesitate to get hand-cuffed by the police in order to save the people from this injustice. (Quoted in Nath 2013)

The Samiti grew vociferous in demanding complete scrapping of the project. At the same time, some important leaders were raising the demand for carving out a separate province in order to stall the project, resonating a similar demand made by those opposing the Hirakud Dam. Towards the end of 1972, rumour went rife that Prime Minister Indira Gandhi was going to lay the foundation stone for the project. The Samiti began gearing itself up to oppose the foundation stone ceremony by showing black flags and organizing demonstrations in front of every government office located in the affected area. Soon this led to a rift in the Samiti itself. The Congress elements in the Samiti did not approve of this strategy, stating that it was futile to oppose the dam and felt that instead it would be far more prudent to fight for better resettlement and rehabilitation. It was also felt that nothing could stall the project as the government was determined to go ahead with it. This resulted in the Samiti breaking up into two groups. While the Swatantra Party members and supporters formed the Bandha Nirodh Committee (BNC) to demand shelving of the project, the Congress formed Punarbasati O Thaithan Samiti for better rehabilitation and resettlement. Shifting of positions led to divisions and rifts. Electoral interests harmed the united struggle when the categorical opposition to the dam gave way to demand for monetary compensation or demand for land for land.

The BNC began to form village-level committees to strengthen its base and appealed to people to be prepared to court arrest, or worst, go to jail to sacrifice for the motherland. The misery of the people displaced by the Hirakud Dam was evoked in every meeting to mobilize popular support.

The former king, P.K. Deo, continued to carry out his fight at the Delhi Durbar by raising objections to the dam proposal in the Lok Sabha and mobilizing MPs to sign a petition addressed to the prime minister. Interestingly, the BNC also articulated an alternative plan to tackle the problem of flood and irrigation. It included building of small dams on the tributaries of the Brahmani River and dredging the mouth of Dhamra, where the Brahmani meets the sea.

However, the proposed alternative plan of BNC fell on deaf ears and the survey work went on unopposed. The Punarbasati O Thaithan Samiti, led by Congress leaders, did not oppose the anti-dam activities openly. Prasanna Kumar Acharya, one of the important leaders of the BNC, said they did 'all sorts of mischief to divide and destabilize the movement.'

Meanwhile, the Congress ministry in the state fell and President's Rule was imposed on 3 March 1973. Thus, there was no government in place to listen to people's grievances. Both the state and the central governments appeared to be in much hurry.

Indira Gandhi finally descended on 23 December 1973 to lay the foundation stone. The BNC, as per its earlier programme, decided to demonstrate at the ceremony waving black flags and court arrest. The administration acted swiftly in preempting and foiling the entire effort. It imposed Section 144 of Criminal Procedure Code (CrPc) on the area. Leaders like Balaram Sahu and P.K. Deo were taken into preemptive custody, and some others were not allowed to reach the ceremony spot. The atmosphere of fear and intimidation created by the administration and the police proved effective despite people's resolve to oppose the dam.

Kishore Patra, 73, from village Barakote remembered:

> Prior to her visit, people who possessed licensed guns were ordered to surrender them at the police station. This scared common people not familiar with political protests. Therefore, many people did not come out to participate in the demonstration.

Leaders of the Deogarh local Congress Committee presented a memorandum to Indira Gandhi at the meeting place. The demonstration did not take place. This greatly demoralized the BNC with organizational activities coming to a standstill for some time. It was only towards the beginning of 1975 that the BNC began to reorganize itself by contacting some leaders from Sambalpur to help the agitation move forward. Pabitra Mohan Pradhan, ex-deputy chief minister, also entered the scene, giving a new lease of life to the fledgling movement. A huge procession, comprising thousands of people, marched to the dam site keeping beat to an energizing slogan:

> *Maribu pachhe chhadibu nahin; Budibu pachhe uthibu nahin*
> [We would rather die but not let go; we would rather drown but not yield]

This was happening at a time when a dark ominous cloud had cast its long shadow on the entire country. The authoritarian hand of the central government suspended the freedom of speech and expression and the freedom to dissent for the next many months by declaring National Emergency on 25 June 1975.

Sudhanshu Mohan Patnaik, one of the leading organizers, said:

> The declaration of Emergency was most fatal for the movement. Pabitra Mohan Pradhan, who was leading the movement, went underground. But the police kept track of organizers like us. We tried to keep contact with people but in hiding. No public activity was possible. At this juncture, the Zonal officials in charge of land acquisition went to the villages. They persuaded and threatened people to take compensation and leave land. I remember one incident in Naikul village where a Zonal land officer was trying to give compensation to Rama Pattanaik. He was a DI. When people got the news, they gathered at his place and had fisticuffs with government officials. But it was not possible to reach each and every village. We had to pay a huge cost because of the Emergency.

Of course, construction activity picked up pace when the National Emergency was imposed. Finally, when the Emergency was lifted and elections were held, most of the leaders of the anti-dam movement got elected from the Janata Party coalition. As promised earlier, some of them tried to persuade the governments at both the central and state levels to scrap the project. A few leaders of the BNC even went to meet Prime Minister Morarji Desai to plead but in vain.

The faith in the Janata Party proved to be misplaced. Perhaps, they did not know what Morarji Desai, as the finance minister of India, had said in

1961 in a public meeting on the submergence zone of the Pong Dam on the Beas river in Himachal Pradesh, then a Union Territory.

> We will request you to move from your houses after the dam comes up. If you move, it will be good; otherwise we shall release the waters and drown you all. (Quoted in McCully 2001)

Having tried all kinds of negotiations with the government, the BNC leadership appealed to people not to accept compensation. It resolved that unless people were properly rehabilitated, it would not allow the government to construct the dam.

On 7 May 1978, a huge public meeting was held at Rengali. It was attended by the Union Minister for Steel and Mines Biju Patnaik, the Chief Minister Nilamani Routray and a few other ministers. When Biju Patnaik stood up to speak, people booed and jeered in protest. He could barely finish his speech. Balaram Sahu, secretary of the BNC, had to intervene to pacify the agitated people, who were in no mood to relent. In his words:

> Anything could be possible. If a slight indication was given, they would have even killed all the ministers present. (Quoted in Nath 2013)

However, Biju Patnaik resorted to a rhetorical promise that became his characteristic style in later years. He said:

> I would first take *pakhal bhaat* and *saag* from your huts in the rehabilitated villages and then only the construction of dam would start. (Quoted in Nath 2013)

Nilamani Routray assured that the mistakes of Hirakud Dam would not be repeated here. They made their speeches and went back to the capital. People also listened and went back home believing in them. Immediately after the meeting, the government of Odisha issued a press note outlining the facilities to be given to the displaced people. One of the important points of this press note was that unless proper rehabilitation of people is done, no area would be allowed to submerge under water. That remained on paper alone.

Meanwhile, the construction work of the coffer dam continued and the water level kept rising higher. The villagers nearest to the dam became certain that their villages would submerge in the approaching monsoons.

Without consulting the leaders of the BNC, they took matters into their hands.

On 11 May 1978, they sat on mass dharna at the dam site. This spontaneous action prodded BNC to mobilize people from other villages. A village-level committee was set up to send one person from each family to participate in the satyagraha. Arrangements were made so that villagers could participate by taking turns. As a result, though some people resisted, many went to participate out of fear (Sahu 2012). The situation was rife with tense anticipation.

The satyagraha continued unabated but by now the BNC had decided to abandon its demand for cancellation of the project. Instead, it began focusing on rehabilitation before completion of the dam. Without engaging in any dialogue with the affected people, the government sent Odisha Military Police on 10 June 1978 to the dam site. Next morning, the BNC leaders sent back *satyagrahis* to villages to mobilize more people to shore up the confidence. But before the people from villages could reach, police had cordoned off the entire area and started its operation.

Bhagirathi Penthei and Gagan Penthei of Kadamdarh settlement colony were present on the day:

> On that fateful day, there was a great gathering of people as well as of the police. The police told the gathering to send their leaders for discussion. But most of our leaders were already arrested. Then the police ordered the gathering to disperse otherwise there would be lathi-charge. There was din and bustle all around. People could not understand what the police announced. Then suddenly, Iswar Pradhan hurled shoes at the police. They in retaliation lobbed teargas shells. It got all smoky. People thought the smoke was from bombs and they began to run helter-skelter. Policemen then began chasing and lathi-charging people. Some sustained injuries from blows, others got injured in the stampede that ensued. Many people were arrested and could come out on bail only after 10–20 days. Afterwards the policemen went around all big villages of the area to arrest the rest of the 'disturbing elements'. Gurusulei, the biggest village in the Pallahad sub-division, bore the maximum brunt of the police operation. Our village had actively participated in the satyagraha at the dam site. One or two months before the start of the satyagraha, the District Collector had once come to persuade us to leave the village and to accept the compensation being offered by the government. In that meeting, Narain Pradhan, our village leader, told the District Collector: 'You're too young to understand what it means to be uprooted from one's soil.' The collector took umbrage at that and we knew they would retaliate. On 13 June just a day before *Raja* Festival, the police force loaded in 18 to

> 19 vehicles reached our village around 2 pm in the afternoon along with the collector, sub-collector and Tahsildar. The entire village was cordoned off. Policemen began house to house search. All the male members were dragged out and herded in an open space outside the village. Only those who managed to flee to the jungle, smelling police raid, were saved. Even women were subjected to harassment. Some 34 male members were arrested and sent to jail. After 15 days, they were released on bail. People became silent after this incident.

The anti-dam protest collapsed after this severe round of police action. As one of the villagers quoted a popular Odia saying, *Maadoku Mahadev Modhya Daranti* (even the great god is terrified of a beating). The repression of that one fateful day, which put an end to the resistance, continues to fester in their memories.

In most interviews in other villages, Gurusulei appeared in different versions of the resistance stories; sometimes with sadness, sometimes as a forbidden tale. While recalling the acts of police brutality of that fateful day, some would mention a rape incident too. In ancient wars or territorial conquests, the history of human civilization is replete with the sexual assault of women. And later it got used in the war of development. The evasive silence of the people of Gurusulei neither acknowledged nor denied the incident. The villagers got quietly drawn into the old overpowering silence and became quiet forever. It's a collective pain they seem to bear along with all else that came their way.

Thrown into the Wilderness

Chaamu jaha dele harase
Paau paau gola borose
Baachi baachi dele padiya
Shraban maaso re bhaange nadiya
Emonto bhuin
Chaakunda bunile uthai nahin. (Kabi Jadumani Quoted in Mahapatra 2006)

[He gave it with glee, the king
But a year went by waiting
The land that He chose with such care
In the wet months, coconuts shatter there
Land for show
Where not even grass will grow]

The dissenting voices had been violently suppressed, and the affected people were left with no hopes but to wait for the day when they would have to leave their lands, villages, rivers and goddesses. They had to leave behind everything dear to them; everything that sustained them materially and emotionally for centuries.

Tormented with all-consuming uncertainties and worries, many families, especially of the middle peasantry, hurriedly arranged marriages of their daughters. The fear that no one might be keen to marry a girl from the families of submerged area (the submerged destitute) added to their anxiety. Thus, many young girls got married in their teens.

The transition also brought some aspirations to the fore. Land-owning families preferred to accept land as compensation so that their world would not descend into chaos. Meanwhile, the landless began hoping they could own some land and live like pradhans who were land-owning peasants and also higher in the caste hierarchy. For the first time in their lives they were seeing a possibility of owning at least three acres of irrigated land, or six acres of un-irrigated land, as was promised in the rehabilitation package. Sudhanshu Mohan Patnaik explains:

> It was understandable why some people emphasized on proper compensation and rehabilitation. Most of the land belonged to 20–25 per cent of people. The landless—mostly jhara, dhoba, khajria, pana, hadi and so on—were another 20–25 per cent. Others had land but it was not sufficient to meet expenses for the upkeep of the family. For example, one family had 2–3 acres of land but had five sons. It was as bad as being landless. So when it was announced that each family would be provided with 6 acres of cultivable land and 50 decimals of homestead land per family, people with small land holdings or no land actually became hopeful that they would lead a better life. Those in favour of proper compensation and rehabilitation were clear too. Pabitra Mohan Pradhan was skeptical and kept saying that better compensation is chimera. It has proved prophetic in our case. We have been completely cheated. The Emergency weakened the movement when it was at its peak. That made it easier for the government not to fully implement the promised resettlement and rehabilitation policy. Even if we presume that the movement could not have succeeded in stopping the dam, we still cannot accept how the government cheated us the way it did.

We went to Kadamdarh colony, which is around 12–13 kilometres from Deogarh, the district headquarters. The place is largely inhabited by jharas—the fisherfolk. As the jeep hurtled through the serpentine, narrow and unpaved road, it felt like a journey into the wilderness and not to a rehabilitation colony where people were supposed to have settled with the promised modern amenities.

When we reached the colony, people were too eager to share memories of their old village, especially those from Gogua. There is always a narrator who carries the story of a community or a common disaster and can recall like none other. Laxman Kumar Penthei, a retired teacher, 72, put facts in some order:

> Our old village was Gogua on the banks of the Brahmani. For jharas, the water of Brahmani was the source of livelihood. We catch fish and ferry people on the waters. You can say we are the river people. When the time came to be evacuated, the zonal officer told us that those who would leave the village first would be provided with one bag of rice each month and would be given good houses, road, electricity, community hall, and water facility. And, most of all, three acres of irrigated, or six acres of un-irrigated cultivable land. We agreed to shift. We thought we had remained backward and inferior by catching fish all our life: *Meena mari helu heena* (catching fish has made us inferior). Now we would become land owning people like the pradhans. With hope in our heart, we shifted to this promised land in the year 1984.
>
> When we reached here, it was almost like a jungle. The area for housing was demarcated for each family. Temporary roads were laid out. There was also a primary school roofed with a tin sheet. Nothing more than that. We who lived so close to water always now had to walk 2–3 kilometers to fetch water. To have a roof over our head, we built up small huts, thatched with straw and twigs. Some of us took shelter under a *mahua* tree, tying a polythene sheet. For the next two years, we managed to survive on whatever we had brought with us from our village and with the compensation money we had got. In 1986, the government allotted six acres of land to each family that was almost 2–3 kilometers away from the settlement across Gohira river. We have to cross the river each time to reach there. In the rainy season, we get completely cut off from our land. But the land was also uncultivable. Even grass did not grow on it. More than 30 years have passed since then, but the government has done nothing to make it cultivable. We are all the time toiling to make ends meet. Where are the resources to make it cultivable? We became pradhans on paper but could not cultivate the land we had. The irony is that we cannot live like jharas anymore. The Brahmani had drifted far away from us. Imagine we now have to go to the market even for a little bit of dry fish.
>
> The only option for us to be able to survive was to cut wood from the jungle and sell it at Deogarh at 15–20 rupees per bundle. If the jungle was

not there, we would have starved. Most of us survive by cutting wood from the jungle till today. We run errands from the jungle past midnight so as to avoid forest officials. Yes, we are aware that it is theft. We return before day break and go to town to sell the wood. The work is so back-breaking that it is not possible to do it on daily basis. Yet, to be able to fill our bellies we cut wood at least 15 to 20 days a month. But if we are caught on our way by the forest guards, our bicycles are seized. We are treated as criminals now.

What we got in reality is nothing but starvation. Thirteen elderly people died of starvation in our colony within the first two years. Managing the family here is so arduous a task. Such is our condition that if we manage to arrange a drop of oil, then arranging a pinch of salt becomes another enormous task, and if salt is somehow arranged, then there is struggle for arranging a fistful of rice.

Earlier, the women did not go to work outside, but now they have to collect *mahua* and pluck *tendu* leaves to earn some money to make ends meet. Some elderly women are having to work at Deogarh town as domestic help for survival, when they should have led a life of rest. After more than 30 years of settlement here, we can only say that our living conditions have worsened.

There is no end to our misery. We do not know what caste we belong to. Since traditionally we are a fishing people, we should be considered Scheduled Caste (SC) or Scheduled Tribe (ST). But the revenue officials do not give us either SC or ST status. Thus we are denied of even basic facilities available to these communities. Now we wonder what we are: jharas or pradhans? SCs or STs or OBCs? Landed or landless?

On the other hand, people of the Pradhan community too shared their tales of woe. When the government offered the option to settle down in the reserved jungle of their choice, groups of villagers went on bicycles with food in their tiffin carriers from one jungle to another to select a place of their choice. They rode from morning to evening in search of good land for cultivation. Those, like the people of Banar, who were unlucky to get suitable land now blame their fate. As one person said:

We chose this land to settle down because we thought it was A-class reserved forest and the soil must have been very fertile because of deposition of humus for centuries. But our hope turned to nightmare after the initial three years when the fertility of the top soil began decreasing. The soil underneath is full of lateritic stones.

An elderly woman laughing at their follies commented:

> Our people were so intelligent in choosing such a nice piece of land that our feet do not get muddied even after heavy rainfall. That is the only benefit we are getting from this land.

If you are pondering over this farce of rehabilitation and compensation that is given in exchange of national progress, we have not yet come to the end. There are categories and categories of hardships, each worse than the other in this story of rehabilitation. There were some pradhans, who chose a piece of land and waited for many years to get to live with a semblance of dignity like pradhans do. In their perception today, they live like the jharas; hence, a notch lower. Let's listen to their story of the Promised Land.

Evicted from Gurusulei, these 40 pradhan families live in the Mahal Marua settlement of Sahargujang revenue village. It is 4–5 kilometres from Batisuan on the Talcher-Pallahara road. Narendra Sahu first gave us a glimpse of the old village:

> Before the Rengali dam came into existence, Gurusulei was the largest village in the entire Pallahara sub-division, having more than 300 families. The village had a high school, a primary health center, an ayurvedic and a veterinary hospital. It was a prosperous village of middle and rich farmers. The average land holding was 7–8 acres of land on the banks of Brahmani and cultivation was the primary occupation. Green pastures along Brahmani supported the cattle economy.

However, rehabilitation brought in many shocks and heartbreaks:

> Around 1982–1983, we left our village. The Land Acquisition Officer (LAO) had prepared the list of households and the dates on which we were to leave the village. In fact, we wanted the entire village to be settled down at one place. But the government could not provide us a suitable patch of land to accommodate all of us together. So the entire village, individually or in small groups, ended up going to 63 different locations. We—40 families—settled down here on the advice of Pabitra Mohan Pradhan. As per rehabilitation policy, each family was entitled to 50 decimals of homestead land but we agreed to accept 20 decimals in the hope of getting 83 acres nearby for cultivation. We chose that piece of land because it was close to our settlement and there was also a *nalla* (water channel) that could be used for irrigation.

> We waited for four years to get that land and did not accept the monetary compensation being offered. But the state government did not do anything to get the forest clearance from the central government (as by that time The Forest Act, 1980 was introduced) for that land! We did not get even an inch. We even approached Pabitra Mohan Pradhan and collected funds to send him to Delhi by flight since he was too old to move in a train. We wanted him to get the clearance from the central government. But that also went in vain. Finally, being undone, we decided to accept money. But the LAO told us that it had been returned and therefore we had to give bribe to get it back. We had begun exhausting whatever food grains we had preserved from our old village and the compensation money we had received towards housing. Many of us collected mushrooms and bamboo stalks from the forest to feed on. We have been reduced to landless people. We survive by catching fish from the reservoir. We have become jharas. Our occupation has changed. Those who were working on land are now moving into the water, casting nets to catch fish. That was in our fate, what could we do?

Both jharas and the pradhans had their little worlds turn topsy-turvy. Some are even amused that they had momentarily hoped for a better life. The driver who was accompanying us from Deogarh shared how he too was a survivor of the Rengali project. On the way from Kadamdarh colony, he got involved and said how any person you accost here in Deogarh has his tale of woe about rehabilitation. He suggested the next destination point to be a roadside rehabilitation colony after having been to one in forested land. It was Srinivaspur.

Living on the Edge

Dalit families who left Bemur came to settle in Srinivaspur. Other than nineteen dalit families, there are two *Chasa* families. The colony is situated on land that was originally a protected forest. Srinivaspur is enlisted as Kalka DPF in government records. The government cleared the protected forest, settled the people and issued a K-Form. However, for de-reservation, the Forest Act, 1980, makes it necessary to obtain the permission of the central government. These people have not been given any permanent record of right over that land. They have been waiting all these years enduring both economic hardship and social isolation. Any outsider entering Srinivaspur raises their hope.

As we entered, a group of people swarmed us, eager to know whether some government department had finally got in touch with them. Their outpouring of problems and appeals for a range of needs was intense. No one ever visits them. Nor does any office receive their complaints. We too had come only to write.

Kaushalya—a daily wage labourer—along with other women shared the woes of having no access to water:

> Water is our biggest worry. There is only one borewell. That too dries up all too soon. That was not the case in our original village Bemur. We do not have a *katta* for bathing. After more than 30 years of settlement this minor problem has not yet been resolved by any government. We are being humiliated and taunted when we go to bathe in the *katta* of other villages.

They collect *tendu* leaves for livelihood. But there is no outlet for sale. The government has not bothered to even find a collection centre for the people who have made such a big sacrifice of leaving their villages and livelihood for the dam to be built in national interest.

> We women collect *tendu* leaves and do seasonal agricultural work, specifically transplantation. We do not have our own *fadi* (*tendu* leaf collection center). We depend on another village for that. But they do not allow us to take *tendu* leaves to their *fadi* because the number of collectors keeps growing.

Each *fadi* is allotted to collect a fixed amount of leaves. If women from another village bring leaves, it cuts into the income of the women whose village is the collection centre. They face daily opposition whether it is about bathing in a pond or taking their *tendu* leaves for sale to earn a bit of money. Abandoned by the government and shunned by neighbouring villages, they yearn for anything from water to registering their existence. They have been living on the edge in this way since 1982.

Dukhabandhu Nayak and Bholanath Nayak earlier lived in Bemur near Gogua:

> Wage work was easily available to us then. But we do not get any work here. Unlike our old village, we are having to walk 5–6 kilometers to get wage work. That too is not always available. You can see how most of the people are present in the village today. There is simply no work available. Though we have been issued K-Form for the homestead land, we do not have any

permanent record of right. As a result, we cannot avail government schemes like the Indira Awaas Yojana. We cannot get loans from any bank. Our children are also not being issued caste certificates. Under the Rengali Rehabilitation Scheme, we were allotted six acres of land but it is upland and not fit for cultivation. We grow black gram, horse gram or *güda dhaan* (a variety of paddy that can grow on upland) in the rainy season. The land is also not properly demarcated. Nobody knows for sure which plot of land belongs to whom. The six acres of land has not been allotted in one patch. There are no irrigation facilities.

The Saga of Endless Struggle, Endless Misery

The rituals of rehabilitation were over for the government when the evacuation process got completed by 1985. Those who had the means, especially the big land owners, went to court and continued with their legal battles. Most others came out on streets to make their grievances heard. In 1986, an organization called Rengali Basachyuta Loka Surakshya Samiti (Committee for Protection of Rengali Displaced) was formed. The committee demanded that the government rectify the list of submerged households, provide all facilities promised in the rehabilitation package and extend all facilities to cut-off villages at par with submerged villages. The committee organized meetings, demonstrations, gheraos of government offices, fast-unto-death, and even blocked the national highway. It continued for two years and in that period managed to force the government to meet some demands. When the committee dozed off, the government machinery also fell into deep slumber.

In 1991, the government declared the Rengali project closed. It came as a shock to everybody. Again in 1997, another committee emerged and continued the struggle. The government also set up another committee to look into the pending grievances of the people. Many committees have been set up over the years, and matters have been looked into from various angles. But no one sees an end to the misery of the people.

The people might have been forgotten but not the land. Whether it is fish cultivation or reaching development to the poor, the government has its eyes on each millimetre of the land they live on and the water and the stones. On the day we met Kishore Patra, he was busy penning down a response to a news item of the day. A fish cultivation project was being proposed in the periphery villages of the submerged area. He showed us the news item and read out his draft of a letter to the chief minister:

Dear Chief Minister,

I am writing this letter to you with a very heavy heart. Perhaps, you must not have heard of us. We are the oustees of the Rengali project, locally called budianchalia. It's a tag we have been living with for more than 30 years, when a big dam was built across River Brahmani. We were forced to sacrifice our homes, land and the river for the larger interest of the country. Since then, there has been no end to our misery. Perhaps it would end now only with the end of our lives. We were promised then by many leaders, including your father Biju Patnaik, that we would be well taken care of. Yes, each displaced family has been allotted six acres of land and it appears so nice on paper. It also looks nice to brag about it as a success story of Rengali rehabilitation package in meetings and seminars. But as they say: one who tills the land knows about the land; he knows that generations of labour goes into making a land cultivable. Most of the land given to the oustees of Rengali dam is not cultivable; even grass does not grow on it.

For the last 30 years and more, only heaven knows how we have been surviving. I am invoking heavens because governments and officials do not care to listen to us. Hundreds of families are still living deep inside the jungles, euphemistically called rehabilitation colonies. They have only been issued K-Form pattas and do not have any record of right over those six acres of land. They are being deprived of getting houses under Indira Awaas Yojana on the pretext that they already have land; their children are being denied caste certificates; and banks are denying them loans. Theirs is a story of denial all around.

Now, whatever good quality land is available in our area lie between 405 feet RL to 410 feet RL. There are as many as 22 villages in them, which are officially designated as periphery villages. People are living in and cultivating those lands. Although, officially it is called acquired land. To rub salt on our wounds, your government has been going on devising plans to hand over those lands to big companies, private promoters and others. Some years back, a plan was chalked out to carry out plantation work on those lands. This was clearly a move to rob people of their only source of livelihood. Was there no other land available in the district for plantation? Has any government ever cared to generate forest that has been submerged in the reservoir? Now we hear that fishing ponds would be dug up on those lands to augment fish production and the land has been handed over to some company from Madras. Why is it that the government always casts its evil eye on the land that is so dear to a poor man for his survival?

Dear Chief Minister, you may find this letter a litany of complaints. However, that is not my objective. I am only stating something obvious and which has always been ignored. Why are we poor peasants, dalits and adivasis

> *always asked, cajoled or forced to make sacrifices for the country and companies owned by big capitalists? Are we not people of this country? Are we not entitled to live with dignity and in peace as human beings? Is there any justice in this country for us?*

As we left Srinivaspur, we were remembering this letter. Rengali is not in the past; Rengali is not forgotten. If administration has not yet issued certificates of de-reservation after 30 years, where do we begin the Rengali story? When each day of their lives deals with the reality of having been dispossessed so entirely, how can we say we are constructing the story from recall? Perhaps by finding it all so surreal, the mind creates an escape route to halt the narration of the story. But even that little bit of refuge was elusive as we looked up at a gigantic construction above us. The sight gave us a jolt.

Yes, we were right under the Ranchi-Vijayawada corridor that was being constructed only a few kilometres away from Deogarh. It is supposed to check the 'Maoist menace' by bringing development to the region. The length of this corridor is 1,632 kilometres. It passes through Odisha covering twelve tribal and backward districts. There's gallons of water—along with everything else—poured into this mega construction. But there's not even a drop of water for the people of Srinivaspur who live under the shadow of this massive highway. While the corridor is consuming crores of rupees, even a few thousand cannot be put aside to dig a pond or make any water harvesting structure. Their little world is overarched by this gigantic construction—a world bereft of work or wages, water or identity proofs. They have been waiting for more than three decades for the government to look at their way. And the government is doing precisely that. By constructing the corridor, it aims to draw people living in areas prone to left-wing extremism to join mainstream society. The disease of gigantism not only lingers, the disease gains proportions too. The disease that will eat up the forests, rivers, stones and sand, and it will try eating up the earth.

As we left Srinivaspur, a man furtively gave us a photocopy of his K-Form to pass on to the advocate in Deogarh, so that he could apply for the de-reserved certificate. The corridor looming above us watched mutely. If only these dams and corridors could speak, they alone would testify that the oustees of the Rengali Dam project still live in hope.

Paani toh nadiyon ko lauta hee dena chahiye
Aur theek hisaab lagaakar kuch kuon aur taalaabon ko bhee
Aakhir mein agar fir bhee kuchh talchhat bacha reh jaaye
Toh hamaare gaanv ke andhe Ram garib
Naapit umr sattar saal aath maheene
Ke lotey mein usey daal diyaa jaaye
Uska lota bharne kee fursat ab
Kisi ko nahin hai gaanv mein. (Uday Prakash)

[Let the waters be returned to the rivers
And after some calculations, to wells and ponds
And if at all a little remains
Let poor blind Ram's pot be filled,
Who is exactly seventy years and eight months of age;
Nobody has time for him in the village]

Notes

1. Banka Behari Das was the state finance minister when the proposal of the Rengali Dam was mooted. He was initially enthusiastic believing in the benefits of the dam. Later in his life, he was disillusioned seeing the misery and distress of the people. He became very involved in people's struggle for proper rehabilitation. In this autobiography he portrays his involvement in the movement as an act of repentance.
2. The late Bholeswar Sahu was a high school student from Gogua village, which was the centre of resistance. His PhD thesis from Sambalpur University was based on the experience of Rengali oustees. He was a keen observer of many meetings being held in the village and later shared reflections about the movement.

References

Das, Banka Behari. 1998. *Sangramar sesha nahin*, Published by Ramesh Chandra Swain, Bhubaneswar.

Kundera, Milan. 1981. *The Book of Laughter and Forgetting.* London: Penguin Books.

Mahapatra, Jadumani. 2006. *Chakunda bunile uthai nahin.* In *Jadumani Granthabali*, ed. Chakradhara Mahapatra. Cuttack: Friends Publisher.

McCully, Patrick. 2001. *Silenced Rivers: The Ecology and Politics of Large Dams.* London: Zed Books.

Meher, Gangadhar. 1910 (2006). *Vedavyash*, First Published in Sambalpur Hiteishini from 26/11/1910 to 03/12/1910. In *Gangadhar Granthabali*, ed. Raghunath Meher. Cuttack: Bidya Prakashana.

Nath, Golak B. 2013. *Development, Displacement and Rehabilitation: A Study at Two Points in Time*. New Delhi: SSDN Publishers and Distributors.

Sahu, Bholeswar. 2012. *Socio-Economic Profile of Displaced Households*. New Delhi: SSDN Publishers and Distributors.

The Imperial Gazetteer of India. 1908. Vol. IX. London: Oxford.

CHAPTER 4

Jai Gandhamardan

Heaven is a forest of miles and miles of Mahua trees
And hell is a forest of miles and miles of Mahua trees with a forest guard in it.
—Muria saying

It was mid-March; the sun had begun to blaze. We were on our way to meet villagers who had participated in the anti-BALCO protest in the 1980s to listen to their stories and share their memories. We were also eager to know what has been happening to their lives and the region today. We camped at Nisarga Nivas, an ashram built on the foothills of the Gandhamardan by the Gandhian freedom fighter Alekh Patra. During the entire period of the anti-BALCO struggle, Nisarga Nivas worked as a meeting place of activists to decide the actions and programmes of the movement.

We began our journey on bikes around mid-day. We passed through the jungle en route to the villages. Sal trees had shed their leaves in the forests; tender leaves of light red-green were shining in the sun. *Palash* trees (flame of the forest) were full of blood-red flowers. The smell of *mahua* flowers was intoxicating the air. People, at some places in the forest, had cleared the ground around big trees to collect them. All of them love and compete with each other to devour *mahua* flowers—from bears, cows and monkeys to men. As we approached the village, paddy fields were swaying gently with the breeze in full glory of green.

R. Padhi, N. Sadangi, *Resisting Dispossession*,
https://doi.org/10.1007/978-981-15-0717-5_4

When women were returning from the fields to their huts, we met them in the community hall or in front of a veranda or on the village road under the shade of a big neem tree. We told them that we had come to hear their stories about the struggle against BALCO and it would open up conversations. Despite their tiredness, they were eager to go down memory lane and express their emotions so freely. Most of them spoke in fragments, jumbling up the time, place and people; perhaps it did not matter to them to stick to the linearity of the story or they were not used to telling an account that way. Or, perhaps because their memories had been corroded by the travails of routine life. After all, it all had taken place almost thirty years back. Or as they put it, it was at the time when they were just married or when their children were too young. They had become grandmothers by now. Some looked at it as a glorious tumultuous period in the past, indicating towards the mundane stillness of life now. Some women fought back their tears; the nostalgia seemed overwhelming at times. Their memories had become as sacred as the mountain, a part of their lives.

Memories were replete with endless collective actions they were part of. So the stories of gherao of a thana, or stopping of a BALCO's vehicle or an encounter with the Collector, *padayatras* and processions would feature frequently. One such story kept coming up time and again. It was about Jambabati Bijira who laid down her small children and herself on the road before the company vehicle. Their faces lit up when they talked about it. There was a sense of pride in the recall. It symbolized their bravery; their commitment to protect their source of livelihood and to protect their *Dangar Mahapuru* (Mountain God)—the Gandhamardan.

The Myth-Laden Mountain

This is the story of the majestic Gandhamardan mountain, which was protected from being blown up for bauxite way back in the 1980s by its people. The name evokes abundance of nature and the valiant people's resistance. Gandhamardan is part of popular culture and folklore, of beliefs and gods, of politics and spirituality. The people who protected this mountain are ordinary folks who draw their succour from their mountain and their forests and gods. The mountain range is a rich source of a variety of forest produce, including medicinal plants, providing livelihood for those living around it, mostly adivasi and dalit people. The perennial streams flowing from Gandhamardan sustain agricultural activities of the region all through the year.

The mountain is in the west of Odisha bordering Chhattisgarh. It stands at the juncture of three districts: Bargarh, Balangir and Nuapada. The Nrusinghnath and Harishankar temples are on either side of the Gandhamardan. The archaeologist G.R. Bhandarkar had written how the Nrusinghnath temple 'is situated at the foot of a hill, and is surrounded on all sides by one of the thickest jungles of the Central Provinces. A streamlet gurgles close by, the water of which is regarded as sacred, and at five places accumulates itself into five pools, called Kundas. The trees and shrubs, with which the hill is overgrown, are so tall and numerous that even at mid-day the sun-light that filters through their foliage is hardly stronger or brighter than that of the morning outside the jungle' (Quoted in Senapati and Mahanti 1971). It is believed that an adivasi couple—Jamuna Kandhuni and Hari Kandha—discovered the statue of Nrusinghnath while digging the soil for roots. They installed it in the temple; their descendants live here till today. Since these temples house their cherished deities, they are a popular destination for the majority of the god-loving people in the region. The Kapiladhara stream flowing between the two temples is considered sacred. A total of twenty-two perennial streams connect to the Sukhtel and Ang rivers, which in turn empty into the Mahanadi. Over 250 rare medicinal plants and herbs are found on the slopes of this mountain. It is, indeed, a wonder mountain.

People ecstatically recall the story from the Ramayana when Hanuman was flying with the mountain with the fabled *Sanjivini* plant that would resuscitate Laxman. As he flew from the Himalayas to Lanka, a part of the mountain fell off, which came to be known as the Gandhamardan mountain. A play that was performed numerous times in the region as villagers began campaigning against BALCO dramatized the myth-laden Gandhamardan: God has taken the incarnation of Nrusinghnath to kill the demon Mushika here, the Kandha couple discover the statue of Nrusinghnath, a simple adivasi boy becomes Saint Poet Yugdas with the blessings of Nrusinghnath and so on.

The flat surface of the mountain, as is characteristic of all bauxite-laden mountains, had once seated an international centre of learning known as *Parimalagiri Mahavihar* (Mishra 1987).

It is supposed to be the same famous Parimalagiri referred to in Buddhist literature. Hiuen Tsang in his writings too makes its reference as *Polo-molo-kili* (Mishra 1987). Some ruins of stone structures are still found on the plateau top. So, there is a contending claim to the origin of the medicinal plants and herbs; they seem to have been brought there by the Buddhists. In the 1940s the Geological Survey of India first recognized the bauxite potential at Gandhamardan. In subsequent periods, the Odisha Directorate of Mines along with other organizations continued exploration-evaluation programmes in different phases of bauxite deposited in the hills (Geo 2007).

BALCO Sneaks In

Whence came this BALCO Asura,
Choking us all to death?
What can I do?
My mind is unquiet.

The forests will die,
No water or air will flow.
Without forests or trees, how can I stay?
Where can I go?

Saag and leaves we gather,
On twigs and trees we live,
Which these shameless ministers
To this Asura want to give.

I am a mother of three,
I never knew such anguish.
I long with these two eyes to see
The company soon perish. (Gangadhar Sahu)[1]

This quiet little laid back town of Paikmal in Bargarh district became the centre of resistance for the entire region and the *andolan*. When you turn left from the main Paikmal square on the road to the Nrusinghnath temple, the ruins of BALCO can be seen on the right side of the road. The dilapidated offices and quarters are entwined with creepers and plants. There is moss and dampness spreading ceaselessly on the abandoned project. If you happen to ask anyone around about these ruins, you would see the pride on their faces and in eyes with which they tell you how this was once the

BALCO office. These are the relics of the struggles—the mute witness to show the extent to which BALCO had proceeded. Lingaraj Pradhan wrote:

> It is easily imaginable from its sheer size the amount of project work that had already been completed. A huge water tank, a series of flats and a club house were about to be complete. A few motor vehicles, abandoned and rusted, were lying strewn around the premises. This indicates how far the project had progressed. A road had already been laid to the top of the hill for vehicles of the company to move. 540 tonnes of bauxite were already excavated and transported. Earthwork of 3 km of the proposed 26 km railway line from Lakhna railway station, Kalahandi to village Manbhang had been completed. According to company's own estimates an amount of Rs 32 crores had been spent. The juggernaut of the project work was rolling on amidst the din and bustle of 1,000 permanent, temporary workers and officials. And the population of the region had resigned themselves to accept it. They were shocked, fearful and helpless. In such a situation, only a handful of people believed that the project could be successfully stalled by the mass resistance movement. This holds one of the important keys to the secret of the success of this movement. (Pradhan 1996)

The public sector company Bharat Aluminium Company (BALCO) entered the Gandhamardan area most unobtrusively. It had already exhausted the reserves of Amar Kantak—a mountain in Madhya Pradesh—for its plant in Korba. It applied for bauxite mining in the year 1976 and got 953 hectares on lease in 1981 from the Odisha government. Within another two years the company got the provisional clearance from the environment ministry. With the foundation stone laid in May 1983, construction work started soon and with great speed. In 1985 work on mine development and the construction of the ore crushing plant also began. Test mining had also begun (PUDR 1986).

When there was such an abundance of myths and legends in the area, the newly arrived company did not hesitate to help itself to add to the myths. It spread the word that the demon Mushika was still trapped inside the mountain and BALCO was the saviour that would kill the demon and thereby put an end to *Kalyug*. In this clash of myths, the people could see through the self-proclaimed saviour company. For them, Gandhamardan was their only Protector. It is the source of their subsistence. The convergence of these two worlds—the spiritual and material—inspired them to lead the anti-BALCO movement. Perhaps, these are not two separate worlds for them, rather an integrated whole. They protect the mountain; the mountain protects them.

People began to mobilize along two strong sets of belief: the religious affinity to the mountain was equally matched with their determination to protect it and its habitat. Sixty-five-year-old Diamond Bhue, leader of the Kandha Samaj, lives in village Laudmal of the Mithapali panchayat. He recalled:

> We had been demanding a dam to help us with irrigation since a long time. In the early eighties, when the government began the work on Manbhang dam, I worked there for two years. We used to think that even though the fruit orchard Madhuban on which three to four villages depended would be submerged, the reservoir water would irrigate the entire Mithapali panchayat. One day Swamiji[2] came and told us that the dam was being built to supply the water to BALCO. 'It is not for the irrigation that you are hoping for. The Company would blast the entire Gandhamardan to extract bauxite. Now, you choose: you want Dam or Gandhamardan.' It was only then we realized our mistake. If Gandhamardan would be no more, how could we live? The streams would die out and our hope for irrigation is also meaningless.

BALCO wanted to mine 213 million tonnes of bauxite from the mountain. It perhaps underestimated the fact that the mountain being rich in its bio-diversity was also the lifeline of livelihood for over a million people in the region. We met Renu Mohar from village Lohasingha, who was very active in the *andolan* as a young woman. Her family members were busy weaving the colourful and exotic Sambalpuri fabric. It would travel to outlets in Bargarh and Sambalpur and from there to the outside world. She works in an NGO. She recalled:

> BALCO came to construct its offices and to do mining. Our people quickly organized and resisted. There are so many reasons. The gods Harishankar and Nrusinghnath are close to our hearts and religious sentiments. Not only that ... we draw many benefits from the herbs and medicines found in this area. The abundance of plants and trees and water is unique. You will not find a place like this anywhere. We get a wide range of forest produce. There were many meetings and *padayatras*. We resolved that neither will we let any mining happen nor let anyone enter the area. The mountain is ours. The forests are ours too.

The Moment of Reckoning

> There is a moment that arrives. However, prepared you might be since long, it is that moment that decides. You can even call it providence. Worldwide, the entire of the early 1980s was witnessing a growing consciousness around issues of environment protection. The Chipko movement gave a clarion call for everyone to become conscious of their forests and environment. When we got to know about the entry of BALCO, it took very little effort to spread the word because Gandhamardan is the lifeline of the people and the most sacred part of our lives.

This is how Prasanna Kumar Sahu, who is known as Swami Swamabesh today, recalls the 1980s when the movement started. When BALCO entered his familiar terrain; he left his job in Sambalpur University and became one of the leading figures in the movement. He lives in the Kapil Muni ashram at the foothills of the mountain.

Right from the beginning, people became aware of the dangers to the environment and habitat. Ghanshyam Sahu, a seventy-year-old man from village Baidapalli said:

> I am a peasant ... so were my fathers and grandfathers; and, so are my children. We know the streams flowing from Gandhamardan are sources of our lives. No scientist is needed to make us understand this. The streams are there because the mountain is there, forests and trees are there. We know it is trees and forests that bring rains. So, if forests and jungles disappear, there would be no rain; if the mountain is blasted, streams will die out. The entire area will turn to a desert. We peasants will die too. So the movement was to protect the mountain, the forests, trees and streams. You people call it environment movement. Yes, the Gandhamardan movement was an environment movement. Environment and livelihood are inseparable.

According to Lingaraj Pradhan, some spontaneous incidents played a role in sparking off the simmering anger and discontentment:

> The foundation stone of the project was laid on 13 May 1983. Two incidents occurred on that day. One, a leaflet was circulated in the name of a few local notables at the meeting place of the foundation ceremony. The leaflet had drawn attention to the facts of adverse effects of the project on people and the environment. They (the signatories of the leaflet) had threatened to immolate themselves, if the project were not stopped. Secondly, when the

> then Chief Minister and Minister of Mines were returning via Padampur, the local college students pelted stones at them. Many students and youths were arrested on that day. (Pradhan 1996)

Discontentment had been brewing in the countryside. Thinking of BALCO as such a mighty entity, people wondered how they could go against the government. The machinery and big equipment that BALCO brought to the mountain caused fear and intimidation. For them, BALCO and the government were one. Therefore, the 13 May protest affirmed their belief in active resistance. Village meetings and *padayatras* began in the villages; also, meetings and discussions happened in Sambalpur University and Sambalpur town.

Pankajini Rout from village Koknara, who was one of the most active students, is an ayurvedic medical officer today. She has a patch of land at the base of the mountain where she plans to grow herbs and plants for ayurvedic medicines. When she met us at the foothills, she escorted us over the mountainous path for over a kilometre. We walked amidst the plants and trees in single file on a path worn out by others. The earth was bathed in sunshine as far as the eye could see. The million hues of green resplendent with the sunshine were heady. The fragrance was at times overpowering, at times elusive. If you get lost in the beauty and the aura, there are plants tugging at your feet almost as if speaking to you. Settling down in the small thatched shade, Pankajini Rout recalled:

> I was a student of the Ayurvedic medical college in Paikmal when the movement began in 1982. There were so many who inspired us in those days. I remember Prasanna Sahu, Niranjan Bidrohi, Gautam Biswal, Asutosh Patnaik, Lingaraj Azad and many others who would organize meetings in and around Harishankar village. Our people are both religious and spiritual. Their relationship with the environment and the land was also related to their love of the mountain and their god. You see the perennial streams and Ang and Sukhtel rivers are part of the ecology. It became our duty to protect the mountain. There was so much of pollution and destruction already happening because of the construction and mining. We could see for ourselves that the area would be reduced to dust and no plants or animals could survive, leave alone people.

Curiously, the point at which BALCO did its test mining in 1983 was named Happy Point by the company. At that spot, large quantities of red mud had been amassed after the test blasts. When the rains came, the mud fell into the Kapiladhara stream, which runs down the mountain and emerges next to the Nrusinghnath temple. The stream turned red as it gushed down. Panic gripped everyone! A few such freak incidents galvanized resistance too. Nature had played its own game to awaken the people.

Recalling this incident, Renu Mohar said:

> Anything to do with the mountain and environment filled us with awe because we worshipped the mountain. When people going to the temple saw the Kapiladhara stream turning red, they thought that the mountain was bleeding. Some of them spread alarm that the end of life had come. It was this fear and panic that bound us to each other and made us become one. We became even more determined to save it. Each such incident strengthened our own identity with the mountain. We saw ourselves as the protectors of our only protector—the mountain. BALCO was the destroyer; it was the *asura*.

Recall is mediated sometimes by the Kapiladhara stream spewing blood and sometimes by an NSS (National Service Scheme) camp that took place. The stories and events are aplenty in people's minds. Small newsletters like the *Gandhamardan ro Sandesh* helped us trace the sequence of events.

The Simmering Rebellion

The first village meetings took place in Manbhang, Lukupalli, Bikram Nagar and Monikel on 16 August 1983 (*Gandhamardan ro Sandesh* February 1987). That very night a huge gathering took place at Mithapalli village. The seeds of resistance were getting sown, yet the deep dread of the government and the ruling party filled people with hopelessness. By September, awareness camps were being organized in different parts of Jharbandh and Paikmal blocks. A call was given for a huge meeting in Jaamseth village on 2 October 1983, which was also Gandhi Jayanti. Representatives from several villages came and resolved to carry out an organized movement. This was a milestone meeting. They submitted a memorandum to the Sambalpur administration on 12 October demanding the removal of BALCO from Gandhamardan (*Gandhamardan ro Sandesh* February 1987).

By the beginning of 1984, the anti-BALCO struggle was able to rouse the consciousness of thousands of people. Thousands of signatures demanding the removal of BALCO were collected and sent to the Lok Sabha speaker to draw the attention of the Indian parliament. Memorandums were also submitted to the Paikmal Block Development Officer (BDO) and the Padampur Sub-Divisional Officer (SDO) on 7 and 16 June, respectively.

The confidence to voice opposition grew automatically. The fears of a huge prestigious public company and the government began to dissipate. Those conscious of the massive work ahead of them travelled day and night speaking to villagers and holding small meetings. This growing opposition had to be channelized into a mass movement. Working day and night in this way, the movement drew the support of youth and students from Sambalpur, Bargarh and other places.

In February 1985, a huge demonstration took place outside the BALCO office. Those who had gathered stopped the movement of BALCO vehicles that were plying up and down. Some say almost 50,000 people were present. Slogans like '*BALCO asura murdabaad*' and '*BALCO asura hum nahin darta*' rent the air.

The movement progressed rapidly. A seven-point charter of demands addressed to the Prime Minister on 7 July was covered in most national dailies. As word spread across other states, the movement evoked much solidarity along with the attention. Meanwhile, the efforts of getting organized and giving a form and face to the *andolan* were getting consolidated fast.

On 17 July 1985, the Gandhamardan Nrusinghnath Surakshya Parishad was founded at a meeting in Paikmal. On 19 August 1985, the Gandhamardan Surakshya Yuva Parishad (GSYP) too was founded by nineteen youths. After almost two years of the students' protest against the laying of the foundation stone, they were organized. There was no looking back as resistance spread like wildfire across the forests and hillocks and the villages tucked inside.

Villagers across the region became one with the movement. Each event became news; sometimes, its repercussions would go a long way in building unity. Renu Mohar recalls the moments and incidents that revved up the resistance:

> Once the idols of the Nrusinghnath temple actually disappeared. No one knew who stole the gods! It created much panic and we thought they are out to get our Gods too. Some even thought that worse was to follow. But after some days the idols were replaced too. Then again one day the Garuda Stambha (pillar) in the Nrusinghnath temple collapsed entirely because of the blasting the company had started in the mountains. It was like an

> earthquake and its tremors were felt in the entire region. People were shocked. Emotions were running high and everyone was both angry and upset. No doubt it was a warning that even our temple would be destroyed. Therefore we always called it *asura*. *BALCO asura murdabaad!*

When the idol went missing, the police searched the house of Ghasiram Mallick, the Kondh priest of the temple. The police dog sniffed its way straight to the BALCO office! The humiliation of Ghasiram Mallick enraged the Kondh community and nearly twelve to thirteen thousand Kondhs from districts of Balangir, Kalahandi and Sambalpur gathered to start a *yagyan* in the temple. This incident helped deepen the anti-BALCO sentiment and the Kondh community became more involved in the movement (Concerned Scholars 1986). Pankajini Rout told us how such incidents drew people close to each other and strengthened the collective resolve:

> It was not just fear or hysteria. The consciousness we gained is with us till today. Earlier we thought it was *dangar* land only. In the struggle, we became conscious of the Gandhamardan region and its environment and habitat. We faced countless threats and intimidation. When Janaki Ballabh Patnaik came visiting, we protested. Almost 200 of us were arrested. Thirteen of us were arrested once again in Bargarh. Our studies were affected; but our education was already happening. We began to understand our small world and through it the universe too. We looked at ourselves and our people with pride as people from the Gandhamardan region.

The NSS Camp

No account of the anti-BALCO struggle seemed complete without some or the other story around the NSS camp. This two-week National Integration and Eco Development Camp was inaugurated at Nrusinghnath on World Environment Day. The year 1985 was also declared as the International Youth Year. Around 300 students participated in the camp; some came from neighbouring regions like Madhya Pradesh, West Bengal and Andhra Pradesh. The theme sent by the concerned government department was environmental security. The camp aimed for students to interact with ordinary people and learn from them how they relate to the ecosystem and protect it. And they did!

Dr Arttabandhu Mishra from Sambalpur University, who was the programme coordinator of NSS, recalls:

When the idea first came that we can place some of our students from the campus with adivasi families, I went off on my own with my driver. But nobody co-operated! Some were apprehensive of students per se. Some asked, 'how can university students be comfortable in our simple dwellings? Where will they sit or rest? There is no table or chair.' It was a blank refusal. Nirupama was one of the most active students on the campus. When I asked her to go and try convincing them again, she achieved it in one single visit. Even all those families who had initially declined got persuaded by her. I don't know how she did that. Fifteen students were placed in different villages for five whole days. NSS rules allowed non-student volunteers. So there were an equal number of volunteers from Chatra Yuva Sangharsh Vahini staying in the villages as part of the placement program. This unique combination worked like magic.

Prasanna Sahu, who was already campaigning in the villages, said:

We wanted the youth to intermingle with the village folk and learn about environment and livelihood. They were asked to observe and note down various aspects of life in the mountains. They were given note pads and pens. They were cautioned not to show off their own knowledge or lecture adivasis. You know how university students can be! We also forbade the use of *paan*, cigarettes or beedis. Boys were asked to wear only lungis or half pants. Shoes, socks, full pants or full sleeve shirts were not allowed. Each student was supposed to take a packet of sweets for the children and some rice, potatoes and onions for a week. Girls were expected to become involved with women's work all day long and boys with whatever the men were doing. Some boys even went in trucks and worked as loaders during the day or went to the jungles to collect and cut wood. At night they would have meetings that were organized by the Vahini volunteers.

For many, this experience became a turning point in their lives as an entire world so different from theirs opened up before them. We met them.

Anuradha Purohit, who had just retired as a school teacher in Sambalpur, went into raptures as she recalled those few days:

I stayed with a family in Manbhang. Nirupama was in Baidapalli in the house of Ghasiram Mallik. She would work in the paddy fields while I would go out to collect *mohuli* flowers. Bhabani Nial was so young then, maybe he was in plus two. He would leave with the men folk in a truck to do brick work and construction work. Early morning, we would go out to collect *bodda saag* or sometimes the leaves of drumstick trees. That was the time to

> get to chat with the girls and women in the villages. We would cook the *saag* and have a tummy full of *pakhaal bhaat* with it (fermented rice) for the whole day. The air was so clean and there was so much oxygen that our appetites were insatiable. We ate lots! Then I would leave with the women to collect *mohuli* flowers. We would separate the petals upon returning. Then we would turn to the older seeds that have been drying in the sun since some days. It was hard work splitting them into halves. They get oil from the seeds. Every bit of the *mohuli* is useful. Old women would share with us about the place and the culture and all that the mountain gives them. Their knowledge and wisdom was immense whether it was the ways in which they protect the mountain or about the plants and herbs. We came across herbs like the *asit phool* that they used for abortion. They would be in tears so often sharing their hardships. They might seem calm immersed in daily chores. But when they begin to talk about current realties, their pent-up pain and sufferings would surface. They would narrate their worries and problems with a heavy heart. It was as if to say that their sorrows were many and now BALCO had come to deepen their distress. I do not know how time flew while we were there. The bonds remain till today. When I went to Mithapalli in 1987 to see the play, I had just got married. They became so emotional. They presented me with sarees and sweets like *chaaro monji khoja* and *adishaas*. They said it is their married daughter visiting them and she simply could not return empty handed.

Nirupama Barapanda was going to retire soon as the principal of a college in Sambalpur. She narrated:

> I was in the house of the Kandha Samaj leader Ghasiram Malik. He was the *dishari* or village priest and lived in Baidapalli at the foot of the mountain. His was the strongest voice against the rapid progress being made by the company. Being the village priest, everyone would listen to him. We were given tasks to ask questions in specific areas. Anuradha's task was to find out about the medicinal herbs and pants and how much had got destroyed already. I had been asked to see the mining activities and the damage caused already. We would be taken to the top of the mountain and shown all these herbs and plants. We learned to identify them and know their benefits for different ailments. We were shown the Durgei stream near Manbhang and explained how the water is becoming less and why. Ghasiram Malik was so clear of the purpose of our visit and took much interest in our exposure and learning. I remember how he took us around those orange orchards. We had never seen orange trees nor such big oranges! Some of the trees were already dying. That is the area where you can see the Manbhang dam today.

> Niranjan Bidrohi, Asutosh Pattnaik and others would come and hold meetings in the evenings after we were over with the day's work. The meetings were held in secrecy. We had to keep distance from the goondas, *dalals*, contractors and Congress supporters who were there in every village. We never ventured alone anywhere.
>
> The camp experience brought everyone together as they stood firmly against one entity—BALCO. Some students who had come for the NSS camp stayed back to work full time in the movement.

As Arttabandhu Mishra recalls:

> I went back to collect the students. The scenes at the time of farewell were unforgettable. Those who had refused me to house students a week ago were in tears as they bid goodbye to them. They kept telling the students that this is their house now. They gave them food for the journey. On the last day of the camp at Nrusinghnath, we were taken by surprise when a big group of villagers with whom students had stayed paid us a visit with their local leaders. They joined us for a meal. They said that they want to keep students with them and bear all responsibility. Those from the Vahini stayed back with them.

The NSS camp became a turning point in the lives of the youth. No wonder that the formation of the Gandhamardan Surakshya Yuva Parishad took place within a few months of the camp.

Visit of the Himalayan Sadhu

On 25 December 1985, 150 people, including 70 women and 20 children, started satyagraha in front of the BALCO office to stop the work. On 26 December, 200 people, including 80 women and 20 children, stopped the entire work of BALCO. Police detained 150 of them and arrested 69 people, including 15 women, 12 children and all the important leaders of Yuva Parishad (*Gandhamardan ro Sandesh* February 1987).

Sunderlal Bahuguna, the renowned environmentalist and architect of the Chipko movement from Tehri Garhwal, arrived at Nuapada on 6 February 1986 for a week-long tour of the area. Arttabandhu Mishra recalls:

> In the village right after the Anga bridge, people greeted him by breaking coconuts and washing his feet with coconut water. He was furious and asked me what we were doing to him. I begged him for forgiveness. You see he

> might be an environmentalist or my fellow member from the National Advisory Committee. But how would people understand that? For them, he was a sadhu from the Himalayas. That is the propaganda that had reached them. At times one used to feel there was no place for science. Right from the beginning it was such that whether it was from the environment point of view or the protection of Gandhamardan for its sacredness, the end was the same for people of different persuasions. And there was place for all. He was given some slices of apple on a plate. He pushed it aside saying that these apples had eaten up their land back home. He was delighted instead to have guavas. He climbed up the guava tree outside the house and plucked many.

Sundar Lal Bahuguna addressed a series of meetings in villages across the region. In February 1986, a two-week-long satyagraha took place. Many people were arrested, including adivasi women. Alekh Patra refused to take bail and was in prison for seventy-one days while Rayadhar Lohar remained confined for thirty-six days. The Bargarh sub-jail, which has place for only ten or eleven people, was packed with people from the anti-BALCO protests. Later GSYP organised a *padayatra* from Harishankar to Nrusinghnath, covering a distance of 120 km in eight days. It was led by the Sarvodaya leader Madan Mohan Sahu. Altogether about 987 people, including 479 women, were arrested only in the year 1986 (PUDR 1986).

Sundar Lal Bahuguna's visit gave a big fillip to the movement. It put tremendous pressure on the Odisha government. When he returned to the north, the campaign picked up active solidarity in Delhi. There was much lobbying among MPs to bring up the discussion in the parliament.

In May 1986, the Department of Environment and the Mines Department at the centre reviewed all aspects of the situation. Even then, they hesitated to put forth any conclusive views. The departments simply referred it to the prime minister. This did not deter BALCO from proceeding ahead.

The Theatre of the Oppressed

The play *Gandhagiri* scripted by Prasanna Sahu to pose the dangers to the habitat drew many people into the movement. Some people now recall the play as *BALCO Asura Murdabaad*. Within a few days of it being staged sometime in 1986, the play became very popular and there were performances round the year in all villages.

Prasanna Sahu recalled:

> Word had already spread about a demon named BALCO that would destroy the mountain for bauxite. BALCO had become personified; some thought it was a person. They were ready to kill BALCO to save the mountain. It took a lot of time to create the awareness of the dangers that lay ahead. We reached out to all the villages and did *padayatras* and meetings to spread the word and through that the consciousness. The play was very useful in reaching out to people across the entire region.

The cultural activist Gangadhar Sahu added:

> First the children made the play and took it around. It created much enthusiasm. Then the elders joined in and made the production even more strong. It was all about how the *asuras* were plotting to kill; BALCO was the *asura*. Seeing the play people were urged to fight the demon. They would weep during the play and get up and cheer and dance too when the fight was victorious.

Using myths and stories about the mountain, the play urged people to fight the evil. It was a fight between *dharma* and *adharma*, a fight between holy and unholy, a fight between *punya* and *paapa*. The socialist thinker and leader Kishen Pattnaik, who was one of the leading figures in the movement, commented: The play was a creative attempt to raise the religious consciousness of the exploited local populace into a rebellious consciousness (Quoted in Sahu 1986).

Prasanna Sahu explained:

> People would sit and deliberate on how to destroy the monster. Local MLAs and MPs were shown as characters too. You see, a play is far more powerful than all the speeches we can give. It has to hit their imagination. If you simply introduce two or three truths in a play with a hundred myths, people get the truths. They are motivated to come and watch and bring others with them. They get excited and talk about the play for a long time after it is over. After that, they become determined to take the message around.

A vast repertoire of songs began to be sung in rallies and *padayatras*. Gangadhar Sahu, who has composed most of the songs, recalled:

> One day, while going to a village in the forest road, I met a woman who was collecting sal leaves and tooth sticks. I talked to her about BALCO; dangers awaiting all of us, if the mountain is blasted. She told me 'I am a mother of three children. My husband has died. But I am being able to sustain my children by collecting leaves and tooth sticks from the jungle. Then what would I do, if Gandhamardan is destroyed, if the forest disappears?' That struck me and I wrote a song keeping her feelings in mind. I went on writing songs and *bhajans* (devotional songs) after this and sang them in meetings. My work was to gather people by singing and then our leaders or comrades gave speeches. I have observed that it is women and children who were attracted most by the singing. I have seen elderly women cry when I sing *bhajans* and touch my feet after the meeting. I felt so embarrassed and, at the same time, happy too: they have awakened to the danger posed to the Gandhamardan. That is why women and children have participated in large numbers in the movement.

According to him, the participation of dalit women and men was overwhelming as they have a natural talent for dancing and singing. There are some others who carry this rich legacy of memories. Lallo Vivar from Bikram Nagar lives in a simple mud hut with a few utensils as belongings. She was wearing a brick-red *gamcha* when we met her. Her husband too was in an identical *gamcha*. They made place for us on the string cot. The ground had been freshly plastered with mud and there were a few more *gamchas* drying. The forest and the mountain looked majestic shielding their simple lives and their poverty. On hearing that we were keen to listen to her stories of the movement, her eyes welled up with tears:

> You must have heard that we cremated Ruduna only a few days earlier. Alekha Patro used to come and address us all. Those days are over. But how can we forget anything? We saved the mountain from BALCO. And we all became one through our hard work and the songs and the tears. We are the people of the Gandhamardan. Even if there is nothing, there is something that the mountain gives us. Even the poorest of the poor can live here without lacking anything. We have survived because the mountain survived. Those who come after us too will survive if the mountain stays. I can only sing for you. I did not like speeches. Whenever I was called on stage to speak I would ask them to let me sing. And till today I remember all those songs as we brought people together to protect our mountain and our god.

Lallo Vivar went on singing one song after another. When overcome with her emotions, she would take a break and laugh too.

These songs of the Gandhamardan *andolan* were played on loud speakers on festival days, in schools and colleges on certain days and even in wedding celebrations! They were played for years even after BALCO had quit.

THE ANDOLAN INTENSIFIES

Despite intense campaigning and the movement appealing to the government, BALCO carried on with its activities. A strategy was needed to somehow halt this. We were told how Ghasiram Malik one day announced:

> We have to stop the vehicles of the company at the entry point into the mountain. It can be done easily. We have three hundred villages around the mountain. Each village will be in charge of one day only. The villages will take turns to carry on the vigil. That way the burden on any one village will be less. The villagers will simply sleep on the road when the vehicles come. When the vehicles are stopped in this way, the company will go out of its wits. If the police use bullets or lathi, we have to face it. They are killing us anyway by mining the Gandhamardan. So we can face bullets too. But let us try.

In this way, they organized themselves to stop all company vehicles from going to the mountain top. Ghasiram Mallick put up a stone in the middle of the road, put vermillion on it and began worshipping. He named it *Balco khai Devi*—Goddess that would eat up the BALCO. The goddess is still worshipped on the very spot. A tiny concrete structure has been built to give it the look of a shrine. A round-the-clock vigil began, initiated by Ghasiram Mallick, Rayadhar Lohar, Lallo Vivar and Ripunath Pujari by putting up a small camp on the side of the road. They were known as the sentinels of the movement (*Jagrata Prahari*). Villagers joined them by rotation and this barricade continued till BALCO left the area. There were barricades also set up at other entry points like Mithapali, Baidapalli and Salepalli.

On 1 June 1987, more than 3,000 people held a protest demonstration outside the BALCO office and demanded that BALCO leaves Paikmal immediately. They asserted that if BALCO did not leave the place within six months, the movement would occupy all its offices and buildings (*Gandhamardan ro Sandesh* June 1987). Almost half of those present were women. Many slogans rent the air:

Jaan jaau jaau, jiban jaau! Gandhamardan banchi thau!
[Let our lives go! Long live Gandhamardan!]

BALCO hatao, Gandhamardan bachao!
[Stop BALCO, Save Gandhamardan!]

As the *andolan* intensified in the year 1987, a severe drought took place. Instead of remaining confined to the demand for BALCO to withdraw, the Yuva Parishad responded to the drought situation too with many demands (*Gandhamardan ro Sandesh* August 1987). It demanded that the administration declare Padampur, Patnagarh and Nuapada subdivisions as drought-affected areas. It also demanded the waiving off of agricultural loans and school fees of students, work for able-bodied persons and free food for orphans, physically challenged people, children and pregnant women. It demanded the opening of free kitchens at the gram panchayat level. Activists visited the drought areas extensively to monitor the implementation of government schemes.

The ruling Congress government was under tremendous pressure as the *andolan* intensified. There were frequent physical attacks by Congress supporters on activists of the movement. On 15 October 1987, Shyamabadhu Bhoi—the brother of the MP—physically attacked Swami Gyanananda Saraswati, the advisor of the Yuva Parishad. In protest, thousands of women and men gheraoed the police station and staged a *rasta-roko* (road blockade) *andolan*. The police were compelled to arrest the culprits. On 21 October, a massive candle rally was organized at Paikmal against the goonda raj of BALCO. For the first time, adivasi women and men and youth marched with their traditional weapons, bows and arrows. The MP sent a letter of apology to Prasanna Sahu (*Gandhamardan ro Sandesh* October 1987). The display of traditional weapons in the march led to many discussions within the *andolan* given the diverse range of groups within it.

Prasanna Sahu said:

> We were all ideologically so different and yet were bound by the single aim to resist BALCO. We had *Samta Sangathan*, Congress and Janata Dal among us. In fact, the local unit of Vishwa Hindu Parishad filed a writ petition in the High Court as they too feared that the Nrusinghnath temple will be endangered. At that time, Jay Prakash Narayan's single slogan of 'power to the people' was a powerful appeal to the youth. The Chaatra Yuva Sangharsh Vahini worked tirelessly in this area. The realization that ordinary people should rule impassioned a large section of youth across the country. Kishen

> Pattnaik was a deep influence on the movement. The movement inspired people from many corners. Support poured in from students, professors and environmentalists. They had no self-interest. Letters of solidarity poured in from across the country and abroad too. Sundarlal Bahuguna's visit galvanized the movement when it was most needed. For those of us, coordinating the events and action programmes or negotiating with the government, it was a conscious decision not to favor any one party in the *andolan*. Since the Congress was in power, those in opposition parties had put all their stakes in the movement. But you know too well that political parties cannot work beyond self-interest. In later years, these parties reaped electoral victories. But the *andolan* to save the Gandhamardan remained one.

In October 1987, resistance was at its peak. The plan to stop BALCO vehicles plying to the mountains met with physical resistance in Mithapali. Jambabati Bijira today lives with her family in Dungurpalli. Her husband used to drive tractors for BALCO. He was threatened that his wife is in the Gandhamardan movement and he can lose his job. The couple asked the authorities whether they would not do the same if their place or house was intruded by outsiders.

> I travelled across all villages in the region spreading the word that our Gandhamardan mountain is in grave danger. We did not have to do much to mobilize women. Women did not pause to question or wait to be persuaded. When they heard that the mountain is going to be destroyed, that was enough for them to give up everything else. We thought BALCO was an *asura*. Some called it company but most called it an *asura*. One day we heard that the company was going to begin its work the next day. Vehicles started lining up on the road. We too gathered in huge numbers. People came from distant villages, even the elderly and children. We were fearless. If the mountain goes, nothing will remain. Why should we remain after that? Our lives really did not matter to us. My children were small. They did not sleep that night with the excitement. They waited for morning to come. Then in the morning people started gathering on the road. Some were lying on it and some sitting. But right in the front many of us lay down on our backs. I put both my children on the road and lay down next to them. When the police asked us why we were stopping the vehicles, we said that we cannot give up the Gandhamardan mountain. The police sent word to Padampur to call for more police. The Collector arrived. He tried to intimidate us and said they would get rid of everyone from the spot. I told him that the people are not guilty of anything. Our people are guilty of only wanting the mountain to be saved. I told the Collector, 'If you want to arrest me, arrest me.

> Put me in handcuffs. We have lived our lives. What about these children? What will be their future if the mountain does not remain? The mountain is so old. It gives us so much. I am guilty of protecting Gandhamardan. Arrest me. Put on the handcuffs. Who are we protecting this mountain for, we are protecting it for our children. If you destroy the mountain, there is no future. We might as well die. Even my children can die. I am laying down my children in front of your vehicles. I am lying down too. Please start your vehicles'. I urged them to start the vehicles several times. We were really ready to die. The police were confused. They could see that I was ready to die along with my children. They discussed among themselves. The Collector said what can we do when you are ready to sacrifice your life. He went away. Their trucks and jeeps pulled out.

Listening to her mother, Jambabati's daughter, who was visiting her with her own small child, became nostalgic. She laughed as she also recalled lying down on the road and how sometimes she would look at her brother lying next to her and nudge him if his eyes were open. They waited with shut eyes for the vehicle to drive over them. She said:

> We were all together and with our parents. We were not afraid. We were so small. We were ready to die that day though we did not know what death was. Today I understand it all and I think that it is we—all of us—who saved the mountain from BALCO. If we were not ready to die, there would have been no mountain today.

BALCO's work had come to a standstill. The movement continued to draw support from far and wide. A massive convention organized at Padampur on 1 January 1988 drew more than 7,000 people. People from other parts of Odisha joined in; there was a large presence from Chhattisgarh too. Within a few days, an intensive campaign took off in Balangir district from 12 to 17 January (*Gandhamardan ro Sandesh* February 1988).

It was a people's victory. BALCO withdrew. The MoU was cancelled on 15 September 1989.

The resistance to BALCO triggered a change in the next elections with candidates of the opposition coming to power in both assembly and Lok Sabha. In 1990, the Congress lost the state assembly elections and the Janata Dal came to power in the state.

It is almost more than thirty years now; if mining had been allowed, there would have been no mountain today. Maybe people being enmeshed in subsistence living with an entirely different way of life helped thwart the advent of mining that would have devoured the mountain. Maybe the faith in the mountain filled people with an indomitable courage.

The Bauxite in the Belly

However, the tug of war between the subsistence of the local people and bauxite mining is far from over. As soon as he formed the government, Chief Minister Biju Patnaik proposed fresh mining plans in January 1991. Bereft of any logic, he suggested mining from the Harishankar side will minimize damage.

The GSYP planned a cycle rally to resume the campaign once again. The main organizer, Subodh Panda, recalled:

> It was a challenge to the GSYP. We decided to go on a cycle rally from Nrusinghnath to Bhubaneswar to talk to Biju Patnaik and to raise our protest against the decision. It was 2 March 1992. We began the cycle journey. There were as many as 130 cyclists. Some of them were old too, say 65 to 70-year-olds. It was a seven-day journey. At that time, the Odisha Assembly session was going on. Finally, we met Biju Patnaik near the statue of Gopabandhu in the Secretariat premises with a memorandum. One of our eldest leaders, Rayadhar Lohar asked, 'Biju Babu, you had promised us to bury BALCO if you came to power. Now you have decided to extract bauxite from the mountain. Does it mean burying BALCO? You say bauxite will be extracted but nothing would happen to the mountain. Is it possible? If you extract the cerebrum (*Bhasa* in odia and *gudi* in Kosli) from the brain of a person, will she be alive?' Biju Patnaik got angry but said that no mining would take place. He said, 'If western Odisha does not develop, I will tell people that Yuva Parishad is responsible. You ask them'.

Gangadhar Sahu remembers:

> We reached PMG square, Bhubaneswar. I sang a song there: *mor maharaja dangar raja, haschhen mulmul*. Then we were invited by the CM Biju Patnaik. He met us at a place near Gopandhu statue in the Secretariat. After discussion, I sang a song:
>
> *Sunantu ahe Bharata sarkar, milu nahi khaibaku ahara ...*
> *Bauxite pain kete bhavana je, bikuchha Gandhamardana*
>
> [Listen Oh Government; We have no food to eat.
> About bauxite you are so keen; You are selling the Gandhamardan]

During Biju Patnaik's tenure, mining plans remained buried. When in 1996, J.B. Patnaik became the chief minister and announced mining could begin from the Balangir side, thousands of people came out in protest and put a halt to the project yet again. One of the strengths of the anti-BALCO movement is the presence of independent organizations and social formations who are opposed to bauxite mining irrespective of which party comes to power (Pradhan 1996). Therefore, any attempt to mine Gandhamardan is till today met with widespread resistance.

The reader might wonder what happened to the hundreds of women who had sustained the struggle throughout. With the retreat of BALCO, most women retreated to the drudgery of their routine lives except occasional participation in anti-liquor protests. They remained excluded from the calculations and manipulations of electoral politics. They lament the opportunistic manner in which most male leaders entered electoral politics. Pankajini Rout is apprehensive of the immediate future:

> The fight was against BALCO. But after BALCO left, there has been no social progress. All our male leaders barring a few entered electoral politics. The daily oppression of women in the villages continues. Nor are they able to stand up against violence and other social evils. Gandhi wanted the revolution to last long. The liquor shops did not disappear with the coming of independence. Sadly, the *andolan* here became quiet after BALCO left. We have to be mindful still. The tiger has been wounded. Everybody knows the wealth that is here now. We know their eyes are on the bauxite still.

Ever since the 1990s, self-help groups have proliferated in the region. It keeps women busy meeting their targets. Pankajini Rout reflects:

> The government propaganda about women's empowerment is bogus. No empowerment has happened through SHGs nor NGOs. Why do people have to migrate to Andhra Pradesh and Tamil Nadu? They work in construction sites and brick kilns in Bhubaneswar and Cuttack too. The government is now aggressively promoting corporate interest as development. NGOs and SHGs backed by company funding are doing everything, knowingly or unknowingly, to dismantle people's capacity. They call it grassroots work and that these are 'collective' initiatives for 'capacity building.'

Upon asking whether the bonding among women has continued since the movement, Jambabati Bijira holds the SHGs responsible. In her words:

> Now every woman is trapped in this SHG or that and I think these SHGs are being funded by companies who have their eyes on the bauxite of Gandhamardan. How will we fight together against the company when we are receiving money from them? Women actually think the government is helping them earn. They do not think there is need of any *andolan*. I was asked to help and maintain accounts. I refused. After that I was sidelined. I do not want any loan from the government. I do not want to be part of any group that gives me debts. When I said this, I was told that I am doing things against my own interest and women's interest. I told them it is only in the interest of the companies and the government that they give us loans. That also divides us women. Everybody is being destroyed. This is *kalyug*. There is lack of belief in anything. The SHGs have tied down everybody and broken our unity. I am not so popular now for having adhered to my beliefs. But I am protected by Lord Nrusinghnath.

BALCO was a single-entity public sector company and the people had stood up against an elected government. But as long as the bauxite is in the belly of the mountain, the eyes of the entire corporate world are on it. Raj Kishore Seth recalls the events that followed:

> In the year 1995, we got to know that a company called Intercontinental Resources Ltd. is going to mine bauxite from Gandhamardan, especially from Harishankar side. Once again, we began to organize people. On 1 January 1995, we organized a mass meeting in the Khaprakhol high school field. Some 5,000 people participated in it. We gave a memorandum to the government demanding (1) stop mining; (2) build small check dams to utilize the stream water for irrigation; and, (3) develop mechanism for protection of medicinal plants of Gandhamardan. Subsequently, a series of meetings and camps were held at various places: 19 August 1996 at Lathor mass meeting and an activist camp at Kapsipali. We also organized a cycle rally from Khaprakhol to Patnagarh and gave a memorandum to the sub-collector, Patnagarh. In one of the meetings at Harishankar in the year 1997, 7,000 people had gathered for two days to discuss the future course of the movement. The play *Gandhagiri* was enacted there.
>
> In 2005–2006, an aerial survey was made. In protest we organized a mass meeting at Tankpani. Gandhamardan Surakshya Yuva Parishad, till date, is organizing two annual meetings i.e. on 19 August (the foundation day of GSYP) and 1 January. The first was organized at Nrusinghnath and the second at Harishankar.

The bauxite-hungry *asuras* have been restlessly waiting; their masks change, sometimes it is NALCO and sometimes it is Vedanta. A visit by senior officials from NALCO in March 2007 caused massive protests on

1 April and 3 May. When BALCO got bought over by Vedanta,[3] the news put the people on alert. They are only too familiar of people's resistance to Vedanta's mining plans in the neighbouring district. In September 2010, Prasanna Sahu gave a memorandum to the president and the prime minister. The GSYP swung into action again and held a massive protest against Vedanta on 1 January 2011. Meanwhile, Prasanna Sahu is busy working on a draft legislation that can protect the mountain forever. He said:

> For whatever good reasons the MoU was cancelled by the Government of Odisha in 1989, those reasons have not changed. So, why should there be constant effort to get at the bauxite? We need some legislation that protects the mountain forever. And we will get it.

CRPF was deployed across the region from 2010 onwards. The threat of possible mining operations and the awareness of Maoist presence hold many people in check, including agents who collect medicinal herbs and plants for ayurvedic companies. Frisking and checking two-wheelers and buses became routine to create intimidation and terror.

On 28 December 2010, Madhav Singh Thakur and Ramesh Sahu were killed by the SOG and CRPF as they were returning home on a motorbike. Madhav Singh Thakur had, a month earlier, questioned the fresh mining plans when the CM visited the area. Some suspected the mining lobby to be behind these deaths; others attributed it to the pressure on Bargarh police to produce statistics of encounter deaths.

Thakur was once an active member of the local BJP unit. Ramesh Sahu was a small shop owner. The Odisha Human Rights Commission took *suo moto* notice and demanded a police report. The Bargarh SP went on record stating how the deceased had strong connections with the Maoists and they were killed in an exchange of fire with the security personnel during a combing operation in the forest bordering Chhattisgarh. Local BJP leaders punctured the story, claiming both were active BJP members who had nothing to do with the Maoists.

Both Paikmal and Jharbandh remained deserted and local people mourned these two deaths as the bandh call given by the GSYP was a complete success. Just as the idols gone missing had bound the people in their attachment to the Gandhamardan mountain, these killings brought them together. They know too well that the mountain is still not safe. The *asura* is on the prowl, hungry for bauxite. CRPF and the paramilitary dominate the region even as we write this chapter.

On 24 July 2012, while going out on the routine chore of fetching water from the tube well near her house in Vindhyabasini colony, a twenty-year-old woman was harassed by some jawans. She managed to outwit them and fled for her life. This incident created a furore among the local residents. When we met the young woman, she said:

> They caught hold of my hand. I struggled to wrest it free. They pressed their boots on my feet. They threw some money into the vessel I was carrying. And one of them said that he was my husband. They began dragging me by force. I was petrified. I told them that I am coming with them and pointed in one direction. When they started walking, I fled in the opposite direction towards my house. I ran all the way without looking back. My hand was hurting and also my feet. My bangles had broken. I could not speak for a long time.

The local people were enraged. The Paikmal Nagrik Committee mobilized people to insist that the police register her complaint against CRPF. Lulu Samal, a youth activist, said:

> People's own grievances against surveillance and daily frisking were getting unbearable. There had been daily harassment of workers, vendors, hawkers and practically anybody who walked the road. Buses are searched for naxalites. Two wheelers are stopped and checked as if we are moving around with bombs and explosives that they can detect to stop a war! CRPF jawans are everywhere. They freely help themselves to people's chicken and eggs. They can pluck anything from the vegetable gardens. They can stand in front of a *paan* shop and empty out a jar of biscuits or salted snacks. How much can people tolerate? So many people came together because this incident was the last straw. Initially, the SDPO of Padampur refused to register a complaint against the CRPF. But the large presence of villagers gave them a scare. They were forced to do their duty.

However, the CRPF Commandant, along with his men, swooped down on the woman's house in full force and cordoned the house. They negotiated with her husband and brother-in-law to withdraw the complaint. The woman said:

> Within two days, around 50 CRPF jawans came to our house and stood all around. Their head spoke to my husband at length. We called the local people again to immediately come to our house. Had it not been for the local people, I do not know what would have happened. I have been married since a year only. My parents and in-laws are worried. How long can we stay here? We are migrants. We will again rent a house and take up work somewhere else. We are wage workers. It is easier for us to move than pay such a heavy price for staying here.

Saving the Gandhamardan for livelihood has not ruled out distress migration within the state and outside. Today, there is heavy migration from these villages to the brick kilns of Andhra Pradesh and Karnataka. Western Odisha is in the grip of a deepening agrarian crisis, peasant suicides and distress migration. The migration from the areas around Paikmal is higher still. Their hardships are aplenty, but their nostalgia nourishes their sense of identity with the mountain. And people are still ready to rise if any threat is posed to the mountain.

Notes

1. '*Muin kain korsi go...*' a song composed by the Gandhamardan cultural activist Gangadhar Sahu. He was inspired by the account of a woman lamenting the loss of the mountain if bauxite mining were to take place. The songs composed by him for the movement are popular till today.
2. Prasanna Sahu, one of the leaders of the movement, is referred to as Swami Swamabesh now.
3. It holds a 51 per cent stake in BALCO, while the remaining 49 per cent is held by the government of India.

References

Concerned Scholars. 1986. *Bharat Aluminium Company: Gandhamardan Hills and People's Agitation*. Sambalpur.

Gandhamardan ro Sandesh. February 1987. Sambalpur.

Gandhamardan ro Sandesh. February 1988. Sambalpur.

Gandhamardan ro Sandesh. June 1987. Sambalpur.

Gandhamardan ro Sandesh. August 1987. Sambalpur.

Gandhamardan ro Sandesh. September 1987. Sambalpur.

Gandhamardan ro Sandesh. October 1987. Sambalpur.

Gandhamardan: A PUDR Report. 1986. New Delhi.

Geo, E.A., and Gallo, P. 2007. *Summary Report*. Gandhamardan Bauxite Deposit.

Mishra, A.B. 1987. *Mining a Hill and Undermining a Society: The Case of Gandhamardan*. New Delhi: Centre for Science and Environment.

Pradhan, Lingaraj. 1996. *Samiksha 96 Odia o Odisha*, Bhubaneswar: Bikalpa Sandhani Manch.

Sahu, Prasanna Kumar. 1986. *A Comment by Kishen Patnaik on the Play Gandhagiri*. Sambalpur: Gandhamardan Surakshya Yuva Parishad.

Senapati, Nilamani, and Bhabakrushna Mahanti, eds. 1971. *Sambalpur District Gazetteers*. Chandrasekharpur: Gopabandhu Academy of Administration.

CHAPTER 5

The Conch and the Missile

Wherever one sits, the earth bears the burden.
—Durwa saying

Wearing a simple white vest and a white dhoti, he sits half-crouched with his rugged right hand gripping the handle of an umbrella as if it were a walking stick and his head is covered with a worn-out piece of cloth with fading green stripes. He is facing the camera and fervently asserting that they wouldn't leave, come what may:

> We won't leave. We won't leave our land. It is just not soil for us. It is a land of gold. We get everything from this land. The government supplies just kerosene to us. Let it stop (his voice rises and his lips quiver). We will manage with castor and mustard oil. But we won't leave our land. (He suddenly tries to rise up balancing his body by tightening the grip over the stick and fumes with anger). Let them kill, let them kill me. I am showing my chest to the bullet. The government has got everything with it: guns, bullets, swords and forces. We have only our conches and brass plates. If the government wants to loot our land, it can do so only over our dead bodies. Till then, we won't leave, we won't leave. (*Voices from Baliapal* 1989)[1]

R. Padhi, N. Sadangi, *Resisting Dispossession*,
https://doi.org/10.1007/978-981-15-0717-5_5

This 'land of gold'—the Baliapal and Bhograi blocks—lies in the extreme northern corner of the Balasore district along the Bay of Bengal. River Subarnarekha criss-crosses the expanse of this land before emptying into the ocean. Through her long course, the river brings both sorrow and happiness to people living in its vicinity and beyond. And this, the river has been doing for centuries. When she swells up in the monsoon, she ravages the entire area, leaving a trail of destruction all around. But then, she also enriches the soil with natural minerals that make it fertile. Local people believe 'what Subarnarekha takes away in monsoon; she gives it back a hundred times more in summer.'

The fertility of the land, so nurtured by Subarnarekha, has made this region prosperous. While reminiscing on the movement, Sarada Giri, a leading activist of the movement, stressed upon the fertility of the land:

> The soil here is so fertile that we can easily make a living even with a tiny piece of land. Everything—rice, ground nut, cashew, betel, vegetables—grows here. When during the movement days, the government cut off our supply of kerosene, we produced oil out of cashews and lit our earthen lamps to manage light for ourselves. For us, to save our land was a question of life and death. Take me, for example, my husband is ill; he cannot do any physical labour. I have got six *gunthas* of land (24 decimals). I cultivated it on my own and did the additional work of husking paddy in other people's houses. Just doing this much I managed to send my children to school and college (two sons and two daughters). Slowly I also started *paan* cultivation on another piece of land.

Subarnarekha has yet another gift for the local people. Her estuary is the bread basket for nearly 30,000, mostly landless, local fisherfolk.

Bhubana Patra from the fishing community was in the forefront of the movement despite being landless. In his words:

> Fishing from the estuary of Subarnarekha is our source of living. Neither did we ever have an inch of a *patta* land then; nor do we have it now. We do not even have any record of rights over homestead land. Still, this is the land we are born into. Our umbilical cords are buried in this soil. It is our *Bheetamati*, our mother. How can we allow it to be dismembered?

Flowers bloom here
Throughout the year
Spring smiles,
Humming bees
Move around

In maddening breeze
Branches are laden with
Red, ripe fruits.
The baby-sun leaps out
To the heart of the sky
From the dancing blue
Waves of the sea.
The fish of Life
Swims across the Subarnarekha
Tender red leaves turn green,
And yellow
Throughout the year. (Nayak 1988)

But this land of gold is not without an underbelly. A tiny piece of land or a fruit-bearing tree is precious, to be protected and guarded like any treasure. Any transgression to disturb this relationship can lead to prolonged legal battles, which sometimes becomes so acrimonious that it leads to fistfights, resulting in breaking of legs and skulls.

Pushpanjali Nayak has depicted this bitter rural reality in her novel *Matira Praharimane* (*Sentinels of the Earth*):

> Sapani, an old widowed woman of 60, gets into a dispute over a mango tree with her neighbour, Siria Pradhan. She sells the silver jewellery gifted by her late husband in order to bribe the revenue inspector to secure her record of right over the small piece of land, where the tree stands. Agara Mallik, a marginal dalit peasant fights with Hari Sahu, a landed Sahukar, over a small piece of land and both land up in hospital. (Nayak 2004)

A Gift

The then chief minister Janaki Ballabh Patnaik made a grand announcement to the press upon his return from New Delhi in July 1984 that he had brought a gift of Rs 300 crores for the people of Odisha from the centre. However, he did not divulge any details about the nature of this 'gift.' About a month and a half later, the people of Baliapal got the first glimpse of this multi-crore gift, when Chintamani Jena, the then MP from Balasore, informed in a meeting at Jagai College Hall that the central government was going to establish a big defence facility in a coastal part of the state. Three months later, the chief minister visited Baliapal and declared that a National Missile Test Range would be set up in the area.

During election meetings a year later in 1985, the chief minister kept assuring that, 'None of you would be displaced for this.' He explained that all they had to do was to stay inside when there was a siren, signalling the launch of a missile and come out when there was another siren, indicating the finish of the process. He insisted, 'In no way, your work would be disturbed.'

When an old man asked him what if his daughter-in-law were to feel labour pain just when the first siren went out. 'How am I supposed to take her to the hospital?' The chief minister couldn't answer him.

People had little understanding about the exact nature of the project till then, nor did they have any idea of its pros and cons. They even did not know about the extent of area to be acquired for the purpose, or the actual number of villages to be affected.

A few days later, when a sheaf of papers relating to the project reached the office of the District Collector (DC) in Balasore, a clerk working there got to see these confidential documents. The documents revealed that a total of 126 villages of Baliapal and Bhograi blocks were to be acquired for the project and a radar station was to be set up on top of Swarnachud hill at Nilgiri. He shared this crucial bit of information with some people. After that the news spread as swift as lightning. It was then that the people realized 'the gift was nothing but a recipe for disaster.'

Some school teachers took initiative and formed an informal protest committee. They even organized a few meetings. The committee became inactive within a few weeks, as the leading members of the committee were supporters of the Congress. All of them buckled under the pressure from the party. Since most of them were in government service, pressures from authorities also worked.

Gadadhar Giri, a popular leader, then began mobilizing his local Janata Party elements to build up a movement against the project. At this juncture, Gananatha Patra, a central committee member of Unity Centre of Communist Revolutionaries of India (UCCRI-ML), happened to meet Gadadhar Giri in a train. Subsequently, they also had three more rounds of discussions and agreed to work together despite their ideological and political differences. They held a series of meetings in various parts of the area in October 1985.

Giri also mobilized state-level Janata Party leaders to come to Baliapal.

During the puja vacations, students of Baliapal and Bhograi formed the Anti-National Test Range Students' Forum. It even held demonstrations before block headquarters. This had an inspiring impact on the elders of the locality to go beyond their political affiliations.

As the movement gained momentum, a wide range of political groups and individuals came forward to lend their support. The movement came to absorb all sorts of views and tendencies for the protection of *Bheetamati*. A slogan emerged in unison: *Maati laagi party naahin*. This means there would be no divisive party politics in the interest of saving *Bheetamati*.

Uttar Baleswar Khepanastra Ghati Pratirodh Committee (North Baleswar Anti-Missile Test Range Resistance Committee or KGPC) was formed in December 1985 with 229 members, representing all villages of the affected area. Members of various political parties were on the twelve-member steering committee. Sarada Giri was the lone woman member. Besides Gadadhar Giri, eight of the members were *paan* traders and three belonged to the landed peasantry.

A Fishermen Front was also formed with the support of the Institute for Motivating Self Employment (IMSE), a voluntary organization working in Bhograi. Similarly, Bhabani Bhuyan, an activist of UCCRI (ML) from Puri, initiated the Women's Front and worked towards organizing women. Even today, women of Baliapal remember her fondly. While Giri led the steering committee, Patra guided and worked through these mass fronts. Initially, Dr Radhanath Rath, editor of the leading daily Samaja, was also part of the campaign.

The Conch

When Biju Patnaik went on a tour to Baliapal after the devastating flood in October 1985, he gave a call to women to blow the conch or beat brass plates to alert people of any imminent danger from external forces, as was traditionally done at the time of floods.

Giri also thunderously declared that if the government established the test range, it would be done on only his corpse. Just as he finished, a few conches blew in response. Since then, the conch became their preferred and prominent tool for communication to alert people. It came to symbolize the resistance against the proposed missile-test range. The sound of conch symbolized their voice of unity.

Minati Jena, recalling her experiences about the power of conch in uniting and inspiring the people to fight, said:

> I was 19 or 20, when the anti-missile test range movement began. I had just got married then, but I was not yet a mother. Whenever there was a call, we used to come out of our houses with conch shells in our hands and begin marching towards Kalipada or Baliapal or Balasore. In every rally, dharna and demonstration, we held the conch in our hands throughout. It was the only weapon we had. No axes, no sickles. Our slogan was: *Take Our Lives, But Not Our Land.* I remember thousands and thousands of men and women, old and young and children used to pour onto streets hearing the sounds of these conches.

The use of conch helped mobilize women in thousands. Thousands of women stood as shields before the gun and lathi-wielding policemen. That served as a formidable barrier. As Bhabani Bhuyan recalls:

> The conch is generally blown three or five times on auspicious occasions like marriages, child-births or at the time of puja. So we made it clear that if someone blew it more than five times, it would be signal for danger. It would then continue till the danger was identified. The blowing then would generally spread quickly from one woman to her neighbour and from her to the entire village, and then from village to village until all other villages had not joined in. The administration was afraid of the these poor, illiterate conch-blowing women. The police felt ashamed about not being able to breach the wall that we women erected before them to enter the area and they would often take out their frustrations by passing snide remarks like, 'Men of Baliapal are using women as their shields.' It's not like that we were merely being used as shields by men, we were the equal partners with them in this collective struggle to save our land. Active male members of the movement always gave priority to us and compared us to Goddess Durga. We were even addressing meetings and were always at the forefront and all this was happening very spontaneously.

The sound of conch had an exhilarating effect in inspiring ordinary souls to overcome personal sorrows in their lives and come forward in this fight for saving their collective future. It motivated them to jump into the vortex of the movement, which for them had by now become a movement meant for their survival, for securing the future of their sons and daughters and *their* sons and daughters. Subhadra Jena, who is employed in a school now, recalls:

> After my husband's death in 1979, I went back to stay with my parents. Since my husband was working in a school, I got employment in the same school on compassionate ground. I was not very regular at my work. When

> the movement began in 1986, I got involved in it. My parents also encouraged me to participate in it. I was 30 then. There were many women in the movement. We were moving from village to village and mobilising people to protect our land. Whenever there was a call, we went and participated in it. It felt good, a kind of a feeling of *desh seva*. After the movement was over, I came back to my school. By then my job had also been regularised. Other comrades carried on in their lives, choosing their own respective paths. Young girls got married and settled down in their lives too. I get to meet them once in a while. We share stories of the movement. When my husband was alive, we had adopted Alekh Dharma. I even got a Sunya Mandir (Temple of Void) built to honour my husband's wish. Now I spend most of my time in school and in the service of God. I feel at peace with myself.

In Baliapal, the call of the conch played magic in mobilizing the young and old, women and men. The movement transformed many people; it gave a sense of purpose. Also, the determination to protect *paan* cultivation bound them together, irrespective of caste or class. Be it *paan* chewers or cultivators, the *paan* has been the source of inspiration for many a struggle in other places too. Even the *paan* has a history to tell.

THE BETEL

The introduction of betel leaf, *paan*, to the area of Bhograi-Baliapal, came to alter its social chemistry. It was the people of *Barajia* caste who first brought this particular plant to this area from nearby Bengal in the early twentieth century. However, it did not spread as fast as they expected. It was believed by many people then that betel cultivation would bring along bad luck and eventually result in the extinction of their entire clan. It was only when traders from Benares began sending their brokers to buy *paan* leaves from this locality and marketed it as *Benaresee patta* that the cultivation slowly picked up. Initially, rich and middle peasants from upper-caste background took the lead. Its cultivation needs constant tending by skilled labourers. Local people liken it with the caring of a kid or attending to a daughter-in-law, who has come home for the first time after the wedding.

As *paan* cultivation grew, a class of local *paan* traders also emerged. They developed their own supply network in far-off places like Delhi, Agra and Bombay without having to depend on the Benares traders. The quality of *paan* from Baliapal-Bhograi impacted these markets such that the demand always outgrew the supply. This is especially true of Bombay. The technique of turning green leaves into yellow was known only to traders from Benares until then. It was Purusottam Behera who brought the technique to this area. He narrates his experience with both pride and fulfilment:

> In 1969, I started trading in *paan* leaves. Dama Padhiari of Kalbasa was doing it before me. In those days, people from Benares had the monopoly over this trade. Once I went to Benares on a business trip. I was most surprised by what I saw there. While our ten baskets of big size *paan* fetched only Rs 400, there one basket of yellow *paan* was selling at the rate of Rs 340.
>
> It made me understand and learn the technique of turning green leaves into yellow. My *paan* owner also had a tent business and I made friends with his workers and started working there as a fitter. There I learnt about the people who knew of this technique. I approached them. I did not tell them that I was also a *paan* trader. I asked them to provide me work. They agreed but with the condition that only food and shelter would be provided until I learnt everything. I worked there for four months and learnt the whole process in that time. Coming back, I began imitating this process at Baliapal. We call it *jhaliba*. I gave a new name to our yellow *paan*, *Jagannathipaan*, or, in short, *Jaggipaan*. Before the Baliapal movement, 187 workers worked with me. All of them learnt this technique. Now, 80–90 of them have become *paan* traders. That is my greatest happiness in life.

After the local traders perfected the technique of *jhaliba*, they urged small peasants to cultivate *paan* in their homestead land for expansion of production. Soon, some people from fishing communities and lower-caste landless peasants began cultivating *paan* on sandy land carved out by the receding sea. Unlike upper-caste families, where it was a taboo for women to work in *paan baraja*, here women and children worked in the *baraja*. Slowly, the widespread cultivation of *paan* began to have a sort of trickle-down effect. All sections of society were able to benefit from it. It is for all these reasons and more that the *paan* was able to galvanize the rebellion against the National Testing Range (NTR) project of the central government. The *paan* as a symbol of resistance has a history in the surrounding districts too.

When the price of *paan* had increased during the phase of the Non-Cooperation Movement at Mahala haat near Kendrapara district, freedom fighters had tried to control its price by giving a call to the people not to buy it. On 15 February 1922, Dama Nayak and Turti Lenka protested against an increase in the rate of *paan* and fought with Netra Malik, who was in-charge of the *paan* trade of a local landlord and got arrested by the police. This infuriated the locals, who gheraoed the police and got them released.

On 30 July 1938, when the State of Dhenkanal introduced the licence policy to be able to earn more revenue and acquire monopoly over the *paan* trade, people once again came out in protest. The Dhenkanal State People's movement gave a call to withdraw the licence system and appealed to people not to chew *paan*. Within months, this led to a full-scale agitation against the State of Dhenkanal. Baishnaba Pattanaik, one of the leaders of the movement, reminisces:

> A momentary incident like boycott of paan led to the historic Dhenkanal Praja Movement of 1938. It was like the beginning of Great Mahabharat War from a small incident. (Mohanty 2001)

At this point in history, the *paan* had to confront the missile. The moment had come when no political party could ignore the anti-missile movement.

The Missile

As the movement was growing in strength, the embarrassment for the Congress at the local level was increasing. The Janata Party heaped all blames for the proposed NTR on Congress. In retaliation, the Congress refuted the blame by asserting that it was, in fact, during the Janata Party regime at the centre that the decision to have this project here was taken. The mud-slinging on each other continued, reducing the issue to the question whether the project should be located here or somewhere else. The larger issues of war and peace, the issue of Indian defence (seen as a holy cow and considered a sacrilege to speak against it) and the issue of people's say in it became secondary. The stand of Janata Party, which was most active in the movement, kept shifting from time to time. Nilamani Routray, the ex-chief minister of Odisha and an important leader of the party, endorsed the setting up of the missile test range but suggested an alternate place. He said:

> Strategically, and otherwise, Andaman would be the most suitable place for setting up this proposed missile test range in order to strengthen our defences in that part of the country and for enhancing our strategic command over the India Ocean region. (Rout 1986)

On the other hand, Biju Patnaik tried to be tactical in vain. He kept suggesting the shifting of the project elsewhere. But he did not spare the opportunity to project himself as an anti-war crusader too:

> I am considerably disturbed about starting an exceedingly high-cost test range under the aegis of the defence ministry ... How can such a concept be compatible with crusade against nuclear proliferation, if you engage yourself in building vehicles for nuclear strikes? How would the prime minister of India defend himself as the saviour of human race while simultaneously preparing for a nuclear war? May I appeal to the prime minister to review the entire matter afresh. One defective Russian reactor has already created havoc: Must we also participate in the ultimate crime of destroying life on the planet? When millions of men and women all over the world are on the march to protest against every form of tools and vehicles that may lead to nuclear holocaust, would our government consider it amiss, if tens of thousands of people of Odisha join their hapless brothers and sisters of Baliapal to prevent planting of seeds of a nuclear war? (Patnaik 1986)

At the local level, activists of UCCRI (ML) argued that the NTR was part of the Indo-Russian Treaty and strove to posit the Baliapal movement as an anti-war movement. They gave slogans: *Want Peace, Not War* and *Want Land, Not NTR*. To the question of shifting the project, their response was 'neither here, nor elsewhere.' The civil rights organization Ganatantra Adhikar Surakshya Sangathan (GASS) made consistent effort to raise the issue of peace and disarmament. It organized screenings of the film *The Day After* to spread the message of the dangers of a nuclear war.

But how did the local people respond to this issue?

Interestingly, the film *Voices from Baliapal* captures quite a range of responses (from *Yes* to shifting to Andaman to *No* to nuclear war) from people after they watched the film. A cryptic comment came from a fisherman when he asked, 'I do not understand why do they want a missile range, when the government is always avowedly talking about peace and disarmament abroad? Why play the saint, if you are not?' But what ultimately became the stance of the movement is articulated by Brindaban Raj, president of Khepanastra Ghati Pratirodh Committee:

> Ours is an independent country. In the struggle for freedom against the British, many of us went to jail and faced batons. What does this freedom mean, if we are not even consulted before taking a decision to set up a test range on our land? Can the government of a free country decide to arbitrarily

> evict us? But ... if the government of India is adamant on its stand, then we are also adamant that *WE* have decided that *WE* will never allow them to build this range here ... We will not let them enter our land. (Raj 1990)

JANATA CURFEW

In February 1986, the government of Odisha issued phase-wise eviction notices to villages through newspapers. In response, Gadadhar Giri led a delegation of 300 members to Bhubaneswar to meet the chief minister. The meeting could not take place because the chief minister by then had left for Delhi. The Student Front held a demonstration before the Collector's office and submitted a memorandum to the President of India. But even this did not deter the government from continuing to issue notices.

Later that month, the committee gave a call of gherao of all the offices of Revenue Inspectors of the area, prompting the officials to lock the offices and leave. Agitating people pasted their memoranda on doors and walls of these locked offices. The Student Front declared janata curfew in the entire area. Messages were sent to villages to keep a watch on the movement of government officials. Thus began the retreat of the government machinery and advance of people's power. The incident of 2 March 1986 was a turning point.

It is still alive in people's memory:

> I still remember the day we gheraoed the collector. Thousands of people had gathered ... the collector was made to walk from Kankadapal, where a meeting was held. After sometime police forces also reached. When the collector was about to leave, we asked him, 'You are taking away our land, where shall we and our children live? Can you give us the similar kind of fertile land that we have?' He assured us, 'Mothers, why are you worrying? Now I am leaving but I will do something for you. If I fail, I will leave my job and go elsewhere.' (Chanda 1998)

Gananatha Patra, who played a leading role in the movement, analysed this incident from the point of view of people's initiative and its import in the future course of the movement:

> News reached that DC Ishwar Chandra Dash, ADC Bansidhar Mohapatra and SDO Benudhar Mishra had gone towards Chaumukh in a jeep. It was immediately decided to gherao them. When [I] banged *thali* (brass-plate) to

> alert people, thousands and thousands of conch shells began to blow in tandem, reverberating the air by the synchronic sound it produced. It went on and on. A centre of control was established and directions were given to block all entry points like Kalipada, Jamakunda, Kachua and Panchupalli by forming a human chain.
>
> At Chaumukh the officials were asked to get off from their vehicles and walk. The wireless was disconnected. People had gathered at village squares so that it would take much time to walk down 9 kilometres to reach Kalipada. There was just one kilometre to reach when news came that SP Susil Pradhan was present at Kalipada with massive contingent of police force. The human chain at Kalipada was not letting them enter. People caught hold of two policemen with wireless sets, who were trying to sneak in riding a motor-cycle. The SP was all ready to break through the human chain by using tear-gas shells, lathi-charge and bullets anytime. When we heard this we left the SDO free and told him to inform the SP that the Collector and others were arriving safe. If the SP tried to break the human chain, the lives of the Collector and others would be in danger. With this instruction to pass he was let free. He ran so fast as if he was participating in some race competition. It had a good effect on the SP and he refrained himself from taking any further action. The Collector reached Kalipada safe. By that time there was a sea of people there. People were agitated but remained under control. They showered the Collector with questions, which he fumbled to answer. By the time the Collector left Kalipada, it was already three in the morning.
>
> On that day, the entire proposed area of the NTR had turned into a battleground. Conches were blowing the whole night and the sound of which was making the adrenalin flow in our veins to make us resolute in our fight. People carried Petromax lights on their heads, lightening up the entire area. It is interesting to note that top leaders like Gadadhar Giri and Brundaban Raj were not present on that fateful day. Still, thousands spontaneously joined in. Seeing the success of this radical action, we immediately decided to launch the barricade movement. (Patra 1996)

Baliapal had seen people's resistance in 1954 when the Odisha government planned to dig the Ambchua-Dagara canal. It would have diverted the course of the Subarnarekha River and prevented some villages getting washed away by the river. People of Chaumukh, Dagara and other villages would have been displaced. Many more would have been cut off and trapped in an island between the river and the sea. The affected villages began an agitation to save their land under the leadership of Praja Socialist Party leader Pyarimohan Das. When the agitation intensified in the year 1955, the government clamped Section 144 on the entire area and arrested the active members of the agitation. A local person filed a petition in the

Odisha High Court challenging the government's decision. The court gave a decision in favour of the people and ordered the government to stop digging the canal (Sahu 2013).

Bhabani Bhuyan who was a key organizer of the marches against the missile test range recalls:

> I remember one incident. It was 5 June 1986. The sun was blazing. Nearly six to seven thousand women and men marched to Balasore, nearly fifty to sixty kilometres from Baliapal. Some of the women were carrying their children and a bag of *mudi* [puffed rice] in the hand. Women would take a dip in any pond that came on the way along with their clothes as the heat was intolerable. When they reached the Balasore station, one gentleman asked, 'Mothers why have you brought these children with you?' One woman answered, 'Janakia would take our lands and villages, and what would you feed the child with?'

There was a similar march on 18 April 1943 by the drought-affected people of the area, popularly known as the Hunger March. It was an innovative protest against colonial rule, and the leader of the march was a twenty-three-year-old youth Durga Shankar Das (A Smaranika of Durga Shankar Das 2016). The challenge then was to save the people from hunger, and today it was to save *Bheetamati*. The conch and the barricade became the symbols of people's resistance.

THE LAXMAN REKHA

A tin plaque was hung on the barricade at Kalipada, which read: *The Land Is Ours, The Sea Is Ours, Government Go Back.*

The barricade was not just a physical structure to prevent government vehicles to pass, it was also a dividing line between the State and the people's power. 'So the barricade that people had erected at Kalipada was sort of a *Laxman Rekha*. It was the most important thing in the Ramayana that was unfolding in the anti-missile resistance movement of Baliapal,' remarked Amulya Behera, a potter and a cultural activist.

The twin brothers Kusadhwaja Jena and Nabaghana Jena were very active on the Youth Front. Both had been sentries at the barricade as long as the movement lasted. People fondly called them Laba-Kusa, Jaga-Baliya or Jay-Bijay. Kusadhwaja Jena recalls:

> I remember it was GP who first proposed the idea of barricade. It was passed in a meeting of the leaders of various fronts. The first barricade was finally erected at Kalipada. The resistance committee also accepted it. We had a system of rotation (*pali pratha*) to defend the barricade. At least 30 men and women were guarding it at any given point of time. Each village had to supply 5–6 people each day. Subsequently, similar barricades were also put up at Panchupally and Kachua.

The years in the movement have left behind some scars. His twin brother Nabaghana Jena speaks at length:

> We are twins. He is younger to me. That is why people call us Laba-Kusa. We are landless but I had a motorcycle repairing shop and him a cycle-repairing shop at Kalipada. Both the shops were in proximity to each other. The shops were our only sources of living. When the need came to protect the land, we readily accepted the role of gatekeepers. Even before the movement, I had a good relationship with Giri. Whenever he came to our area, he always used to sit in my shop. He inspired me to contribute to the movement in whichever way I could. As we got more and more involved in the movement, we hardly had time to run the shops and shut them down. After the movement was over, Kusa could not revive his old shop at Kalipada. I shifted elsewhere. This is mainly because when Giri passed away, some local leaders of the Janata Party got involved in nefarious activities taking advantage of the barricade. When we exposed it, they became hostile. My brother could never counter the hostility to open his shop again.

The barricade was an innovative experiment in a popular struggle. It immediately caught national attention. Researchers, activists, political leaders and important personalities swarmed the Baliapal and Bhograi areas. Everyone was keen to understand, appreciate and imitate it. The movement suddenly had generated a lot of curiosity among different sections of society.

About this barricade experiment, researcher Sujata Patel writes:

> Baliapal closed itself out and its people established a *de facto* control over their land. The movement's committee became the 'government' and the enforcing law and order agency. This started the internal siege of Baliapal. (Patel 2001)

The absence of state machinery created a void and the committee had to take charge to solve day-to-day disputes. *Vichar*, a traditional village system of arbitration, was resurrected to handle this. Eight members of the steering committee were given the responsibility for eight gram panchayats to hold *vichar* sessions to settle disputes; other four members acted as arbitrators. This had a miraculous effect on bringing down police cases in the area notorious for land disputes and resultant criminal suits. It also had effectively checked entry of law-and-order machinery into the area. The blockade continued. Even the CM had to cancel his tour thrice due to popular resistance.

In retaliation, the state government imposed economic blockade by stopping the supply of PDS items like kerosene, sugar and so on to the area. Still it could not break the resolve of the people. People made do with castor and cashew. The fisherfolk helped in bringing kerosene from nearby Digha town of West Bengal. Tactics of economic blockade had miserably failed. Frustrated, the government then played another dirty game to create fissures in the movement. It declared to scale down the project area to fifty-four villages. An attractive rehabilitation and resettlement package was announced to lure away people from the movement. Leaflets detailing the rehabilitation and resettlement packages were air-dropped. It included a model village for the displaced people and nine industrial units (a spinning mill, a *vanaspati* factory, an oil mill, a leather industry, an agricultural tool factory and four other projects) were announced, which were to be taken up by Industrial Promotion and Investment Corporation of Odisha (IPICOL) to take care of their needs of employment. But this also could not make any significant dent on the unity of the movement.

The people vehemently opposed it, saying, 'Spinning mill is a death mill, weaving mill is entrance to NTR,' and also destroyed the foundation of the model village.

Art in Resistance

As the movement gained ground, local people began to use available cultural repertoires–song, poetry, drama and musical drama–to deepen the struggle and to spread the message far and wide. Not only local people but also poets, dramatists and writers of Odisha joined in. Many people still remember Gaurang Rout's street play, 'We Want Peace, Not War.' He shares with us his journey and the experience of staging the play at Baliapal.

After completion of M.A. from Utkal University, I did not accept any job. I had a passion for drama and started working with Anweshan, a cultural group associated with SUCI. I was not a member of SUCI but stayed in the Party office. Owing to some differences, I left the Party office and stayed at the Bhubaneswar Railway Station. At that time, reports on Baliapal were in newspapers. Two things struck me. One was displacement of thousands of people from an area known for betel, paddy, fish and greenery. Another one was war. Because missile test range means war, that too atomic war. The shadow of the cold war was still lingering We were aware of the horrors of Hiroshima and Nagasaki. Then I wrote the street play 'We Want Peace, Not War.'

Along with the young artists of Anweshan, we started rehearsals of the play at Bhubaneswar Secretariat Club. One day, Sushil Roy came with an invitation from Brajanath Rath to make a play of Fakir Mohan Senapati's short story *Daka Munshi* and to stage it at Balasore on the occasion of the great writer's birth anniversary. In fact, the invitation was for Narayan Pati, the founder of Anweshan. But by this time, he had left for Bombay. I told Roy that I was not competent to do that sort of play. Instead, I told him that we were rehearsing another play. He came and watched the rehearsal for some time and disappeared. After half an hour or so, he came back and told us to get ready for Baliapal to stage this play. At that time, Braja Rath and others were going to Baliapal. So we could go with them and they would arrange everything.

We were youths. We immediately agreed to his proposal without thinking much. We packed our bags and carried our *dholak* and *harmonium* and left for Baliapal. When we reached Kalipada gate, the Pratirodh Committee did not allow us to go in. Braja Rath and others went into the area. The Committee made a condition that if the play was in support of the movement, they would allow us. Hence, members of the Committee would watch the play first. We felt terrible. It is a play, what is this business of supporting and opposing. Still, we got ourselves mentally prepared and began the show.

To be honest, I had written this play but had not seen Baliapal. But our inspiration was Sachi Routray's poem '*Chhota Mora Ganti*' and Binod Nayak's '*Gramapatha*.' I had imagined Baliapal as a land of betel and fish, a land of greenery. Now, I don't remember the lines. But other lines are like this:

Baliapalara Bhai ho! Bhogarai Bhai!
Lahu luha dhali tuhi gadhilu dunia
To suna duniare lagigala nian
Ma aakhi luha tote karuniki bai
Mo Baliapala Bhai! Bhogarai Bhai!

[Brothers of Baliapal and Bhograi!
The world you made with tears and blood
That world is up in flames
Don't the mother's tears drive you insane?
My brothers of Baliapal and Bhograi!]

I have marked that when we sang these lines women wept. Once, one of them fainted.

You know both state government and Central government were interested in the project–Janaki Patnaik at the state and Rajiv Gandhi at the centre. We showed them as king and monarch in the play in the model of Moghul Tamsa. But people could easily identify them. Listen to these lines:

Suna Sunare suna
Rajanka ghosana suna
Baliapalare kshepanastra heba sthapana
Sahe tirish khanda gan heba uchhanna

[Listen Listen Listen!
The King has proclaimed!
Baliapal will have a Missile Test Range,
Will destroy one hundred thirty villages!!]

We had put in an evil character in the play. His business was to persuade people to leave land, to disturb the movement. Rai (now cine actor Raimohan) was playing that role. When people saw this character they jeered at him, hurled abuses at him. At times, people got so carried away that they came to the stage to beat Rai.

At the end of the play, there is a slogan: We Want Peace Not War, Long live Human civilization. On that day, when we ended the play at Kalipada gate, hundreds of people watching the play began chanting the slogan. Then, hundreds and hundreds of conches began to blow and people ululated to felicitate us. These sounds and sight are still etched on my memory. That day, I realized what was meant by people's art and what it meant to be a people's artist.

After this, this play was staged 50–60 times at many villages and marke places of Baliapal and Bhograi. The play had so much impact on the people tha the DG police called me to the police station and threatened me not to stage the play. I did not listen to them. Though, I had to pay a heavy price later in life.

Purusottam Behera, though known for his pioneering role in bringing the technique of turning green *paan* into yellow, is equally recognized for his songs and musical drama 'Maharakshya kshyapanastra.' He said:

> Just before the beginning of the movement, my wife passed away. I started writing songs to console myself. When the movement started, I wrote patriotic songs on Baliapal. People love to listen to songs and memorize them more than speeches. I kept writing on the happenings of the time. For example, when the Government declared rehabilitation scheme and industries for employment or when we decided to form *Marana Sena* or when Gadadhara Giri died. I don't remember the lines of these songs. The notebooks were lost in the 1999 super cyclone. I remember when Gadadhar Giri passed away; we added a scene in the Geeti-natya, where Parvati is berating Lord Shiva for taking away Giri's life. Shiva is consoling Parvati that he will take birth and lead the peace movement in the 21st Century.

Death of a Leader

When the movement was at its peak, Gadadhar Giri passed away on 13 January 1987 in Delhi. The news left the entire movement shocked and numbed. The loss was huge; some even thought he might have been poisoned. He was maintaining a fine balance between the steering committee and various fronts. Soon after he was gone, the coordination between the committee and fronts broke and a gap began to emerge and widen; a sort of tug-of-war ensued to claim the leadership. On the other hand, his rather untimely death proved to be a heaven-sent gift for the government and the pro-NTR Congress elements to weaken the movement. Taking advantage of this situation, the state government offered a tripartite talk between the CM, the opposition leader and the committee. But the talks failed to yield any consensus.

The administration made many attempts to forcibly enter the area, in vain. On 3 February 1988, the Collector announced his intention to enter but was prevented by about 20,000 people. On 8 May, Operation Baliapal was put into effect. Magistrates were asked to accompany the Collector and a 5,000 to 8,000 strong force of Orissa Armed Police was moved about five kilometres away. But the Collector was dissuaded by senior officials (PUDR 1988). On 25 May 1988, the DC of Balasore declared that they would enter the area forcibly by breaking the barricades erected by the villagers. He reached the area with massive police force, ambulance, fire-brigade and a team of doctors for any emergency situation. The movement gave the call for a human chain at Kalipada to defend the barricade. Nearly 25,000 people had gathered at Kalipada by daybreak and lay on the road, blocking all traffic. Basanti Pila, recalling the incident, says, 'One incident that I particularly remember was that someone very influential had visited our area. Conches were blowing and we were all rushing to Kalipada. There were thousands of women. We all lay on the road, from the canal to Kalipad on a stretch of 2-3 kilometres.'

Seeing such resolve among people, the Collector and his armed forces had to retreat. People had once again proved their unity despite all machinations and threat of violence on the part of the administration and bickering among top leadership.

After this incident, the government made no further attempts to break the barricade. Also, the movement did not go on offensive for scrapping the project altogether. A stalemate continued.

By mid-1989, the air was rife with imminent elections. Political parties were bracing up to face the electorate once again. At this juncture, the Janata Party demanded to lift the barricade for election campaigns. The committee dominated by elements of the Janata Party readily agreed to the demand. A hope was generated that the project would be scrapped if Janata Party came to power. Finally, the barricade was lifted in November 1989. Thus, the *Laxman Rekha* that people had drawn to protect themselves from the evil designs of state power suddenly disappeared.

Although all governments remained ambivalent about scrapping the project, none dared to push for it at least in that area. Thus, the fertile soil of Baliapal-Bhograi, its rivers and paddy fields, its *paan* and fruit trees remained alive; and, its women, its fisherfolk, its peasants and *paan* traders had succeeded in saving their *Bheetamati* not only for themselves but also for their children.

The proposed missile test range did however come up some sixty kilometres away from Baliapal at a place called Chandipur. And now it is spreading its tentacles there.

Twenty-five years is no small time. The youth of that time who have become old recall the stories of how they protected their *Bheetamati*. But the young are in search of a future in distant lands only. Today, the youth are leaving for places such as Surat, Visakhapatnam, Hyderabad and so on that seem to be greener pastures. Amulya Behera said:

> It is just not the lure of money that motivates the young to go outside; it's a question of value system. Being a packer in some tile factory or being a hotel boy in some city hotel is seen as more dignified by today's youth than to toil in a field and earn livelihood from agriculture.

Arjun Charan Barik, a youth leader of the movement, reasons it out:

> Except *paan* cultivation, all other forms of agriculture are no more sustainable here; fish catch is also dwindling, resulting in meagre earnings for fisherfolk. And this is the primary reason which is pushing the youth to move out.

The coastal district is witnessing other developments too. The government is planning to set up fourteen ports on the coastline to export minerals and import materials for mineral-based industries. These ports will be set up from Chaumukh at the mouth of the Subarnarekha River to the Bahuda mouth in Ganjam district. It is the turn of the villagers of Chaumukh, who now face the threat of being uprooted for the proposed Subarnarekha Port. Such development swallows up not only the people who will be thrown out of their habitats but also the land and the jungles, the paddy fields and the *paan barajas*, the rivers and the beaches.

Note

1. The documentary *Voices from Baliapal* was made by Vasudha Joshi and Ranjan Palit in 1989. It was one of the earliest documentaries on people's resistance to displacement in India.

References

A Smaranika of Durga Shankar Das. 2016. *Mahan Swadhinata Sangramai Durga Das Ae Matir Santan*. Bhograi.

Chanda, Basanti. 1998. Published in *Odia O Odisha*: Sameekshya '98 - People's Struggle in Post-independent Odisha and the Role of Women.

Joshi, Vasudha. 1989. *Voices from Baliapal*. A Documentary Film.

Mohanty, Baishnaba Charan. 2001. *Pana O Priyatama*. Bhubaneswar: Capital Students Store.

Nayak, Pushpanjali. 2004. *Matira Praharimane*. Cuttack: The Cuttack Trading Company.

Nayak, Samarendra. 1988. *Baliapal* in *Aau Chup Nuhen*. Balasore: Subarnasri Prakashani.

Patel, Sujata. 2001. Community, Identity and Politics: the Baliapal Movement. In *Community and Identities*, ed. S. Jodhka. New Delhi: Sage Publication.

Patra, Gananath. 1996. *Baliapal Kshepanastra Ghati Birodhi Andolan: Ketoti Analochita Diga* (Anti-Test Range Movement of Baliapal: Some Aspects Not Yet Discussed. Published in *Odia O Odisha*, Sammeksha '96; People's Struggle in Post-independent Odisha).

Patnaik, Biju. 1986. Letter to the Prime Minister, dated 2 June, 1986. *The Other Side*, August.

PUDR. 1988. *Bheeta Maati: A Report on Baliapal Missile Base and People's Struggles*. Delhi: PUDR. August.

Raj, Brundaban. 1990. *For Baliapal! A Handbook*. Kolkata: Unnayan Publications.

Rout, Nilamani. 1986. Baliapal Test Range and India's Defence. *The Other Side*, August.

Sahu, Narayana Prasad. 2013. *Hero of the Anti-Ambchua-Dagara Canal Agitation* in Biplabi Samajvadi Pyarimohan Das. Balasore.

CHAPTER 6

Chilika Teere

'Fish,' he said softly, aloud, 'I'll stay with you until I am dead.' He'll stay with me too, I suppose, the old man thought and he waited for it to be light.

—Hemingway, 2004

Passengers on the Howrah-Chennai rail route chatting nonstop over peanuts and hot tea go into a stupor when the Chilika Lake appears. They watch mesmerized from the windows as the train rushes through a few kilometres of magic scenery. This natural beauty of the lake has inspired poets, writers, artists and filmmakers alike. It was this train journey that inspired Gopabandhu Das to write about Chilika in the 1920s in *Bandir Atmakatha*. Radhanath Rai's *Chilika*, an epic ode to the lake, lives even today in the hearts of many. Godavarish Mishra's *Kalijai* also immortalizes the lake for the imagination of the people. It is in this way that Chilika has become an integral part of Odia nationality.

The lake and its natural habitat is a much coveted holiday destination, a honeymoon retreat or even a weekend escape from the daily grind of life for many. The temple of Kalijai, situated on a tiny island in the middle of the lake, draws daily many of the god-loving people of Odisha. The Irrawady dolphins on the Satpuda side draw many tourists. If a weary soul is able to rest a while and lighten one's heavy heart, it is simply because of the thriving aquatic life underneath the water surface that has kept the

R. Padhi, N. Sadangi, *Resisting Dispossession*,
https://doi.org/10.1007/978-981-15-0717-5_6

ecosystem intact. With sunshine illuminating the vast expanse of hundreds of square kilometres and penetrating deep into the lake bed, there are millions of creatures underwater ceaselessly performing a range of activities. Migratory birds fly from Serbia, Russia, Mongolia and other parts of Central Asia and Europe to their destination—the wetlands of Mangalajodi on the northern side of the lake. These birds fly thousands of miles to the Nalaban Island because the abundance of aquatic life here becomes food for them and the marshy wetlands provide ideal nesting ground. Local guides, armed with a tattered copy of Salim Ali's *Book of Birds*, help tourists identify as many as they can see of the 165 different species that populate the wetlands. These birds intermingle with the local birds, from November to March each year, and then fly back to the seas—from Caspian to Aral and many more.

You are likely to recall the name of Chilika as the largest brackish water lagoon in Asia from geography lessons in school. Yes, it is a rare wonder on this planet where the sea water rushes in to meet the water from a number of streams and rivers. Spread over more than 110 square kilometres, the lake touches three districts: Puri, Ganjam and Khurda. During the monsoons the lake expands to 1,165 square kilometres, and at the height of summer, it shrinks to 790 square kilometres. The sheer length of the lake from north to south is over seventy kilometres. It is separated from the Bay of Bengal by a sixty-km-long strip of marsh land and wetlands.

This alluring landscape and its shimmering waters hide many deep secrets. And darkness and sorrow too. Invisible to the world outside or the teeming tourists who come daily or the prayer-muttering pilgrims live almost three lakhs of dalit fisherfolk in 135 villages. Chilika is home to them; their modest dwellings dot the Chilika coast and are scattered inland too. Fishing is their traditional occupation. Living in abject poverty, they have fought many a tough battle to protect their fishing rights from predators in many avatars. The film *Chilika Teere*,[1] which was released in Hind Cinema in Cuttack in 1977, evoked the pathos of this exploited community. It depicted their gruelling poverty, back-breaking labour and myriad hardships. As they deal daily with money lenders, community tensions and local goons, the film builds to a climax. The protagonist Raghu, who is a rebel, leads the village to rise up against the manager of the fishing company who buys their produce. The film went on to become a legend.

The lives of fisherfolk across the seas are marked by abject poverty and exploitation. In *Chilika Teere*, Raghu addresses a gathering of villagers:

> There is no dearth of fish and water in Chilika. Yet we are always so deprived. The fish trader cheats us in weighing the fish. They suck our blood and discard us like prawn shells. How long will we tolerate this? (*Chilika Teere* 1977)

Soon the fisherpeople of not only Raghu's village Sujanpur but also from nearby villages rise in revolt against the traders. See the resonance in the manner in which the protagonist in a Mexican film addresses his fellow beings:

> Friends, how long do we have to put up with this slavery and poverty? Who of you in any given year earns more than 40 centavos a year? Who can feed their families with so little? Who has money for medicine? We all know it's unfair, but we know it doesn't have to be this way. A few exploiters take everything to satisfy their greed. They did not make the sea, the rivers or the fish, and they didn't make the canoes, boats or nets either. Nor did they make us. They didn't give our arms the strength with which to work or anything else. Why can't we exchange our fish with those who breed cattle, with those who harvest corn, or with those who make fabric? Who prevents this change? Those with money have taken over the boats, nets, transport. They control everything and they pay us whatever they like. We know what happens for eight months of the year, when there is no fishing. And when we can fish, they take half for the boats and the nets. The exploiters pay us six centavos for a kilo, and they pay the chief his share plus two centavos per kilo. They resell it for 3 centavos with ice and for 12 in crates. If it costs 26 centavos, they sell it in Mexico City for 80. Poor folk elsewhere can't eat fish and we can't eat vegetables. Poverty is not the law of nature, nor is it God's law!
>
> The exploiters are strong because they unite to exploit us. They agree to pay us the same, and shackle us all with the same chains. Let's unite, as only then will we be strong enough to protect ourselves. We ask only for what is rightfully ours, the fruit of our labour! (*Redes* 1936)[2]

The people of Chilika knew the sweat and toil that goes into earning a square meal a day. But when the 1990s arrived and stirred up the economy in a frenzied manner, Chilika was not spared. The 'poor' state that houses this natural beauty became greedier of high profits from private investors. When commercial prawn cultivation began, big money reared its ugly head and, with it, its bulging muscles. Tata was the most prominent predator that the fisherfolk chased away. However, the fishing mafia dominated by upper-caste Odias and money bags from other states tightened their stranglehold. Venturing into the rough sea in the fishing season became a question of life and death.

Contending Claims

Mountains, hillocks, lakes and rivers abound in stories narrated over generations. Indeed, the line between fictional accounts and historical facts is thin. Chilika is no different. There is a fourth-century legend about the pirate king Javan Raktabahu, who came to plunder Puri. He anchored his fleet of ships very surreptitiously off the coast and waited for the opportune time to strike. But the sea washed up the refuse and debris from the ships to the shore, thereby warning the people of the imminent attack. People fled the town with all their belongings. When Raktabahu entered Puri and found it abandoned, he raged in anger. He concluded the sea had betrayed him. So, he led his army to wage a war against the sea itself. As his army advanced, the sea kept retreating. But there came a moment when the sea too rose up in retaliation. It surged back and flooded the shores, destroying the entire army of the pirate king. When it finally settled down, what emerged from it was the Chilika lagoon. Since then, local people live reassured that Chilika can always fight off any predator.

Chilika is believed to be protected too. The deity of the fisherfolk is Ma Kalijai, whom the fisherfolk invoke whether on the waters or in deep sleep. There is a story when an impressive flock of flamingos alighted at Chilika. As they walked on their long legs in a disciplined military manner, the army of the Raja of Khurda mistook it to be another army and fled. The royal family of Raja Harisevak Mansingh was mighty relieved as they had suffered much loss. He thought that Kali made them victorious (*jai*) and thus named the goddess Kalijai. Wherever her name comes from is for lesser mortals to figure out. It is true that the storehouse of hair-raising tales of the fate meted out to those who incur her wrath has lived generations. Chilika has been a coveted and contested space since centuries and continues to remain so.

In 1997, when the royal family of Parikud tried to sell off a portion of the lake along with Ma Kalijai, the organization of the fisherfolk—Matsyajibi Mahasangha—rose in resistance. Anadi Behera, one of its leaders, recalled:

> In September 1997, the royal family of Parikud tried to sell part of the Kalijai hillock to a retired sub-inspector called Mahapatro. They planned to sell 14 acres and 80 decibel of land for Rs 70,000 to build a luxury hotel. We were stunned with disbelief. Who can dare to sell a goddess and a hillock? The deity residing there is our sacred goddess. We have fed her our *pakhaal bhaat* and *poda macho* (fermented rice and roasted fish) every single day with our own hands. She has been with us forever in our happiness and sorrows. From disbelief it was collective outrage. We set out to retrieve both Ma Kalijai and the hillock. This incident brought all the fisherfolk together. We started an *andolan* and thousands converged there in boats. We stayed there and did a *yagyan* (sacred fire) for four days to sanctify the temple. The state government was forced to cancel the lease. Chilika is home to the fisherfolk. We won that struggle.

Once more, myths and legends reinforced their truth, as the protectors of Chilika fended off modern day pirates.

To Whom Does Chilika Belong

Seventy-five-year-old Hadibandhu Ghadei, a member of the Durga Primary Fishermen Co-operative Society, lives in Banpur. He was among those who had their *sairats* (fishery sources)[3] around the Nalaban Island that got declared to be a bird sanctuary under the Wildlife Protection Act in 1972. Perhaps his was the first generation that forfeited its traditional fishing rights. He recalls:

> We had our lease area near Nalabana; it is the area that lies between Gurubai and Anlakuda. The names of these *janas* were Kathapentha, Boranganasi, Baruan and Godhi. It is far from our village where we lived. In the fishing season, we would go and stay there for days to do fishing. When the government declared the bird sanctuary in the Nalabana area, our *janas* were taken away from us. No compensation was paid. At that time, we were not so conscious; we could not gather courage to fight the government. We also did not have money to enter any legal battle.
>
> Like daily labourers, we go to Chilika every day for fishing to support our families. If we fail to go even one day, the entire family starves. How can we fight the government legally? Court cases cost so much money.

When tourism promised to fetch revenue, the government snatched away the livelihood of the fisherfolk. They, along with their progeny, had to fend for themselves like the group of young men who were intently listening to our conversation. They work as daily labourers in Balugaon and Banpur. He continued:

> The bird sanctuary was meant to protect the Australian birds. The government was more eager to protect birds from Australia than the fisherfolk of India. That is also fine. The government must have got some aid from Australia for this. Why did it not share the money with fisherfolk who lost their livelihood and futures due to a bird sanctuary?

The sorrows of the fisherfolk never seem to end. After the sanctuary was made, another disaster struck them. Whatever leasehold area was left, the nearby non-fishermen villagers forcefully occupied those lands and started prawn cultivation. The fight to hold on to their *sairats* became perilous:

> Our villages were involved in the Matsyajibi Mahasangha. The government did not give us protection despite meetings, appeals and agitations. The non-fisherfolk were allowed to seize our rights. But now see what is happening. Within one and a half years, all the prawn *gherries* have been demolished. We welcome this because we have wanted an end to prawn cultivation. But how could the government do it so swiftly now? Now that they are out to put an end to illegal prawn cultivation, they are throwing us out of the waters too! The Chilika Development Authority (CDA) is destroying our *khandas*; they are seizing our nets and equipment. As a result, fisherfolk are losing thousands and thousands of rupees. Once again there is an attack on our livelihood.

We were trying to peep into the history, but the present was in too much turmoil. Illegal prawn cultivation was being brought to an end by the government after many years. What was the grand plan this time? Tourism was our best guess.

Anadi Behera had asked us to meet him at the statue of Gandhi on the main Balugaon road. There were many questions we had in mind while waiting for him. Does one begin with the Sorana firing or go further back to the history of the fishing co-operatives? He soon arrived and took us to the office of the Matsyajibi Mahasangha. Any dilemmas about where to begin were put to rest as he placed the proposed new bill of 2017 on the table. He said:

> The central question is: who does Chilika belong to? And even today that is under dispute. In any case, there had always been caste hatred and we were looked down upon. We were the untouchables. But today everybody wants to do fishing as it brings big money. Even the powerful and rich no longer think it is a profession meant for untouchables. They have finally rallied

> together behind this bill. What happens to our traditional rights? We have always maintained that the land is yours but the fish is ours. From 1959 itself our traditional rights as fisherfolk had been protected by Leidlaw.[4] Only the fisherfolk with traditional rights on their *sairat* obtained them on lease. We were the lease holders always. But this new bill is changing the very definition of fisherman itself. According to it, everyone is a fisherman! The government is taking away our traditional rights as fisherfolk.

Even before the co-operatives were made, the people of Chilika enjoyed full access to the fish, dependent on it for their livelihood since generations. The non-fisherfolk lot from villages also enjoyed fishing rights, albeit in a limited manner, who could fish for their own consumption. The fisherfolk community paid a royalty (*chulimunda*) to the Raja of Parikud or the Raja of Khallikote depending on the area that had their *sairats* or the allotted fishery grounds.

During British time, the fisheries of Chilika were also under the control of various zamindars, who leased out the fisheries exclusively to the traditional fisherfolk of the area and collected royalty. People belonging to Keuta and Nolia castes were catching fish from Chilika, whereas Khatia and Kandara bought the fish and sold in nearby villages. This continued until World War II. When the zamindari system was abolished in 1951, the people got the lease directly from the government of Odisha (Upadhyaya 2013). But the hold of the zamindars and mahajans remained; consequently, indebtedness and poverty remained. The earliest primary co-operatives were created in 1926. However, the nefarious practices of cheating and intimidation by caste Odias persisted.

The Fact-Finding Committee on Chilika Fisheries constituted by the government has observed:

> The land belongs to the Revenue Department and the traditional fishermen are the leaseholders to fish and hence only the traditional fishermen have the sole right over the lake water. This they have enjoyed from time immemorial and they seem to have documents to this effect from the days of the Maharajas. Caste-Hindus (meaning the non-fishermen) have forcibly occupied the land and water or have taken the water rights on a sub-lease basis. The caste-Hindus use their social, economic and/or mere physical muscle power to retain hold over the land and water and also to acquire more land. The traditional fishermen are increasingly realising this social and economic subordination and want to regain control over their traditional rights and to change this subordinated status. Village level opposition to this subordination

> and efforts at regaining control over their traditional rights have led to physical conflicts and to law and order problems. There have been continuous occurrences of bloodshed over these issues. The unequal competition between the traditional fishermen and others to gain control over resources will only increase as fishing becomes more profitable and as more and more people with capital to invest are allowed to enter the area. (The Report of the Fact-Finding Committee on Chilika Fisheries 1993)

Officially, the fishing community has always lived below the poverty line for decades. They eked out subsistence from what the fish fetched them, especially rice for the household. And indebtedness was part of their lives. Fisherfolk have always been forced to sell their fish to the moneylenders who would sell it at higher rates to agents from outside. So the possibility of making any profit was always curbed by the same sahukars.

As Anadi Behera recalls:

> It was only from 1974 till 1990 that we had exclusive rights. Till 1980 we were able to eke out an existence with debts that the community would always be able to pay off. Fisherfolk are always poor; but the waters give us enough to look after our families. But there began a lot of intrusion from many corners of the country. People came to trade fish in Chilika waters from Tamil Nadu, Bengal and Kerala. From 1980 till almost 1993 this coercion and domination kept increasing. It was in the eighties that we began hearing about prawn export and cultivation.

Prawn cultivation began in Chilika during the 7th Five-Year Plan under the Economic Rehabilitation of the Rural Poor Scheme (ERRPS). In the years 1984–1985, 25,000 acres of water-land was identified in Chilika for economic rehabilitation of some fisherfolk. Out of this, 300 acres were distributed for prawn cultivation. As the prawn cultivation proved lucrative, the mafias got the opportunity to enter Chilika. The primary co-operative societies were floundering and landed up borrowing money from moneylenders of Brahmagiri, Puri and so on to deposit lease money. At times, they were also sub-leasing their own fisheries to moneylenders. This opened up the route for moneylenders to begin prawn cultivation in Chilika (Report by Manabika Adhikar Sangathan 1999).

The world around was changing; the economy was taking a big turn. The 7th Five-Year Plan coincided with a big development in the global scenario. The promotion of aquaculture to meet the global demand for fish came in the guise of a Blue Revolution. In the mid-1980s, the Asian

Development Bank and the World Bank, along with other international outfits, began investing millions of dollars into promoting aquaculture. Private entities began exporting prawns, harvesting huge profits by striking clandestine deals with co-operatives. The hold of the moneybags and the fishing mafia on the local fishing community tightened.

As one of the most active members of Meet the Students, Nirakar Behura, explains:

> How did the upper caste and the big business enter into fishing in the eighties when the upper caste had always regarded fishing as an occupation of the lower caste? It is significant to reckon here that capitalism operates on the logic of investing capital wherever huge profits are guaranteed from the principal amount invested—be it the market for fish or the activity of sweeping and cleaning, or the bazaars of Africa or America. Therefore, when the demand for the *bagda* prawn became high in the global market and its price escalated fast, the entry of small and medium industrialists as well as big capital grew exponentially. (Behura 1996)

With the demand of *bagda* prawns becoming the most coveted export item, the ruling party in power too saw dreams. It ushered in its much favoured corporate body.

Resisting Tata

In 1986, the J.B. Patnaik government proposed to lease out 1,400 hectares of area to a company that would be a joint venture of the government of Odisha with the Tatas. This spurred the Janata Dal to don the mantle of the rescuer. Most dramatically, the Janata Dal leader Biju Patnaik took an oath with a handful of water from Chilika and swore to get rid of the Tatas. The war cry by the party *Chilika bachao, Tata hatao* reached all villages. No wonder that all five assembly seats in the Chilika region went to the Janata Dal in 1989. Once in power, the party dropped its mask as swiftly. In 1991, it openly invited Tata for a mammoth prawn cultivation project. The deal was the same but there was a renaming of sorts under the guise of 'development.' Thus, the joint-sector project called the Chilika Aquatic Farms was planned near Panaspada and Gola villages of Brahmagiri block in Puri district. It was a Rs 20-crore project that included a hatchery in Puri, a processing plant on the Bhubaneswar-Puri road and a feed mill.

The people of Chilika, along with many organizations and individuals, came together and formed the Chilika Bachao Andolan. The *andolan* attracted attention to the imminent takeover of Chilika waters by the Tatas and drew solidarity from across the country. The many forces within the movement were from differing ideological persuasions but were united with one objective: to throw out the Tatas from Chilika. And they did.

Over twenty young students from a group called Meet the Students from Utkal University left for the region to work among the fisherfolk in resisting Tata:

> We were young and full of zeal to understand the roots of social inequality. We used to have intense discussions organized. There were people who inspired us like the late Gandhian freedom fighter Manmohan Chowdhury, the founder of *Pragatibaadi*, Pradyumna Bal, the revolutionary poet Rabi Singh and many others. In a meeting held in June 1991, we urged people to join us. Among those present, Chittaranjan Sarangi joined Meet the Students and became an integral part of it. Almost 8,000 people *gheraoed* the Odisha Assembly on 20 September. The mobilization was done largely by Matsyajibi Mahasangha. The three-year lease to the fisherfolk's co-operatives was going to expire on this day. (Behura 1996)

The huge turnout at the assembly along with thousands of people from Matsyajibi Mahasangha energized the young students. They became hopeful of campaigning across the state. However, leaders of Matsyajibi Mahasangha were wary of the alliance. Mistrust got expressed as allegation of NGO funding for the rally was made against a leader of Meet the Students. The latter continued to work in the eastern side of Chilika in the name of Chilika Bachao Andolan. On 22 January 1992, the *andolan* appealed to the Office of the Revenue Divisional Commissioner (RDC) against the advance possession of land given to the Tatas by the government. On 2 February, the RDC issued a stay order declaring the transaction as void and warned Tata not to try entry as the land was under dispute. But the company continued to advance its plans. This intensified people's resistance.

On 14 February, there was a furore in the Assembly and seventeen MLAs cutting across party lines created hell for the CM. This was triggered by press coverage by Karantidarsi Yuva Sangam exposing Tata's illegal encroachment and the unauthorized embankment construction. The fisheries minister had to admit that no formal lease had been given to the Tatas. But he remained noncommittal about the illegal encroachment and the construction of the embankment (*Chilika: Voices of the People* 1993).

Everyone—from children to the elderly—participated in protests and sat at the barricades they set up near Gopinathpur village to block the entry of vehicles or personnel from Tata or the administration.

Gobinda Behera, who was the convenor of the Chilika Bachao Andolan, recalled:

> The construction of the embankment near Gola was in full swing. People marched and took over the Tata-occupied areas, hoisted a flag and declared a 'Janata Curfew.' There were so many from outside the fishing community. There were students and people from Puri and Bhubaneswar, who gave us hope and energy. We were almost 5,000 in number that day on 16 February, determined to break the embankment and reclaim the land. On 7 March women marched to the embankment and began breaking it. Within a few days, the number grew. Thousands of people would march to the site to break the construction. We could not break it. These were symbolic actions. There were platoons of police and goondas roaming the area always. Tata had hired all these antisocial elements to break our struggle. The police were with Tata too. We set up a gate to stop all Tata vehicles. The atmosphere was charged all those days. We were ready to die to save Chilika. On 28 March, eleven platoons of police descended on us, and began a severe lathi charge that took us unawares. There had been no provocation. Many people ran helter-skelter. Many were injured grievously. Almost 70 people were arrested. Among them were women and children. They also picked up the university boys and girls. The villages went quiet. On 4 April, they arrested Chittaranjan Sarangi.

Even as the news of the arrests spread, there seemed to be no reaction to the police crackdown by any progressive organization. Unlike present times, there was a dearth of people's lawyers who could immediately offer legal support. The only support came from students again who gheraoed the District Collector of Puri and demanded the release of all those in jail. They were all released on bail on 9 April. Some of the cases continue till date. Very soon, the *andolan* organized itself again and lobbied for support. Some 21 MPs signed a letter to the prime minister urging him to restrain the Tatas. There was also an appeal made to the environment and forest minister. The *andolan* organized *padayatras* and reached out to all villages to keep up the fight. At a high level meeting in August 1992, the then environment minister Kamal Nath ordered an enquiry for environment clearance that was still pending. The resistance and the solidarity actions and the media coverage made Tata withdraw quietly. The company incurred heavy losses. And yet again, like a flock of disciplined flamingos, the fisherfolk and the people and the students came together and made a different army flee.

However, extensive prawn cultivation continued.

STRANGLEHOLD OF OUTSIDERS TIGHTENS

On 31 December 1991, the government declared the new policy, which for the first time divided Chilika into capture and culture sources. The traditional methods of catching fish were curbed drastically. This policy also earmarked a percentage from both the sources for the non-fisherfolk of Chilika. Out of the total of 47,000 acres, 27,000 acres were reserved exclusively for fisherfolk for capture and 20,000 for cultivation. Out of this, 14,000 acres were for non-fisherfolk and 6,000 acres for fisherfolk. This established the legal rights of non-fisherfolk for the first time in the history. Once that happened, big money and mafia claimed almost the entire of the lake. Although they were allotted 14,000 acres, it was an entry point to slowly take over the lake. They spread their base and took over almost 75 per cent of Chilika. Though, they were only supposed to do fishing, they entered all other areas. The two policies introduced in favour of the outsiders by the Odisha government first hit us hard. We knew we had been cheated by the government. (Anadi Behera)

Three primary fishermen co-operative societies filed writ petitions in the High Court challenging the 1991 fishery policy of the Odisha government. The High Court ordered the formation of a committee to independently investigate into the facts and status of fishing rights of the traditional fisherfolk. A retired professor named Ghanshyam Das headed the committee when it was formed on 26 April 1993. The committee was also expected to look into the operations of the fishing mafia and what ails the ecology and environment of the lake. Within three months, the report was ready. It was indeed a rare government acknowledgement. For the first time, the presence of fishing mafia and their links were made official:

Mafias are attracted to 'hot money' which comes through prawn trade. They are the persons with money and muscle power, who by enticement and intimidation exploit the poor fishermen and non-fishermen. The induction of the mafia to the lake dates back to early eighties when culture fishery started. The mafias have been inducted by the third party sub-lessees or by encroachers. The third party sub-lessees take either verbal or written lease illegally from the regular lease holders of certain fishery sources for prawn culture by paying an exorbitant lease amount and they are, by and large, absentee landlords who operate from Puri, Bhubaneswar and Cuttack. It has come to the notice of the committee in course of its field visits in the lake that some of these absentee landlords comprise important politicians or their relations, bureaucrats of standing, and moneyed people, who apparently have a lobby with the government. They are there for minting money, as no other alternative investment by payment will give them such a relatively high

> and quick return as that of prawn farming. They make a huge investment by payment of subletting fees, purchase of prawn seed/juveniles, capital investment by way of pen-enclosure, provision of watch and ward for the culture source, transport cost, handling charges, etc. It is but natural for them to see that their investment remains safe and intact and yield an income in time and as such, their *modus operandi* is mafia operation. Indeed, the mafias are recruited by them both from outside and locally to provide the necessary watch and ward service at the culture sources point. Sometimes the mafias also take sublease of some fishery sources for themselves and operate them for prawn culturing. The mafias are playing havoc today in the lake as they have become the real monarch and determine the fate of the poor fishermen. It is learnt that they are armed with deadly lethal weapons like guns, revolvers, AK-47s and bombs. They symbolize encroachments and all acts of illegalities in the lake areas, terrorise the local people and want to have a grip over fishery sources. (The Report of the Fact-Finding Committee on Chilika Fisheries 1993)

Once money bags and muscle power became the modus operandi, even fisherfolk became indirectly complicit. By leasing out their plots to non-fisherfolk, they paved the way for mafia domination. Soon those dependent on leased-out resources became vulnerable to coercion and violent takeovers. Thus, most depositions made to the Committee appealed for freedom from the tyranny of the fishing mafia. Those at the helm of affairs in Bhubaneswar looked the other way. Their own coffers would dry up otherwise. The stranglehold of the mafia on the area tightened as never before. Chilika, once more, was under siege. With their bombs, and their guns and their greed, newer versions of pirates and plunderers kept appearing relentlessly, wave upon wave.

Police Firing at Sorana

Three whitewashed busts under a small thatched canopy at the entry of the village remain as tragic reminder of the events of 29 May 1999. That night, Pramila Behera, Banchhanidhi Behera and Lingaraj Behera from Sorana were killed in police firing. Sudarshan Behera from Bhusandapur and Digambar Behera from Jagulipadar were also killed. When collective resistance of the fisherfolk had peaked once again, it was brutally crushed. Let's trace the events that led to the Sorana firing, when the fisherfolk took to direct action in dismantling illegal prawn *gherries.*

Based on the Committee report, the Odisha High Court delivered a verdict on 23 November 1993 that upheld the rights of the fisherfolk. The Court banned prawn cultivation and held the government responsible in preventing the entry or proliferation of mafias. Nothing much changed on the ground.

On 27 June 1996, the revenue minister reported in a meeting held with the chief minister that illegal prawn cultivation was taking place in almost 20,000 acres in the districts of Puri, Khurda and Ganjam. As a result, by September, notice was served to dismantle all such illegal *gherries*. A programme named Operation Clean Chilika began in October under the supervision of the Puri Collector. He was in charge of clearing 14,000 acres of the total area under forcible occupation. The Sub-Collector Dharmananda Dalai, directly in charge of the operation, was transferred within 24 hours. That was the end of Operation Clean Chilika (Manab Adhikar Sangathan 1999). Yet another public interest litigation was filed in the Supreme Court by a Gandhian named S. Jagannath. On 11 December, the Supreme Court banned prawn cultivation in Chilika and ordered the dismantling of prawn farms and *gherries*. Next year on 5 July 1997, members of the Matsyajibi Mahasangha met a parliamentary delegation that had come and registered protest against continuing prawn cultivation and lack of access to their fishery sources.

The persistent demands of the Mahasangha to free Chilika of the prawn *gherries* and implement the High Court and Supreme Court orders were going unheeded by the government. The victory of the Mahasangha in preventing the sale of a portion of the Kalijai island had galvanized their energy and unity. As Anadi Behera recalls:

> The collective action against the selling of Kalijai had revived our movement. In 1999, we intensified the struggle to free Chilika. People were in despair. There was no fish left. There was emptiness all around. *Jana maana sunyo hoi golaa*. If we were to survive, the prawn *gherries* had to be dismantled.

The months of March and April in 1999 saw organized resistance building up. Over 3,000 fisherfolk with 300 boats gathered to take up the clearing of the prawn *gherries* on their own by 24 April. This happened at Barkul:

Seeing the gathering of fishermen, the district administration of Puri and Khurda came to talk to the Sangha and promised them that the eviction campaign would begin on 28 April in Khurda and 2 May in Puri districts. But the Sangha did not swallow the sugary promises of the administration and began direct action on 24 April. They cleared around 1,500 acres of land by destroying big prawn gherries in the Krushnaprasad block. Meanwhile, it was declared that the Puri collector would come for discussion and Sangha should not take law into their hands. The administration arrested 67 fishermen and confiscated four boats at the tail end of the campaign. They were forwarded to court on charges of dacoity. On 27 April, some 5,000 men, women and children blocked the National Highway at Balugaon for five hours demanding unconditional release of arrested fishermen. (Manab Adhikar Sangathan 1999)

The cry to free Chilika of the hold of the mafia reverberated across Odisha and outside. The massive demonstration was unprecedented and made breaking news. The administrations at Khurda and Puri were compelled to dismantle *gherries*, but the big ones owned by the influential were left untouched. The Mahasangha announced in a press conference in Bhubaneswar that they were exhausted of the manipulations of the government and would resort to direct action again.

Braja Ghadei of Baulabandha village from CPI (M) recalls:

Our situation was becoming more and more tragic. We could neither feed our families nor move around in the waters. The local moneyed men had forcefully occupied our leasehold areas and expanded it more. They would take over 20 to 30 acres. The *gherries* would sometimes stretch up to 5 km from the village boundary. Chilika Matsyajibi Mahasangha appealed to the government, the district administrations and everyone who mattered. We appealed to the courts for remedial measures. Nobody heard us. Gradually, the resentment smouldered more and more compelling us to take direct action. In 1999, representatives of 145 villages met and decided that we need to demolish the *gherries* ourselves. When our leaders gave the call, we all rose up in unity. Our lives depended on freeing Chilika. We were ready to risk anything to stave off starvation. The Mahasangha intimated the district collectors of Khurda, Ganjam and Puri. They began their operation from Balugaon and destroyed some *gherries* in the Parikuda area. After the second day of operation, we halted at Sorana in the evening to decide the future course of action.

On 29 May 1999, the people cleared up 1,000 acres and destroyed 11 big *gherries* belonging to Baradihi, Nairi, Tarapi, Baulabandha and Balia of Khurda district. Around 11–11.30 pm, the District Collector along with police forces reached Sorana. They woke up the leaders who were fast asleep and threatened them not to continue the operation. The leaders replied that they began this operation as the administration did not do anything. They were forcibly put into police vans. Word spread that the leaders were being taken away. As the news spread, people woke up from their sleep and rushed to block the vehicle in which their leaders had been held captive. They blocked the path of the vans and a terrible clash ensued.

A woman named Magi Behera in Sorana who was present that night narrated:

> After the day-long anti-gherry operation led by Mahasangha, our leaders were resting in a room. Food was served for the people who had participated in the operation. Suddenly, 10 vehicles with armed police along with mafia reached the spot. They arrested the leaders and took them away. As the leaders called out to the people, hundreds of people came and blocked the vehicle in which our leaders were kept. There were women and children and the elderly too. In the darkness, police lobbed teargas shell and opened fire. The mafia sprayed chilli powder and glass powder loaded in small pipes all over us. With our bodies hurting and eyes blinded, we crawled to block all the vehicles. We saw Pramila Behera of our village lying on the ground hit by a bullet on her thigh and writhing in pain. We bandaged her wound with a piece of cloth. As we moved ahead, we found three more people. They seemed dead. When police tried to take our leaders, we started beating up the police. They used lathis on us. Then they left with the dead bodies and our leaders too. It was the administration that killed and incarcerated us, yet we were held guilty and had to face police charges for years.

It was not just the police that descended upon them that night. There were men who were brought in by the non-fisherfolk or mafia. The two terms are interchangeably used. The police began using lathis, hurled tear gas shells and opened fire! Four people died on the spot. And another person died after four months of being hit by a bullet on his chest. Sixty-seven people were arrested, slapped with false cases and later released on bail.

Mahadev Behera from Sorana from the Matsyajibi Mahasangha recalled:

> At that time the CM Giridhari Gomanga declared Rs 100,000 compensation for the deceased and Rs 20,000 for the injured. Till date, Lingaraj

> Behera who died after four months has not received the compensation and his mother has been approaching me since then. The government set up an enquiry committee headed by P.K. Tripathy and suspended the Collector. After some time, the Collector got a promotion. And the Commission concluded the killing to be justified and held the deceased responsible! This is the justice done to us!

Pramila Ghadei, a CPI (M) activist, was eager to share about the protest against the police firing:

> We went for the *rail roko* programme in Bhubaneswar. Around 2,000 women participated in it. It was mostly women. We packed some food and went to Bhubaneswar a day before the programme. We stayed overnight on the platform. Around 6.30 or 7 am, we sat on the rail lines and did not allow any train to pass. We occupied the tracks and refused to move. It continued for three hours or so. Soon, the police arrived. They persuaded us to withdraw. But our leaders and CPI (Liberation) leaders insisted on continuing. Finally, more police arrived and started lathi-charge around 11 am. People ran here and there out of fear. Many people had their legs and hands broken. They were taken to hospitals. We reserved buses and came back home late at night. I could barely move for days as one of my joints was injured.

Everybody was shocked. The CM Giridhar Gomango was quoted in newspapers, he admitted that he was 'kept in the dark about the incident.' That reflected the combined power of the district administration along with the upper caste and business sharks. They had come to rule Chilika. The lake that sustained the fisherfolk, the dolphins and myriad other creatures, with legends of its power to protect itself and its people, stood helpless when corporate greed and state oppression gripped it with its tentacles. The mythical flock of flamingos could perhaps only capture the imagination and scare away lesser evils. This was a whole new beast altogether. And Chilika was gasping for breath.

The Choking of Chilika

You are killing me, fish, the old man thought. (Hemingway 2004)

The non-fisherfolk and the mafia got emboldened to let loose a reign of terror and intimidation. Systematic attacks on the fisherfolk and on fishery resources became a pattern from the 2000s.

Bansidhar Behera from the co-operative society in Gopinathpur said they had been able to protect their fishery sources. He said:

> Our *sairats* are in our control you can say. But it has not been without a struggle. We had to fight hard to recover 600 acres in 2001 when the non-fisherfolk took over. We had no option but to use force and muscle power to fight that battle. This is how the administration and police leave us to our means. I too have been behind the bars when we resisted the mafia. False cases on villagers are a common story here. Even now we have to be on watch all the time. Once April comes, they all march in. It is most dangerous to be alone in the waters without protection. So often a fisherman has been found with his hands and legs tied to the boat and mouth stuffed with a potato. The boat would be left drifting. Sometimes there are stab wounds too. They loot all the catch and flee. The sea monsters are on the prowl all the time.

The people of Gola village have been struggling since fifteen years to reclaim their *sairats*. They are mired in endless litigation and police cases. In the late 1990s, conflicts were breaking out in many areas. An upper caste dominated village called Panaspada barred them from accessing their own Bhabania *jana* and snatched their boats. First information reports (FIRs) were registered. The people were able to resume fishing in December 2000 in the presence of police security and the Tahsildar. But they were attacked again with hand-made bombs and guns. Twenty-two people were hospitalized with bullet wounds. This case continued for ten long years. Finally, they resumed fishing (again under police protection) at the end of 2011. This did not last longer than a month as fresh attacks were made on them. A fisherman was hacked and his leg was burnt. The case is still pending in the High Court. Fisherfolk usually forfeit access to leased *sairats* during these long periods of litigation.

Adikanda Behera from Gola said:

> Our society continues to pay lease money every month but we have no access to Bhabania *jana*. We carry on some fishing activity by setting up *khandas* but Chilika keeps receding. And fishing has become so expensive. We are not being able to even repay loans invested in fishing. After paying for the lease, we have to buy nets. Other equipment is also needed. We used to take loans from *mahajans*—the usual sahukars here in the village or nearby villages. The earlier practice was to sell our catch to them. It was always exploitative. In recent years, companies like Bandhan and SKS have taken their place. They give loans on a weekly basis, charging an 18 per cent

> interest. We might be free from sahukars but these companies are tormenting us in worse manner. Even if we have not met our costs, we have to pay. Otherwise they are at our doorstep! We have no political or economic power to fight against the non-fisherfolk. It is so hard to meet costs of health, children's school fees and household needs. We fisherfolk are always in despair.

Bhagaban Behera from Gola, who was helping us meet people, was in his teens during the *andolan* against the Tatas. He too recalled how they have never been free:

> The people of Gola are caught in a terrible bind. If we risk venturing out, we can get badly beaten up by the mafia. The police and administration are not for us. In December 2001 when platoons of police set up their camp in this village because of the dispute around Bhabania *jana*, women appealed to them to rescue the menfolk from the mafia. Instead, they got harassed by the police personnel. We are the inhabitants of this land. Chilika is ours. But the Chilika is always under siege. You can say it is like Kashmir. Our grandparents have been fighting the non-fishermen, we are fighting the non-fishermen and mafia lobby. Our children are seeing this ever since they opened their eyes. We work hard to give them education; but even they know that all hopes lie in our traditional livelihood and not working outside. We have to win access to our fishery sources.

Large-scale commercial prawn cultivation that pauperized the community took its toll on the lake. Adikanda Behera explains how the decline of fish in Chilika is manmade:

> From Arakhkuda to Satpuda, there are innumerable prawn *gherries* that got built from 1988 or 1992. It is only getting worse. There are non-fisherfolk catching seedlings right at the mouth by using zero-net. Nothing escapes from it. Prawns and other fish that used to naturally reach the areas adjacent to our side do not come anymore. Ever since the embankment of Tata got made, the Chilika has receded a few kilometres from our villages. And then the non-fisherfolk made their prawn ponds. You can walk through the area in summer. All the old systems of *dian* and *uthapani* are over since 12 or even 15 years.[5] If there are no tides coming in, how can there be fish? The interplay of sweet and salty water through the year is no longer there. The water is sweet all the time.

The lake itself is facing a grave threat. The water-spread area started reducing over time due to siltation and other manmade processes. The

32-km long Magarmukh canal that connects Chilika to the Bay of Bengal is near the village of Arakhakuda. This natural opening allows the flow of water and fish from the sea. The inflow of sea water makes the water saline from January to June. For the next six months, the monsoons and flood water make it sweet. But even these patterns are undergoing rapid change. For the fisherfolk of Gopinathpur and Gola, the water is losing its salinity while the people of Arakhakuda are at a loss for the increase. The decline of fish in the lake is already making them travel to distant shores as Agadhu Behera from Arakhakuda village explained:

> We just do not get any fish this side. The fish (juveniles) are collected at the Magarmukh mouth itself and taken away to faraway places. These are clandestine deals. How can we make an earning? Our youth are going to places as far as Kerala and Goa for fishing. They are hired for the fishing season and get Rs 1 lakh for the whole year. After travel costs and expenditure there, a family gets to spend a maximum of five or six thousand rupees per month on an average. If they were to stay here, these families would perish. We can see the lake drying up very fast. The water is salty all the time now. Earlier, the water would rise because of the inflow of sweet water in the monsoon months. And we used to catch fish for three to four months on the elevated portions of Chilika. That was called *uthapani*. But now the natural flow has stopped with no fish coming this way. Since some years now, the seedlings are taken away by the non-fisherfolk way ahead at the mouth of Chilika. Also, when there is no rain, how can there be *uthapani*? The water has been slowly becoming poison since 10 years or more. It may be because of the chemicals used in prawn cultivation; I cannot say about these things. We still depend on *bahani*. When there is high tide, we are able to earn some money. But we no longer get the big fish that we used to because of the *gherries* that have come up for prawn cultivation. We only get *chuna macho* (small fish). How can we survive when everything has changed so much? You see we belong to the waters only. We do not own paddy fields. The fish gave us everything. We built this house and we got our children married. We were able to look after relatives and attend their events. The fish used to yield the money for all our needs. Today our earnings have become unpredictable. Sometimes we fetch 200 or 500 and sometimes 1,000. *Chasa budile barase, bahania budile juare.* (The peasant suffers for a year when the crop fails. Fisherfolk suffer high-tide when the fish-catch fails.)

Agadhu Behera had asked us to reach the village before sunrise when the catch comes in. The shore was filled with women busy buying shares and settling rates. This hectic activity lasts a few hours. Women are also into wage labour. Manika Behera works from the wee hours of the morning to midnight. She said:

> We do some amount of wage work to make ends meet. The men are out all night on the lake. Around 5 am they reach the shore with the catch. That is when our work begins. We clean the fish and sort them out. Then we put them in baskets and walk all 17 kilometres to Brahmagiri to sell. But we have to rush home by 4 pm to complete all domestic chores and cook the evening meal. When there is not enough catch to go to market, we work as loaders. For four months, we work in cashew plants. Our job is to collect and clean. In this way, we generate some income to run our families.

The construction industry that is thriving in the area absorbs hundreds of erstwhile self-reliant fisherfolk. Tuni Behera was in school when the Chilika Bachao Andolan had galvanized her people. She reflects on the old times and feels deeply for her community, especially the women. She said:

> I remember those days in the anti-Tata movement. I was a kid who would tag along. While surging ahead to face the police or administration, the *andolan* people would leave all their bags with me and I would sit and guard them. It had inspired me so much. Even though we were children we became aware during that time what is just and what is unjust. But what we see today is only more widespread despair. Today the domination of non-fisherfolk and boosting of artificial prawn cultivation has affected us women so badly. Since we can no longer depend only on fishing, more than 70 per cent of women in my village go for construction work and loading and whatever else they get. Some men go, but it is women who have to earn for the family. It is not that economic hardships are new to us but the atmosphere is so hostile now. Earlier men would walk 5 or 6 kilometres to buy alcohol. Now there are shops all over because the government wants to earn revenue from us poor people. We urged women not to let men take away their hard earned money to buy alcohol. Drinking is bad but to give money for alcohol is as bad. We got organised and made a difference a few years back. But now the number of shops is even more. It feels so hopeless.

The Uncertain Future

The rich biodiversity of the lake had earned recognition in 1979 as the first Indian Wetland of International Importance under the Ramsar Convention. In 1993, the lake was removed from the Ramsar Convention and placed under the Montreaux record as intensified human activity was altering its ecological character. Indeed, the Chilika Development Authority (CDA) worked hard to contain the damage. By 2002, Chilika somehow managed to climb back to the list of recognized sites. Yet the grand old lake stands today with a heavy heart as it is still an endangered lake.

The prawn *gherries* were once again being cleared up by the CDA as we went around doing our interviews. The CDA seemed to be implementing the Supreme Court orders on wetlands made years ago and the Odisha Marine Fishing Regulation Act (OMFRA) specifications. Wherever we went, people seemed sceptical of the proposed Chilika (Regulation of Fisheries) Act 2017 and what it has in store for the rights of the fisherfolk. The oustees who survived the Nalaban Bird Sanctuary get a sense of *déjà vu*. They have been through this ordeal. In the 1990s, promotion of tourism by setting up the Nalaban Bird Sanctuary had cost many fisherfolk families dearly. Nothing has happened meanwhile to restore hope in the government machinery:

> Do the government *babus* know what is *jana* and what is *khanda*? They have only heard these words. What do they understand about the fishing practices? Now they tell us *khandas* are not allowed beyond 800 meters from shore or from the edge of the village. Have they any understanding of the changes that have taken place in Chilika? Now there is hardly any water 300 to 400 meters from the shoreline. When there is no water, there will be no fish. We set up *khandas* as far as we can walk up to our neck in water. Naturally, fisherfolk will go deep into Chilika for fishing. Also, CDA wants us to use traditional equipment (made of bamboo) to catch fish; no net. Are bamboos any more available in our locality? Generally, we buy it from nearby villages; we don't procure from the jungle on our own. I do not understand what the problem of CDA with *khanda* is. One possible reason is that when tourists come to Chilika to see birds, these *khandas* may be an eyesore for them. Once we lost our livelihood to Australian birds and now to tourism. (Hadibandhu Ghadei, Banpur)

Their relationship with the ecosystem that has lasted since hundreds of years has been through major upheavals. The ecological well-being of the lake is inextricably linked to the livelihood of this vast dalit fishing community. But the manmade dangers that lurk before them are becoming more precarious each day. Even today, they invoke the goddess Kalijai, who has many origin stories.

Myths like to contend with each other, and that is how the story of the flamingos was contended by another story about Kalijai. According to it, once upon a time, a little girl was going to get married and was on a boat sailing from Bankar to Parikud. Suddenly, the boat overturned when it ran into stormy weather and she died. Godavarish Mishra composed a passionate poem on how she became the goddess who resides at Kalijai. It is she who keeps an eye on all boats and crew ever since, and people pray to her for safe sailing. Who knows if it was the power of Chilika or the imagination of the poet which transformed a drowned girl into a revered goddess. The struggles of the fisherfolk for their rights have been thwarted time and again by different enemies. Like Kalijai, they too have been the protectors of Chilika. And like Kalijai, they too have been submerged. And they have emerged each time from the depths, in different ways, transformed.

Notes

1. The title of this chapter has been taken from the name of this Odia film.
2. Made in 1936, *Redes* was directed by Emilio Gomez Muriel and Fred Zinnemann. It shows the daily grind of the fishing community on the Gulf of Mexico. A terrible incident faced by the protagonist instigates a political awakening in him and his community.
3. The upland near the village is called *sairat*. Traditionally, fisherfolk were the lease holders of these *sairats*. With the onset of commercial prawn cultivation, non-fisherfolk forcibly occupied the *sairats*. It became easier in places where the *sairats* were on the edge of their own villages.
4. A.F. Leide-Law was a Canadian expert in fishery co-operatives. He was commissioned by the Government of Odisha to study the critical issues and problems of Chilika fisheries. He made a set of recommendations to implement the co-operative structure in Chilika under the government's *sairat* leasing policy by maintaining the traditional system of community based operations of different kinds of fishery sources. The Chilika Reorganization Scheme, 1959, was based on these recommendations.
5. Fishing Methods in Chilika:

   Bahana: In this method, fisherfolk use many types of nets, such as patuajala, sahalajala, khaingajala, muni jala, fishing in deeper waters.

   Jana: These are shallow areas near the villages. Traditionally, these shallow areas are enclosed by long sheets made of bamboo. Fisherfolk go to fishing in *jana* in the dead of night and enclose the area with bamboo sheets, keeping in view the movement of fish. Generally, this method of fishing occurs during the period from Ashwin (October) to Pausha (December). Now, nylon nets are being used in place of bamboo sheets. Secondly, many of these janas have been illegally and forcibly occupied by non-fishermen of nearby villages and turned into prawn *gherries*.

Dian: It is a small place for fishing near the *jana*. It is enclosed by bamboo from four sides. Some fish jump into the *dian* from the *jana*. These *dians* also have been converted into prawn *gherries*.

Uthapani: These are uplands near the lagoon. In the summer, fisherfolk build small bunds on those lands to trap rainwater in the rainy season. During the rainy season, the trapped water is slowly released into the lagoon, especially in the evenings. Fishes from the lake, especially kantia fish, climb up against the flow of the water. When fishes begin climbing up, the fisherfolk stop the flow of the water from above and catch them.

Chingudi Khati: This method of fishing begins when the water of the Chilika becomes more brackish after the end of the rainy season. An area is enclosed with a bamboo sheet of 100–200 feet and traps are set up at one end. When the prawns move, they get trapped. Now, people are using fine nylon nets called zero-nets and traps to catch prawns. As a result, seedlings are also being trapped, in turn, the catch is diminishing day by day. These fine nets are also blocking the movement of waste and causing siltation.

References

Behura, Nirakar. 1996. *Odia O Odisha: Sameekshya '96 and '98*. Vikalpa Sandhani Manch.

Chilika Teere. 1977. An Odia feature film.

Chilika: Voices of the People. 1993. A Report Published by Chilika Bachao Andolan Krantidarsi Yuva Sangam.

Hemingway, Ernest. 2004. *The Old Man and the Sea*. London: Arrow Books.

Mafiamalini Raktambu Chilika. 1999. A Report of Manabika Adhikar Sangathan (MAS), July.

Redes. 1936. A Mexican Film.

The Report of the Fact-Finding Committee on Chilika Fisheries Submitted to the High Court, Orissa. 16 August, 1993, Cuttack.

Upadhyaya, Kunjabihari. 2013. *Wayward Chilika Bancha Andolan in Odishara Jana andolana*. Balasore: Jeevan Sangram Saraswata Trust.

CHAPTER 7

The Kia in Rage

Jaha ku jie rasila kia phula pari basila
[The one whom the heart desires
Exudes the fragrance of *kia* flowers]
—Odia saying

The quiet coastal plains of Odisha abound with many hidden treasures that bring with them many secret stories too. As the years flew by, one of the stories got pulled out to the gaze of the world when evil eyes descended upon that land. This is the story of the rare *kewda*, or *kia phullo* as is known locally, that gave a tough fight to one of the most pampered corporate houses of the state—the Tatas. It is a kind of screw pine that grows in wild abundance around Gopalpur and Chatrapur in Ganjam district. As Chatrapur station approaches, passengers on the Chennai-Howrah railway line can see these wild bushes. These are the *kewda* bushes that have seen holiday crowds heading for Gopalpur-on-sea, *babus* rush to the district headquarters in Chatrapur and buses with dreamy-eyed students ply to Berhampur University.

Growing wild on the hedges of paddy fields or along the pathways to the villages, the long tapering leaves of these bushes that spill out gesturing wildly to the wind seem to be clasped by a powerful hand. They need no tending, no fertilizer, no pesticide and no water. They only give

R. Padhi, N. Sadangi, *Resisting Dispossession*,
https://doi.org/10.1007/978-981-15-0717-5_7

and give in joyous abundance, especially in the monsoons. Anyone who breathes in the scented flowers is transported to another world, even if momentarily so. The only rival to be feared is the monkey. They descend upon the bushes as they love to eat up the buds as soon as they sprout. Therefore, one has to guard the bushes round the clock. The only thing monkeys are scared of is loud noise. People use toy guns and fire crackers to scare them away. They only knew how to fight monkeys that coveted their *kia phullo* until the Tatas came and picked up the real guns. They were not after the flowers but wanted the land on which the flowers grew. Everything changed overnight; the flowers, the people and the land were all under public gaze as event after event followed. It was the beginning of the great steel rush in Odisha—the land of peasants, fisherfolk and forest dwellers. And the world got to know about this sleepy area and its quiet and flourishing *kewda* trade with distant lands that has been continuing since decades till today.

The people who live here cherish the land as their livelihood is tied up to it. Being one of the most fertile regions in Ganjam, the area produces almost 90 per cent of *kewda* in the country. It is concentrated around Chatrapur, Berhampur, Rangeilunda, Jagannathpur and Gopalpur-on-sea. This spot provides all the natural conditions for the bushes to flourish. However, TISCO eyed this area for the many strategic advantages it had for steel production. We bring to you this long and sordid story of steel versus flowers.

The Story of Kewda

The *keora* flower has been one of the oldest forms of perfume that is mentioned in the Baburnama. It also appears in Persian paintings. It is a much sought-after source of aromatic perfumes down the ages. The history of Indian perfumes is linked to the history of Kannauj, Kanpur and Lucknow in Uttar Pradesh that remain the dominant trade centres. This quiet coastal district of Odisha linked up with the trade in the 1920s. In 1924, Adi Mohammed came to Agraram and Chatrapur villages and discovered *kewda* flowers; since then, its aromatic quality spread far—en route Uttar Pradesh and West Punjab. Its extract got known to be obtained from the male species (of *Pandanus odoratissimus*) that is known as *kia* or *kewda* or *keora*. And the perfume is known as *keora* or *kewda* attar that comes from *itr*, the Arab word for perfume. He also established the first hydro-distillation unit. In 1930, Mohammed Ali came to Indrakhi, which is in today's Golanthara block, from Lucknow and also began the production of *kewda* attar and *kewda* water (Reddy 2002). Gradually a few local entrepreneurs got established, and Raghunath Reddy formed the first Regional Kewda Flowers Farmers Association in 1950. Wages for collection of flowers and cost of flowers became regularized with the forming of a committee representing all villages. Till today, the trade continues to be controlled and regulated from Kannauj and Kanpur in Uttar Pradesh. Farmers are dependent on these traders for its sale as well as for the sandalwood oil base, which is so essential for *kewda* attar production.

In the 1980s, the production of *kewda rooh* or *kewda* essence became a turning point by using the same 'Deg' technology. Experts are skilled in the art of controlling the fire and the quantity and rate of distillation without the use of any gadgets. Depending on the month of collection, time of starting the distillation (preferably in the early hours of the morning), the yields of *rooh* vary in the range of 25–40 grams per 1,000 flowers (Reddy 2002).

The traditional method of distilling and extracting maintains the quality of the attar and *kewda* water. In the Deg process of distillation, a huge copper vessel (ellipsoid in shape) is placed on the fire that is controlled by experts. It is covered with a lid that is sealed with clay and cloth pieces. The flowers and water are in the vessel. The vessel has a pipe made of bamboo that connects to a tinned condenser. The condenser is placed in a huge water container where experienced workers sit half submerged and check the condensation rate by the touch of their hands on the surface of the condenser. The fire is regulated by skilled workers; the water around the condenser is changed now and then. When these vapours are absorbed in sandalwood oil, attar is made. The traders come and stay in these distillation units throughout the season. They also provide the cash to the collectors who collect the flowers from the villagers.

A Morning in the Land of Kia Flowers

It was around 5.30 in the morning. We left NH5 near Chamakhandi and went towards P Laxmipur along the canal road. The dark green bushes grow luxuriantly on both sides of the road. The cream-coloured *kia* flowers in blossom were flashing here and there. Men, women and children were out on the roads. Flowers have to be harvested in the early hours as they lose their fragrance with the opening of the calyx. A thin, long bamboo stick with an iron hook on its tip was in everybody's hand. This would help them pluck flowers from taller bushes as well as stand a bit away from the bushes where snakes slither by happily.

These bushes can be as short as 3 feet or loom as tall as 18 feet. There are four rounds of collection that happen, the most intense phase is between July and September. Plucking and collecting *kia* seems to be a sacred activity for these god-loving people. But to pluck *kia* in the morning is a hard economic activity. Qualities like delicate and soft generally associated with flower are not in *kia*. And *kia* is a sort of flower which is hard to touch. The soft and white leaves become green and spiky as they grow outward.

As the day advances, activities around *kia* also grow. Pluckers from fields come home carrying flowers in their bags and baskets and begin to count how many flowers they have plucked. Collectors reach villages on motorcycles and cycles. They move fast from door to door of their clients to collect flowers, exchange a few pleasantries and disappear. Those who have collected a few flowers carry the bunch in their hands to the nearby grocery or pan shop, which is a contact point. Once the collection is over, flowers are carried to the distillery. We met a few who were even taking five to ten flowers directly to the distillery. There are flowers in hands, in bundles, on bikes and on their mud verandahs as the transition takes place so swiftly. The entire morning hours are busy with *kia*. We may call it *kia* time. Everyone is at work: *kewda* growers, *bhatti* owners and labourers, and the landless who are busy plucking and taking the flowers to the distilleries.

We go right into the village where D. Kamraj Borma is sitting on a chair in the village square. His legs no longer support him since his paralytic stroke. He happily tells us about *kia* cultivation:

> *Kia* is the gift of nature to us. It grows wild in our locality; needs no investment; no ploughing; no watering, no application of fertiliser. It only gives. Earlier, it grew wild on the village commons and on the bunds of the paddy fields which worked as green fence. After the Phailin cyclone hit us in 2013, people began to grow *kia* in their paddy fields. For that too, you need hardly any investment. You have to only plant the young saplings. The production of *kia* flower has grown four times today. The rate of the flower is decided by the pluckers themselves on a yearly basis keeping in view the demand of the market. Now, it is eight rupees a flower; 7.50 for the plucker and 0.50 paise for the village level collector.
>
> *Kia* grown on the village commons are generally leased out to anyone from the village. The lease money is decided by the village committee in such a fashion that the lessee gets enough to run his or her family; the committee also earns some fund to be used for the good of the village. You must

have heard that the money earned from *kia* has gone into setting up a school. We started the Chamakhandi High School in 1977, a collective endeavour of peasants' earning from the same *kia* cultivation. Now you can understand why we put up such a tough fight against the Tatas.

In the old days when a rupee was made of 64 paise, 8 to 12 flowers were sold at 1 paise. *Kia* has had a commercial value from the days of our grandparents and their parents. When the rupee changed to 100 paise, it was sold at 2 paise per flower. Then it became 4 paise. The price has steadily grown. Today it is Rs 8 per flower.

The distilleries are agog with life. Copper vessels are on the fire with workers tending to the fire and the cooling of the condensers. A distillery owner narrates to us how his great grandfather has been coming here even before there were proper roads or so many trains. And how they would walk the last few kilometres in heavy rain.

TISCO and People's Resistance

This area became the ideal choice for TISCO to set up its second steel plant after Jamshedpur. The proximity to NH5 and the south-eastern railway route and the promise of the state government to make the Gopalpur port an all-weather port were not all. The Pipalpanka Reservoir Project on the Rushikulya river was planned to provide 60 million gallons of water daily for the steel plant. None of these plans were made known to the people whose land was going to be acquired.

The Memorandum of Understanding between TISCO and the Government of Orissa was signed on 25 August 1995. The notice under Section 4 [1] which informed the villagers that the government intended to acquire their land was issued in December. Guidelines on rehabilitation were sent to the Collector on 19 March 1996. The constitution of the Rehabilitation Advisory Committee took place on 6 July 1996. And the Company constituted its own Steering Committee on the matter on 26 October 1996. At no step in this decision making and decision facilitating process were any of the village representatives consulted. The villagers came to know of the imminent loss of their land and livelihood by newspaper reports, a newspaper notice and a foundation stone laid by the then prime minister Narasimha Rao—each event giving a signal of non-negotiable finality. (PUDR and APDR 1997)

A month before the Memorandum of Understanding (MoU) was signed, the news had reached people in its own unannounced manner as news always does. Many village leaders came together for a meeting on 7 July 1995, and the Ganatantrik Suraksha Samiti (GSS) was made. Many of them belonged to the CPI; there was also a significant presence of the Congress leadership and supporters. Narayan Reddy from CPI was made the President of GSS.

GSS sent its first memorandum to the District Collector on 9 July 1995. That very evening there was a meeting at Palm Beach in Gopalpur between company officials and the administration.

Kamraj Borma tells us how the *andolan* against TISCO started. He ruminates over the struggle and the losses suffered. He has murder charges on him since the last 20 years or more along with some other comrades. He recalls those eventful days:

> Who would tell us what happened at the Palm Beach meeting? The local people were aware of the meeting but not what transpired there. We were still waiting to hear from the administration whom we had met as a collective. But the news was first carried in Pradyumna Bal's paper *Pragatibaadi* and it confirmed for all of us that indeed Tata was coming to the area. And we became aware that Tata would acquire the land with the help of the government.

The project by Tata became too real when a helipad was built to receive the Prime Minister—P.V. Narasimha Rao—who was going to lay the foundation stone. Over 3,000 people from across the villages gathered and protested against the construction of the helipad. Yet, he arrived. A bulletproof dais was made from where he delivered his address on 30 December. The number of protestors grew to almost 7,000 that day. Women and men raised black flags that they had brought hidden in their sarees and pockets; slogans rent the air asking Tata to go back and NO to land acquisition. The first lathi charge took place on the day the foundation stone was laid. The villagers were not deterred. They went back the next day to the spot and demolished the foundation stone.

As will be seen in subsequent chapters, what Chilika and Gopalpur were seeing at the hands of the Tatas would become a *leitmotif* for many other regions of the state that would be resisting private companies. The slogan that reverberated in the protest against the then Prime Minister continued through the 1990s and 2000s in Odisha:

Moribu poche daribu naahin; Jonmo Maati chaadiboo naahin!
[We would rather die than live in fear; We will not surrender our land ever!]

Villagers worked hard at blocking all entries to the area. There was tremendous unity. They put all stakes into organizing and resisting the entry of Tatas.

For almost six months, no government or company vehicle could enter the area as the entry points to all eleven villages were shut out with wooden barricades. Twenty-four-hour vigils were on at the three main entry points to the area: Chamakhandi, Hariapalli and Badaputti.

Narasimha Rao was the MP from here. When the 1996 general elections saw the demise of the Congress in the entire country along with a hung parliament, Rao, who was facing several charges of corruption and scam scandals, won the Lok Sabha seat from the same Berhampur constituency. Maybe basking in the reflected glory of a prime minister choosing their constituency, the people of Berhampur shut their eyes to what was happening to the villagers in the neighbouring block. Or maybe they believed in the promise of development.

As the excitement of elections petered out, a concerted effort was made for land acquisition. On 3 July 1996, the Special Land Acquisition Officer entered Basanaputti with a heavy police force. The people were prepared for a fight. There was heavy opposition. Over 40 people were booked under criminal cases.

The Basanaputti incident and the criminal cases foisted on so many people created tension. The time came to organize a rally to Bhubaneswar to protest against the land acquisition and loss of livelihood; July 23 was the date chosen. Hectic preparations were on. Villagers came forward in huge numbers as word spread to each household. However, in a preemptive bid, on the midnight of 21 July, the police landed at the house of the GSS President Narayan Reddy and arrested him. Over 2,000 people landed up at the Chatrapur police station and blocked NH5. There was a gherao of the District Collector's residence, demanding the release of Narayan Reddy and asking Tata to go back. Despite this heavy-handed move taken by the district administration, more than 5,000 people landed up at the Secretariat in Bhubaneswar on 23 July as planned. The mood was even more rebellious strongly condemning both repression and Tata.

Soon, a police *chowki* popped up right opposite the GSS office in Chamakhandi, which is the old CPI office. And in the absence of any criminal charges that would justify the arrest of Narayan Reddy, those at the helm of affairs in New Delhi decided to invoke the National Securities Act (NSA) on the same day, 23 July. The CPI was sharing power in the centre; the Home Minister was Inderjit Gupta. When the NSA was invoked, he was either powerless or resorted to tacit silence. But he did manage to lobby and get Narayan Reddy released after 52 days.

The struggle to persuade the party to take up displacement and land-grab as people's issues was taking many twists and turns from 1990 onwards. The party was faltering again and again in standing up for *kewda* cultivators and the landless in Ganjam district. The leaders of the GSS left no stone unturned in eliciting support from district to state-level offices of the party. Kamraj Borma narrates how hard they worked to get attention to the crisis looming large and failed.

> We struggled hard to bring the attention of our party; most of us were from the CPI. In 2000 assembly elections, we were keen to put up Narayan Reddy from Chatrapur because he represented all of us in the struggle against the Tatas. At that point in time, the party supported Biswanath Sahu. Narayan Reddy got 38% of the votes while Biswanath Sahu got only 3% share. It became a serious issue in the party because the split resulted in the BJP candidate Ram Chandra Panda securing 43% votes. Three of us were immediately suspended from the party: Narayan Reddy, I and Chandreya Reddy.
>
> We had already made an attempt to pass a resolution demanding the withdrawal of Tata at the district level conference in Kabisurya Nagar just before assembly elections. But we were told that some of us have to sacrifice for the country to develop. We were shocked but did not give up easily. We somehow managed to again raise the issue in the AITUC conference in Berhampur. Then at the state conference in Paradip, we again proposed a resolution that Tata should look for an alternative site. They refused to pass the resolution. Narayan Reddy, Chandreya Reddy and myself were ready to leave the conference because we felt strongly that why do we need the party if it cannot pass a simple resolution against our lands being snatched away from us by the Tatas when we have given our entire lives to the party. Then, Chaturanand Mishra—an ex Minister—refused to let us walk out. He said, 'People die wherever Tata has gone. If we do not pass the resolution, then I too have to leave this conference.' The state conference was thus forced to pass the resolution.

Three weeks had passed since the people had returned from Bhubaneswar demanding the release of their leader booked under NSA. On 16 August, a heavy police force escorted a survey team to Kuanpalli and Narayanpur.

There was stiff resistance by the villagers followed by a severe lathi charge. Many women were injured. When 500 policemen descended on Hariapalli village the next day, women and children lay down prostrate on the ground refusing entry to the village. They were thrashed violently with injuries on hands, legs and eyes. Many had missing toenails.

The police repression grew each day even as the people resorted to peaceful protest in great numbers. Women were injured, and two even died in these peaceful protests.

Badaputti and Chamakhandi were attacked on 19 August. Women were chased, beaten up and dumped into ponds. Sixty-year-old Juna Lakshmi Amma of Badaputti, who got grievously injured, died two days later. The police entered Basanaputti on 21 August and wreaked violence. Fifty-five-year-old Sainee Erama from P Laxmipur succumbed to her injuries on 29 August. Till today the villages remember these women who died resisting. The period from September 1996 to February 1997 was relatively calm. However, company agents were making inroads and persuading people about jobs and compensation.

The tough resistance shown by the people was making the administration think hard about new ways of entering the area.

> A few days back the Annual Shareholders Meeting of Tata took place in Mumbai. On this occasion, Chairman Ratan Tata was specifically asked about the probability of the implementation of the steel project in Gopalpur in the face of stiff resistance from the people's movement. He replied that the people's movement is not so strong and that land acquisition has begun and it would be completed by the end of September. The shareholders asked what would be done if the people's movement intensifies and becomes more intense. Ratan Tata replied categorically that if the people's movement became more intense, Tata would withdraw from the project since the company has never had any project anywhere by affecting or agitating the local people. He gave the example of Chilika to say how Tata had withdrawn from the integrated shrimp cultivation project by respecting people's opinion. (Bal 1996a)

The state government persisted even if Tata made ambiguous statements. Far from withdrawing, the violence unleashed by the state and the company became worse than before. The spate of events that followed in early 1997 shocked the entire state and rocked the Odisha assembly. Narayan Reddy was arrested yet again in February 1997. This time he was accused of ballot snatching in the local panchayat elections. The disquiet was palpable: a crackdown was imminent.

Police Firing in Chatrapur

On 19 March 1997, around 500 police personnel armed with helmets, shields and lathis entered Sindhigaon. The women working in the fields gave a tough fight. When the police said that they were doing an excise raid, the women demanded where the excise police were. As the women continued to oppose, lathi charge started. Word spread quickly, and many more villagers landed up to defend the people of Sindhigaon. The police retreated. It was a severe lathi charge as many women and men were grievously hurt on their legs, thighs, arms, foreheads and eyes.

Even then, without losing courage, the people soon gathered near the road of Sitarampur. They were keen to work out a future course of action as the lies and the ruthlessness of the administration were becoming too clear. Over 400 people were at the meeting. The Collector with police force entered the meeting from the back. It made some people think that they have come to attack Sindhigaon. They rushed towards there via Sitarampur. Soon they were lost in the chaos as tear gas shells were hurled at them. Someone threw a stone at the police in retaliation and then the firing started. The police had come prepared. Many people received bullet wounds.

Twenty-two-year-old Raghu Sethi, *dhobi* by profession, was brutally attacked by the police who entered his house. He gave his account to a fact-finding team from Bhubaneswar:

> I was in my house. Some people came and asked for water because they had pain in their eyes from the tear gas. I gave them water. I remained inside and closed the doors. After a few minutes the police came and knocked on both the sides. When I did not open, they threatened to throw tear gas shells on the roof. So out of fear I opened one door. In the meanwhile the police had broken the lock ring of the door on the other side. Then the police forcefully entered the house. They were about 15 to 20 in number. They rained their lathis on me. I was suffering from chicken pox but they did not care for my physical illness and dragged me to the SP. The SP ordered them not to beat me. Now I am not able to see things clearly in my left eye due to the police assault. The police also hit me on my knees. I am a *dhobi* and the police threw away the clothes which were there for ironing. As a result, I lost a pant and two shirts of a villager. He is asking for his clothes repeatedly... Now also I am frightened. On the first day and the next day of the incident I could not sleep at night. Those two days I was constantly hallucinating the trauma of being beaten. My legs continue to tremble so much. (A Report by PUCL, GASS and MAS 1997)

Firing on a retreating crowd from the back did not miss the wrath of the press at that time. The very next day Chief Minister J.B. Patnaik was compelled to make a statement in the assembly session. He said that it was an excise raid to check illicit liquor! The media was fearless at asking uncomfortable questions in the early 1990s. Why was an excise raid conducted with armed police, fire brigades, an ambulance and the Revenue Inspector?

The Sun Times on 1 April revealed how the state government had asked the Tatas for financial support for the deployment of paramilitary forces (Quoted in A Report by PUCL, GASS and MAS 1997). The targeting of Sindhigaon was planned in the white corridors of Bhubaneswar. The administration had provided full support to TISCO to carry out its technical survey.

Sindhigaon Under Siege

> This was our land. You can see that the Ishwar temple is still there. We visit it every month simply because we cannot keep away from it. Life was good in those years. Staples like rice, vegetables, coconuts and fish were available for everybody. That's the only nice time we had in life before Tata emerged on the scene. We had even made our own school from the money collected from *kewda* production. We never knew what to do with money. We had a co-operative bank in our village that gave us loans. People were unable to pay back. Once we broke down the bank in anger. We said that we do not need money; we do not need loans.

Being so entirely self-sufficient, villagers were militant right from the beginning in not relenting to the pressure tactics of the company and the administration to part with their land. In the face of such sustained resistance, the company began to master many tricks in conspiring with the state and administration. The village had to be reduced to rubble for the Tatas.

It was 1998. Police deployment intensified and camps were set up around the village for months on end. The insistence to weaken the resistance and let the survey work began to find other means. The school was occupied by the police; children could no longer go to school. Water was stopped into the irrigation canals. As a result, peasants of Sindhigaon lost crops of groundnuts. They ran out of drinking water. Many animals died. Sindhigaon remained in the grip of heightened tension. In July, Narayan Reddy had written:

> In the interest of the Tatas, the state government deployed hundreds of armed police personnel on 17 June and was bent upon unleashing bulldozers on the agricultural land and dwelling houses of the people. Armed police forces raided houses. Chaos and lawlessness reigned in the area. It was the day of *Mahalaxmi Snan*—a festival of the peasants. They were in the fields sowing the first seeds of the season. As they began sowing, bulldozers entered the field and began levelling the land. When they protested, the police started a lathi charge. In a brutal show of strength, the armed police entered households as the Collector and SP ordered each and every house to be raided in search of bombs and weapons. Peasants are not terrorists—there were only ploughs and sickles to be found. The Collector was too embarrassed to give any response. After this, the villagers appealed to the Collector and SP to remove the armed police personnel. However, they announced: 'We have come here so that you all leave the village. Otherwise, the village will be destroyed. This is an order from the government.' A protest meeting was convened in the village that day itself. (Reddy 1998)

Many people recall this very eventful day when the clock was ticking fast and furious as they held on to their determined stance of preferring death over eviction. Prafulla Samantara and Ali Kishore Pattnaik of CPM present in this meeting appealed to the district administration to withdraw the police personnel. The Collector seemed to agree to leave the village, but the CM insisted on the eviction as he had given his word to Tata. Prafulla Samantara recalls:

> That day when the police began coming in huge numbers and stood guard all around, we suspected that something dreadful was going to happen for sure. The entry point was the school—it acted like the gate to the village. All the people were inside. This continued for 48 hours. It was so nerve wracking; it was like a war situation. There were sand trenches and police poised with their rifles. It had become clear that police would forcefully enter the village to take over the land if people did not vacate within the timeline they had announced.
>
> The situation was such that the local leaders and leaders from outside present there had to arrive at a compromise. They appealed to the administration to ask the police to leave and instead do a house-to-house check in the entire village in our presence for whatever they were claiming to be looking for—arms or anything else. The Collector was persuaded and it was decided they would come back the next day at 10 am. Indeed, the search for arms was a ruse. When the CPI leader Loknath Chowdhury went to meet the CM that very evening to appeal for the withdrawal of police, the CM

> categorically stated that there would be no compromise. The Collector informed us that the CM has stopped him from arriving at any such compromise. They will wait only another 24 hours and resort to action. The takeover of Sindhigaon by next morning became a certainty.
>
> The CM was determined to use coercion; the people were determined to die in resistance. In sheer desperation I made a phone call to Bhubaneswar urging friends to think how the imminent massacre could be averted. Pradyumna Bal contacted Advocate Guru Mohanty from PUCL. A delegation headed by the veteran freedom fighter Manmohan Chowdhury went that night to meet the Chief Justice around 10 pm. He listened to them and said that the court would be convened by early morning. The Court thus issued a stay order by 8 am the next day. It clearly stated that the police should be removed from the area and no force should be used for eviction! We showed the telegram to the Collector around 10 am. The High Court stay order made all the difference for that day at least.

The police soon began vacating the area. But people faced even more hardships. The company goons found other means to carry out their attacks. The administration finally closed down the school. The villagers were not able to go out on work. Many daily wage labourers going to Jagannathpur and Berhampur had to forego earnings for a few months. The landless were most affected. It was nothing short of an economic blockade.

Meanwhile, the administration also focused on other villages. Patrapur was emptied without much resistance as security forces began occupying the empty houses. Then it was the turn of Badapur to be evicted. As people were refusing to buckle under pressure of police and the administration, Tata resorted to fracturing the unity that held them together. The compensation of Rs 1 lakh for one acre of land was offered repeatedly through agents and goons. The landless were approached separately.

It is no easy matter to sustain resistance. People look up to the leadership; the leadership looks up to the administration. In that war of nerves, cracks begin to show. Some people had been considering compensation even as the siege had continued. Deep rifts setting in within the community seemed bewildering. Nageshwar Reddy who was at the forefront of the struggle and lived in Sindhigaon at that time reflects:

> Constantly we were dealing with inner fights and mutual suspicion on one hand and increasing police presence in our village. While we were being asked to leave the land, we did not know at that time that other people were dividing us. We were becoming enemies of each other. When we began we

> were all anti-Tata. Then some became pro-Tata. They did not dream of becoming pro-Tata ... who was behind them? It was so bewildering ... we did not have the understanding then to figure out who was dividing us.
>
> The police set up camp in and around our village. Even in that tension, whatever we were speaking among ourselves was getting conveyed outside. The administration was with the company to get our land. We were without any leader. Then when we could not handle so many police cases and police camps in our village ... when we saw our own leaders weakening ... we could not continue. Who will guide us? This was the first time we were in *andolan*. Those of us who took compensation were seen as betraying the movement or weakening it. Do we blame the government or the company or our own leaders? Sometimes we wonder if the *andolan* was made to acquire land for its leaders and Tata. Because no one would have shifted if there was no Tata.
>
> All of us were forced to leave the village. We were forced to take compensation. You can say no one used coercion. But no one made a free choice either. Why would anyone want to leave one's village? It was the situation that compelled us. It was the police repression and the false cases that drove us out. They used only that. How could we withstand the repression? And who are the leaders we turn to?
>
> Who is pro and against? How do you decide? Those who were supposed to be pro and collaborated with Tata are still on their land. Those who fought Tata were thrown out and called pro-company. Do not go by what the newspapers say, do not go by what leaders say. But if you listen to me today, someone will tell you not to believe me too. That is our predicament today. We are no longer a community.

Seven hundred families got displaced from Sindhigaon, Badapur and Patrapur; landless dalits from Keapalli and Paikapada were also evicted with the lure of concrete houses in the new rehabilitation colony. The rehabilitation colonies that came up bore the names of the three villages that were razed to the ground: Sindhigaon, Badapur and Patrapur.

Lives Rehabilitated

An alternative plot for the landless is upheld as manna from heaven in development speak. And a promised job seems to equate the loss of subsistence that otherwise works in myriad ways for generations. An entire economy that relied on subsistence was wiped out.

Pradyumna Bal, an eminent writer and founder of *Pragatibaadi*, brought out a series of three articles appealing to the people of Odisha to think for themselves what Tata promises to give and how much exactly does it loot in the process. He vividly calculates the cost of rehabilitation:

> There would be no space for cowshed, goat shed and storing of agricultural implements. There would be no space for trees; fruit bearing trees would not be waiting for them. From being settled cultivators with income from many sources, they will become refugees overnight. The Odisha government and Tata claim to be taking only 6,500 acres. Will the people be provided with that much land of the same quality near the rehabilitation colony? What can be the compensation for a fruit-bearing coconut tree? It takes 20–25 years for a coconut tree like we have in Odisha to bear fruit. And then the tree will bear fruit for 70 to 100 years.
>
> What compensation can Tata provide for a tree that yields income too? Where is the place for a drumstick tree? One-tenth of an acre is two and a half *guntha*. The annual income of the people of this area is more than one lakh per acre of land. The income of a coconut tree varies from Rs 500 to 800 per year. If the income of 50 years of such a tree is settled the compensation would be for Rs 35,000 if we assume that a tree can give Rs 700 per year. Do you know how much a drumstick tree can yield in a year? The flowers bloom into drumsticks three times in a year. The retail traders buy drumsticks and pay them 40 paise per drumstick. Most people have 10 to 15 drumstick trees in their backyards. If a drumstick tree yields two hundred drumsticks in one harvest, it will yield 600 drumsticks in a year. If a family has ten trees, it will sell 6,000 drumsticks a year. This will fetch them at least 2,400 rupees a year. If a drumstick tree yields for ten years, each family will get 24,000 rupees. Will Tata give this money? If income from one acre of double-cropped land is a minimum of 10,000 rupees a year, it would translate into 5 lakhs for fifty years? Will Tata give this? Every house has jackfruit trees in the backyard; the jackfruit is sent to Kolkata by trucks. If every jackfruit tree yields rupees 2,000, the compensation for fifty years will be one lakh... Will Tata give this money? They also produce cashew, mangoes, papaya, brinjal and other vegetables. Compensation for these can be calculated. They are not going to get any agricultural land. Hence, what will be the compensation amount for livelihood of each member of a family needs to calculated. (Bal 1996b)

Kashinath Nayak, who is over 62 years, said:

> I did not have any land in the old village. We shifted to this place around 1998; each person was given 10 decimal of land here. Now I have a house. Then, I used to go to Berhampur town daily for work. I was a mason then and continue to be so today. We worked as masons or carpenters or vendors and, sharecropped some land. That met our requirement of rice. We

> also caught fish from the village streams and rivers. We grew some vegetable in our tiny homestead land. A drumstick tree alone fulfilled many of our vegetable requirement. Most importantly, someone extended a helping hand at any time of need. That is the advantage of living in the village. Here we have to depend on market for everything from rice to fish, from vegetable to *saag*. We do not have that same feeling as colony dwellers. Each family has its own problem. How can we then support each other?
>
> We hoped that we would get jobs in the Tata factory. We have been in hope for the last twenty years. Still, there is no job. We do not know whether we will get it anymore. We are hearing that Tata is offering 7 lakhs of rupees to one family in lieu of job.

Those who were in the forefront of the struggle are today living with the scars of criminal cases foisted on them. Nageshwar Reddy lives in the Sindhigaon rehabilitation colony now. He carefully recalls some of the moments of the collective struggle:

> I was in my late thirties then. I do not know where to begin ... so much has happened. Today I am nearing 60 ... I cannot even say we were proud of what we did. If we were proud, we would not be so divided—each on his own. All that we have in common are these police cases. How do my grandchildren understand why I am an accused in a murder case. Where is the land we fought for? Even then we are regarded as being pro-Tata till today.
>
> We were so confused to find ourselves in jail simply because we did not want to sell out land to a company. I told myself: 'Even Lord Krishna was born in jail. So it is fine to be in jail.' Twenty three of us served sentence for 11 months. There are 18 or 19 of us still. Some people died too in later years. Balaji died, Guru Murthy died. You may say they died of natural causes. But it is this *chinta* (anxiety) that killed them. Tata steel plant was never built but we lost everything.
>
> Those who lived like me ... lost all mental peace. Look at me. At that time I got 3 lakhs for 3 acres. Today the rate is 5 lakhs per acre. I bought a tractor (Laughed loudly). Even I thought I could invest in a tractor and hire it and make more money. But it did not turn out that way. Whoever invested the money in anything only made more losses. None of us are used to that kind of money. We are peasants only (Laughing again). The only worthwhile investment was the house construction that everyone got involved in. We got 10 decimal each. We thought that at least we build a house to live in. But there's no source of earning since then. People have to go to distant

places in search of work. This is in the middle of nowhere—did you see anything here on the way? We are nowhere—anyone can see that.

The landless dalits got houses too. But being agricultural labourers, they have no work or source of earning. You must have seen those empty houses on the way here. They have to eat too and bring up their children. So, many have left for distant places in search of work. What can they do in a house?

Memories are fraught with a sense of resignation. Their accounts are marked by sadness or sometimes even bitterness when they recall the betrayal of the leadership; clearly they communicate the sense of futility of going over events that cannot be altered.

Or, perhaps still there is a hope of getting something from Tata. Then, why mar that prospect by talking about the movement as pro or against Tata. The only grievance till today is about Tata not providing the promised jobs. Otherwise, over the years, they have somehow reconciled themselves to their fate and look at the past as the past only. They have come to terms with the hardships through sheer hard labour.

A landless peasant runs a tailoring unit. He narrates his story and the hardships he suffered:

I was a tailor in Berhampur. We were poor but we were content. My family was engaged in agricultural labour. We used to get fish, coconut, a bit of paddy, *saag* and drumsticks. When the *andolan* intensified, my village people asked me to close shop in Berhampur and stay in the village. We were desperate to get our daughter married since we did not know our own future. That was a mistake. She suffered so much trauma and torture that she came back in six months. Nothing seemed to be working for us. Yes, we got 10 decimal land and I took a loan to build the house. But we had no earning for two or three years. Who will come here to give me orders for tailoring? Everybody was in terrible shape. I had to train my daughter in tailoring too when she walked out of that cruel marriage. Slowly we built our lives. But now there are so many tailors too!

We still manage to make 150 or 200 a day on average. But everything is so expensive. We have to buy every little thing. We are spending more money than before but not eating as well. We had always worked hard. When the Tatas sent us off here, it was a test for us. It has taken many years to settle—it is so hard to describe. Neither can we explain nor can anyone understand.

A suffering soul makes the trauma and hardships of displacement more bearable through nostalgia and longing. So often, it becomes the only way to survive. The old village seems so idyllic in the past. As a woman said:

> There was *saag* in every meal. There was so much fish always. We lived closely as a community. In a sense all of us are poor but some are even poorer. When the fish catch was made, the fish would be sold at one-third of whatever the market rate was. This was done only in the interest of the poor. Nobody could buy more than a kilo. Everybody could have the fish in that way.
>
> We had paddy, coconuts, lentil, *ragi*, ground nuts and the *kewda* flowers that fetched us so much. We all survived, we lacked nothing. No need and no want. Now we need money to buy everything, even *saag* and drumsticks.

Like the people of Hirakud or Rengali, the people who left their villages bear the stigma of being displaced. Within a few months of the razing down of these villages, Tata made a formal announcement of its withdrawal from the project. There was a common refrain of many people we met: why did they have to undergo so much hardship and heartbreak when Tata did not do anything with the land. They got immersed in rebuilding their lives.

The Long Wait

Many years passed. Not everybody had taken compensation money as some kept waiting for the promised job.

Narayan Reddy from CPI won the assembly elections from Chatrapur in 2004. He grandly extended an invitation to the old foe. Tata Motors was facing stiff opposition from the peasant community for its Nano project in Singur in West Bengal. In September 2008, Narayan Reddy welcomed the company to set up its Nano factory in Chatrapur. The same media that had aggressively questioned the police firing at Chatrapur lapped up such dips in movement politics.

Around 2010, Tata revved up the process of utilizing the land that had been acquired and converted it to a multiproduct SEZ. The Gopalpur Industrial Park SEZ was inaugurated by the chief minister on 24 August 2010 without any resistance. The company had already acquired 3,585 acres of which almost 800 acres was government land.

Tata finally began the construction of the boundary wall for its ferro-chrome plant on 1,235 acres of land. The hope of the promised job was rekindled. The construction work went on between 2010 and 2014. Local villagers were engaged to build the wall, thereby forfeiting any access forever to their agricultural land. They provided labour at Rs 150/- per day to barricade their own land from themselves. When construction work got over, they were shown the door.

Kamraj Borma says:

> We could no longer use the name of Gana Sangram Samiti as it was all fragmented and the old leadership had either sat back or become pro-Tata. So we made the Samaja Surakshya Samiti on 31 October 2009.
>
> A total of 3,900 acres were acquired. All those who sold were assured of one contract job per family and that too to make the boundary wall on their land. The peasants who grew *kia* on their own land had been reduced to wage labour.

The betrayal by the company led people to form yet another organization to demand for job and compensation: Tata Ispat Prakalp Prabhabita Chaasi Mancho. When the organization sat in dharna demanding jobs, the local MLA and then the Minister of Education (who is also a land loser) got involved in the process of negotiation. The Tatas agreed to give jobs to 1,800 people in the presence of the Minister. But after a few days, all of them were retrenched on 1 August 2016. Reflecting on the manipulation of the Tatas, Damburu Reddy says:

> The boundary wall took the longest time. Everybody was working on it. When almost 90 per cent of the wall was over, Tata made a clever move. They effectively split our people into two categories, Land labourers and Land losers. The former were landless agricultural labourers and the latter were those whose land had been acquired. This split made Tata get away with accountability to jobs for all project affected people. After the negotiation in the presence of the Minister, we were assured of 1,800 jobs only to land losers. That also did not materialize. A new package was also announced for land compensation. It was increased from earlier two lakhs to four lakhs. And those who do not want job would be given one lakh more. But the hope of job for our youths remained a dream as ever.

Jai Titanium

The mega steel plant—a bilateral dream project of TISCO and Nippon Steel from Japan—did not materialize. Twenty years have passed since Tata eyed this land of *kia* flowers. People in the rehabilitation colonies of Tata lamented their fate. Those who remained in the villages had to fight back for their land again and again. Plans for a 120 MW coal-based thermal plant were initiated by the Dr. Ramakrishna Prasad Power Private Limited (RKPPL) of Hyderabad. On 10 January 2014, a public hearing initiated by the State Pollution Control Board came to naught. There was stiff resistance by the people of Badaputti and P Laxmipur. They had to confront their former leader Narayan Reddy who came with the administration. He had switched sides.

While trying to piece together the narrative of the people's struggle, we kept meeting the children of those who had fought the Tatas for their land. They are in late teens and early twenties. The dread of unemployment haunts them. In early August 2016, we met them outside the boundary wall of the Tata ferro-chrome plant in a dharna. Through the arithmetic of dispossession that the Tatas had begun to master, the number of land losers worthy of employment in its ferro-chrome plant had dwindled to 860 for its construction work, including 86 young men who had passed out from ITI. They were paid Rs 150/- per day as unskilled labour. As soon as construction came to an end, they were laid off on 31 July under the plea that there is no work. A strike that began on 1 August continued for 2 months in vain. Those who the land belonged to and their children had become wage workers. They levelled the land and built the ferro-chrome plant and a boundary wall that alienated them forever from the land of their ancestors. While both the administration and the company stalled negotiations with the people, all Odia dailies proudly flashed the news of Tata Steel's 55,000 TPA ferro-chrome plant in Gopalpur Industrial Park being inaugurated by the Chief Minister on 30 November.

On yet another day, 16 August 2017, there was much excitement as people were getting ready for a public hearing by the State Pollution Control Board taking place in the neighbouring Kanamana panchayat. The Saraf Titanium Park is planning several units to manufacture high titanium slag, titanium dioxide pigment, ferro titanium, scandium oxide, rare earths and rare metal products. It will tie up with Indian Rare Earths Limited in Chatrapur. The public hearing was dominated by the youth who clamped down any voices of dissent. They asserted that the people of Ganjam do not have to go to Surat or Kerala or Tamil Nadu for employment as the first titanium plant in the country would be set up in their own area, in their own Ganjam district! Cries of Jai Titanium rent the air. An April 2016 report given out at the venue categorically stated only 179 jobs would be provided. Yet another generation was being wooed by the propaganda of employment.

There is no end to the saga of suffering of the people of this land. Juna Lakshmi Amma gave up her life trying to save Badaputti from TISCO, which was a stronghold of the resistance. Today, the same village is reeling under the grip of another ominous curse. There are signs of radiation deaths and disease. Many have died of kidney failure in recent years, while several more are being diagnosed of chronic kidney disease. Dead fish are found floating on the ocean waters. Villagers are deeply suspicious of the proximity of a monazite processing plant of Indian Rare Earths Limited (IREL) near the village. Yes, dispossession happens in so many ways. The sandy beaches of Chatrapur and Gopalpur have become the coveted land in the search for non-carbon nuclear fuel by the powers that be. There is uncertainty at every step for the human habitat and the entire ecosystem. Who can say what will happen to the sandy beaches with its casuarina trees, the *kewda* bushes and the marauding monkeys, the *kia* flowers and the coconut trees, the fish and the crabs?

REFERENCES

Bal, Pradyumna. 1996a. *Rajya ebong lokonko lagi na poonjipati nko pain! Pragatibaadi*, August 4.

Bal, Pradyumna. 1996b. *Tata kono neuchi? Kono deuchi? Pragatibaadi*, August 18.

PUDR and APDR. 1997. *Gopalpur: Steel Plant, Displacement and People's Struggle*. A Report by PUDR and APDR. New Delhi. May 1997.

Police Firing at TISCO Project Site, Gopalpur. 1997. A Report by PUCL, Ganatantrik Adhikar Surakshya Sangathan (GASS) and Manabika Adhikar Sangathan (MAS), Bhubaneswar. March.

Reddy, Narayan. 1998. *Tata pain sindhi gaan re ganahatya koribaku mukhy mantra nko nirdesh thila; manyavar high courth nko hastakhap aamoku bonchai dela*. Swabhimaan, Monisho ro bartaboho, July 1.

Reddy, P. Adi Narayana. 2002. *Kewda Flower Processing in Ganjam: An Economically Important Activity in Proceedings of the National Conference on Utilization of Bioresources*. New Delhi: Allied Publishers Pvt Limited.

CHAPTER 8

The Song of the Mali

But there are things which you have said to me which I do not like. They are not sweet like sugar, but bitter like gourds. You said that you wanted to put us upon a reservation, to build us houses and make us medicine lodges. I do not want them. I was born upon the prairie where the wind blew free and there was nothing to break the light of the sun. I was born where there were no enclosures and where everything drew a free breath. I want to die there and not within walls.
Parra-Wa-Sammen (Ten Bears) of the Yamparika Comanches
—Dee Brown, 1970

The winter in Maikanch had ripened. The *malis* (hills) that wore different colours during the rainy and autumn seasons with the crops of *ragi*, maize, *alsi* and *kandul* had been bare. Crops grown on them had been harvested; so also paddy from the tiny plots nestled with the perennial streams. Villagers had the blessings of Dharni Ma. There was no worry for food for the next six to seven months. The *dishari* had fixed the days for celebration of *Pus Parab* marking the end of the harvest and had not dreamt or cautioned any danger to the village. Yet something happened. On 16 December 2000, the police fired upon a gathering of protestors in Maikanch and shot dead three of them and injured a dozen more. They were protesting against the setting up of an Alumina Plant and bauxite mining in their ancestral land. A few bullets pierced the bauxite-pregnant belly of the hillocks, and a few hit the streams running out of the hillocks.

R. Padhi, N. Sadangi, *Resisting Dispossession*,
https://doi.org/10.1007/978-981-15-0717-5_8

Tiny fish playing in the streams found themselves dead before they could hide under the pebbles. And three cows grazing in the hillock also fell to the police bullets. Were the hillocks, streams, fishes and cows participating in the protest? Did they feel threatened by the plant and mining?

Nestling on the foothills of Baphlimali, Maikanch with a predominantly Jhodia-Paraja population is in Kashipur block in Rayagada district. The district was part of undivided Koraput till 1992. In the same year, Utkal Aluminium International Ltd. (UAIL), a consortium of companies, signed a Memorandum of Understanding (MoU) with the government of Odisha to set up an Alumina Refinery Plant at Doraguda by extracting bauxite from Baphlimali. Subsequently, more MoUs were signed to mine bauxite from other *malis* of the areas. This was projected as the panacea for one of the most backward regions of Odisha, in journalistic parlance, the Ethiopia of Odisha. But the people of *malis*—the kandhas, parajas, jhodias and pengos—had different perception. It is their land, the '*dumas*' (spirits of the ancestors) are watching over them; it is their life and livelihood however wretched it may be for others; it is in this land that lie buried many dreams and many memories; many dreams are still alive. Out of this soil are born their cultures and practices. So, in the name of development, when their land, streams, forests and *malis* that they have known to be theirs for centuries are handed over to companies, they rise and revolt to protect their sources of subsistence.

Let us step back in time to have a glimpse of their world.

Fragility of Subsistence and Welfare Work

The people of undivided Koraput, which is also part of the mythical Dandakarnya, for centuries had been content hunting down *baraha* (boar) and *kutra* (wild goat) for food; and fighting tigers to carve a patch of land out of forest for growing food grains. Life was marked by the passing of seasons with their only worries around *bagha*, *megha* and *jara* (tiger, rains and fever) and the joys of dance and dalliance in *Chaiti*. Gopinath Mohanty in his novel *Amrutara Santan* (Children of Nectar) portrays the lives of the people of Koraput, especially the Kandha-Paraja. Written in 1945, his other novel, Paraja, shows the kind of economic transition that was being ushered in by the modern state, leading to a collapse of the entire world of the protagonist, Sukru Jani, who is an adivasi peasant. In order to pay the fine for an alleged violation of law in a forest that he believed belonged to him and his people, he had to mortgage his land to a sahukar. It is a poignant story of the gradual destruction of a community and the entire way of life as seen through his family. The monetization of economy with the presence of colonial administration and the sahukar in the tribal land had spelt disaster for their subsistence living.

With the dawn of India's independence, Koraput proved to be a good laboratory for development. River dams and hydro-electricity projects, mining and industries were set up. People were uprooted from their homes and habitats, and dispossessed from their lands and forests (see Introduction for details). This was a severe blow to their life of subsistence. By the time the 1980s came, their economy had become even more fragile. Massive deforestation and acquisition of cultivable land for mega projects had weakened the economic base of the people, specifically food security.

Reminiscing the 1980s, 43-year-old Gangaram Majhi from Kucheipadar shares the life and livelihood of a landless person. He emphasizes the importance of *dangar* in the economic life of local people.

> When my father died, my mother sent me to my uncle's house because it was difficult for her to feed me and my younger brother. There I worked as a cowherd. We had no land. When my father was alive, he cultivated *dangar* (slopes of the hill) land. When I grew up, I came back to the village and did the same. I also share-cropped some land and managed to have some rice. In the *dangar* we grow *mandia*, *kandul* and maize for food. From that we manage food for 7 to 8 months. But the rest of the months, especially in the rainy months when old food stock is exhausted and new crops are awaited, are really hard for us. We also grow *alsi* to sell and to buy clothes, oil and salt.

When asked if somebody falls seriously ill what he would do, he laughed feebly and said, 'What would I do?' and remained silent. It was sheer helplessness, as if to await death helplessly. *Dangar* cultivation is so essential for their survival that even a landless peasant like Ganga faced the bullets and was injured in the Maikanch firing for protecting the land.

The situation is no better for a marginal farmer like Manohar Jhodia, an activist of the anti-mining movement. He has faced violence, intimidation and threats from company goons. He shares how the unpaid loan from the sahukar by his father pushed him to leave education and become a bonded labourer.

> My father had one acre of land and he also cultivated some *dangar* land. When due to some dispute, some villagers destroyed our crop consecutively for two years, my father stopped my education. I was in class seven. He

> could not manage and I came home to assist him in the field. He had taken some loan from the Sahukar but failed to repay. He was forced to send me to the Sahukar's house to work as a bonded labourer. I worked for two years and came back home. At that time, Agragamee, an NGO started working in Kashipur and I worked as a Communicator for Rs 300 a month. Even with this small amount, our situation improved.

Those who had more land too have their own story to tell. Mukundi Saunta belongs to the old tribal landlord family. With the expansion of the family tree, their landed property was parcelled out, and he now owns five acres of land.

> In our area, how much land you own is not as important as the quality of land. You see, out of my five acres, three acres are of *bhatta* land (upland). We cultivate it once in three years. So, practically, I possess two acres of land. The yield is so poor; two to three quintals a year. On the other hand, the low land produces around 10 quintals of paddy. But that sort of land is less available and most of it is with the Sahukars, traders and politicians. It is true that we do not starve. But we cannot even send our children to a school in a town. Life becomes difficult for us in monsoon time or when the yield comes down due to unfair weather.

The labour of women plays a pivotal role in this subsistence economy. They participate in all sorts of agricultural activities like weeding, transplanting, preparing field and cutting except ploughshare. Animal keeping is another economic activity that women do. Ambai Majhi shares her experience and the role of women in subsistence:

> For us the day begins when the cock crows first. With a bit of tobacco to chew, we leave for the jungle to collect fire wood. We reach home by noon and prepare some *mandia pejo* (*ragi* gruel). Then we carry the food and share with other members of the family who work in the field. The work continues till sunset. In the evenings and at night, women husk paddy and sort out the other food stuff.
>
> We have 5 to 6 acres of land where they grow paddy, corn, *alsi* and *ragi*. We grow edible roots and tubers too. I still do not have money. I simply tend to these pigs and sell them. I manage to sell three or four in a year and get 1,000 to 1,200 rupees from the sale. I have one buffalo. Four cows have died. We have to work to live and survive. If we do not work, there is nothing for us. We will simply die. If one is alive, one has to work.

Once the equilibrium of nature is broken, or the mediating thread is snapped, for whatever reasons—crop failure, deforestation, court cases, marriage or expansion of family, or the death of the only able-bodied person in the family—the disaster becomes inevitable for the individual family. Many seas and continents away, in Latin America, the lives of the Indian communities are the same. In an Indian village in Guatemala, Rigoberta Menchu's sister is going through the many vows and ceremonies that mark a marriage. The young couple vows that their ancestors will live through their children and no rich man or landowner can destroy the children. Yet another vow states how they will suffer, the children will suffer, many of the children will die young because of the circumstances created by white men. But the couple vows to bear it just as their ancestors have borne it. They then vow to be responsible for the children who survive and go on following the Indian ways. There is pain and hardship awaiting the young couple. This fear and uncertainty strengthen the will to survive with back-breaking labour round the year. The community considers it a miracle for a child to reach 5 years of age (Burgos Debray 1984).

In the year 1980, Achyut Das appeared in Kashipur with a missionary zeal to start development work in the most backward villages. Tilonia was his inspiration started by Bankar Roy and Aruna Roy. After extensive surveys in the villages, he founded Agragamee to begin the project. Achyut Das writes:

> Community Grain Bank was the first step to fight against hunger and scarcity of food in Kashipur. For four months from June to September people do not have anything to eat. Wage work is also not available. People don't have money to buy food from outside. *Saag*, bamboo stalks and various roots from the jungle are also not available in plenty. The only option available to people is to eat mango kernel and tamarind seeds. Adivasis are forced to go to sahukars. As a result, they get dispossessed and become bonded labour. (Das 2008)

Agragamee's role in mobilizing people to develop a collective food grain centre had some impact on the exploitation of sahukars. People collectively stored an amount of food grains after harvest in the centre and took it at the time of scarcity. As a result, they did not go to sahukar for loan or as bonded labour. Achyut Das claims, 'in 1981, community grain banks had started in five villages and by 1985 it had spread to 250 villages.'

Despite Agragamee's role, news of hunger and starvation deaths from the region continued to pour in. It drew national attention, and the then Prime Minister Rajiv Gandhi visited the area. He tasted *saag* in adivasi houses to have a feel of the poverty. Following the prime ministerial visit in September 1987, the International Fund for Agricultural Development (IFAD) agreed to extend loan for the Kashipur project on December 1987, and funds were channelled through an organization called Orissa Tribal Development Project (OTDP). IFAD funds began to flow in from May 1988. Initially, Agragamee was part of the IFAD project but withdrew from it claiming that 'the OTDP was not listening to its advice or villagers' feedback.' Finally, the project was closed in December 1997 after an expenditure of 24.4 million USD (around Rs 120 crores) half of which was loaned by IFAD and the rest by World Food Programme. Most of the expenditure went into developing roads and communication networks. Yet again, in the name of mitigating poverty and starvation, the entire undivided Koraput, Kalahandi and Balangir districts were put under the KBK Yojana scheme. As companies began to queue up to Kashipur, people began to believe that IFAD had laid the road for the juggernaut of development to roll—to take away their lands, streams, *malis* and *dangars*. Truly, development is the ruse for the entire dispossession of the self-reliant adivasi peasantry.

Earthworms Rise in the Black Shadow of Companies

Where shall we go leaving our land?
Can we live without land?
We are the earthworms, we live off the earth.
We won't leave our land.

News of handing over their sources of livelihood to companies does not percolate down to the local people so easily. It is not desirable in democratic governance either. But it reaches people in curious ways passing through the ghats and hillocks. The story goes like this:

One fine evening, the *dakua* (one who calls the villagers to the meeting place) of Kucheipadar announces that some big people from the town are coming to the village to discuss something big. There shall be a meeting under the mango grove at the edge of the village. A feast of the goat is also arranged. The meeting begins and the big people from the town declare that the government has been kind enough to set up a big project in their area for their employment and economic benefits. People do not ask about the project nor do they enquire into any details. They silently nod their heads and sometimes utter a monosyllabic answer—hai, hai (yes, yes). They are a people who are not generally used to asking questions, that too, to the big people from the town. The meeting ended, and the feast of the goat began. When people were relishing the goat meat, Ratu, the drunkard, who had been to the hill to collect some medicinal herbs, made a dramatic appearance and screamed at the villagers, 'you ********** fools! You have gathered here to eat the goat meat? You don't know they have come to take away our land for setting up a factory.' Ratu disappeared as dramatically as he had appeared. No one knew where Ratu got this information. But his words sowed the first seeds of doubt.

People began to talk about the project and the loss of land. Their doubts got confirmed when the UAIL project officials started survey work in the name of laying down a railway line.[1] At this juncture, the local MLA Akhil Saunta, who belonged to Kucheipadar, offered to arrange a meeting with the then chief minister of Odisha. Towards the end of November 1993, an eighteen-member delegation from five villages met the chief minister. He assured them of shifting the site of the project. But nothing happened; rather, more and more areas were surveyed. Now, people did what they had learnt from their ancestors to protect their land: to resist.

Each time the survey team appeared on their land, all of them, children and old, men and women, adults and young, rushed to the place with whatever they could lay their hands on: lathis, axes and sickles. No one waited for anyone. It was like chasing away a wild animal that had entered the village surreptitiously. When men tried to seize the survey instruments, women sprayed chilli powder and *Bai danka* (a wild itching plant) on members of the survey team. Even the survey camp was set on fire. The local police station at Tikri got active and tried to arrest people. On one occasion, the police arrested Maharaj Majhi, one of the leaders of the movement. One thousand people gheraoed the thana and forcibly got him released from the police. The intermittent fight between the chilli powder and gun powder continued for more than a year. On one occasion, two officials of Norsk Hydro visited the proposed plant site. When people got the news, they gheraoed them and brought them to Kucheipadar. They were made to sign on a paper that they would not visit the area any more.

Similar protests grew in adjacent project areas like L&T and Hindalco. People developed newer methods to protest and resist. In the L&T area, local people from forty villages quickly formed an organization, Anchalik Surakshya Parishad (Council for Local Protection), to carry on the struggle. The Council put up a check-gate on the way to the hilltop to stop company vehicles and burnt down the company office. In the Hindalco area when the survey work began with the protection of the police, people blocked all roads by cutting down trees and putting boulders. The survey team had to beg people to be allowed to return. Yet, on another occasion, Alai Majhi, a frail, old woman of Barigan, took off her clothes and threw them at the police and dared them to touch her. She declared that he who touched her would marry her!

To shame the Power is a way of Protest. Isn't it?

March for the Mali

The river flows by Ramibeda and Doraguda;
Streams murmur along
Bagrijhola, Kucheipadar
Etched in our hearts are these lands, these villages,
These streams, these rivers
Which we cannot leave behind
We cannot leave

Indal is here with Tata and Hydro
To wipe us out, to wipe us out
All in the name of Development ... Development!
To cheat us, to cheat us
All in the name of Employment ... Employment!

Baphlimali, Kutrumali, Sijidangar—
They are all ours, all ours
Do not, do not allow them to be ruined
Do not, do not hand them over
To the companies ... to the companies! (A song of the PSSP)

When L&T and Hindalco suspended their activities to bide for a more favourable time, Indal (UAIL is locally called Indal) carried on with the cunning of a fox, devising newer methods. The obliged government machinery was mobilized to distribute compensation money for the proposed acquisition of land. Company agents, deviously called communicators, were sent silently to individual households to persuade people to accept compensation money. The government officials and local police station too joined in this surreal exercise. They invented lies; if the people won't accept money, their relatives would get it and the company would take away the land. In this country, these tricks have stood the test of the times. Yes, they applied all the tricks mentioned in the old book on statecraft, 'Arthasastra'—*danda, dana, bheda* and *sama*—to get the people to accept compensation. The tricks worked. Some villagers accepted compensation money. However, it did not work in villages like Kucheipadar and Bagrijhola (of the plant area) which were going to lose the maximum amount of land. Apprehending the larger danger ahead, a process of organized resistance began. Activists from earlier movements like Anti-BALCO Movement, Gandhamardan and Anti-Missile Test Range Movement, Baliapal lent their support. Even, the leader of the Narmada Bachao Andolan, Medha Patkar, visited the area. And, Prakrutika Sampad Surakshya Parishad (PSSP) was formed in the year 1995 to carry the struggle forward. On the other hand, the company floated an NGO called Utkal Rural Development Society (URDS) to win over the 'heart' of the people. It tried to organize free health camps, repair village roads and culverts and distribute plants. PSSP mobilized people to foil these activities. It became a war of nerves. And people's hearts remained unwinnable.

As these local protests gathered momentum, the idea of a unified movement also gained momentum. In the last week of December 1998, a 10-day *padayatra* was organized. It passed from Barigan to Baphlimali to Kucheipadar connecting struggles; connecting communities like Kondh, Jhodia and Pengo ensconced in the many *malis*; and connecting adivasis, dalits and *paikas* of Kashipur. As the *padayatra* went by, the now famous song *Gaan chhadiba nahin, dangar chhadiba nahin* (shall not leave the village, shall not leave the *dangar*) reverberated in the hills, streams and rivers. This Gandhian strategy of *padayatra* along with its adivasi touch had much joy and laughter in it too. Young boys and girls sang songs and danced late into the night despite the day-long trek. As Pramila Majhi, one participant of the *padayatra*, recalls, 'to dance is to heal the body. It takes away pain.' It was also exciting for many for whom the world outside their villages was limited to their weekly haats only (the market).

But the war of development went on relentlessly ...

Company's Trick: All Party Development Committee

Exasperated, the company pulled out another trick from its bag: The All Party Development Committee. Members of all the major political parties—Congress, BJD and BJP—were part of the Committee. The single-point programme of the Committee was to garner support for the project. Incidentally, the members were local traders, contractors and politicians who had an eye on the project to get contracts—small and big. It became a formidable local group in support of the project. It symbolized the unwritten consensus among major political parties of the country about corporate-led development.

This development sprang a surprise on the movement. It also clarified many things for it. Bhagaban Majhi, one of the leaders of the movement says, 'People became clear who our enemies are and who are our friends.'

In a showdown of strength, the Committee went to organize a meeting on 15 December 2000 just when PSSP had given a call for a *chakka jaam* programme at Rapkana square on 20 December. The Committee on its way to the meeting place was stopped at Maikanch by PSSP activists. This resulted in a scuffle, and the Committee went back. It was a sort of defeat for the latter. For they had been ruling the roost in Kashipur, and ordinary adivasis and dalits had dared to challenge them for the first time.

It was a costly challenge. Next morning around 10 am, three platoons of armed police entered Maikanch.

Kashipur Developed into Martyrdom

> Around 10–11 am, sarkari *babus* and police forces reached the village in two cars and three jeeps. Only we women were around. Most of the men were away. They inquired about five men they were looking for. When we told them that they are not here they asked us to call them from wherever they were. We told them that they can talk to us. They refused saying that they want only those five men. They told us to move out and started entering the village. As we refused, they hit us with lathis. Danei fell down. We thought she died. Everyone howled, Danei is dead, Danei is dead. We continued to howl and shout at the police forces. It reached the men. They came rushing down the *malis*. Then the police started firing. Raghunath Jhodia, Damodar Jhodia and Abhilash Jhodia succumbed. Police carried away their dead bodies and some injured.[2]

As the news of police firing reached villages, people kept coming to Maikanch. PSSP activists, who had gone to different villages to campaign for the Rapkana *chakka jaam* programme, rushed back to Maikanch. Receiving dead bodies of their beloved comrades from the police, PSSP arranged the funeral pyre in the nearby *mali* for which they sacrificed their lives. As the pyre was lit, slogans rent the air: Long live Raghunath Jhodia! Long Live Damodar Jhodia! Long Live Abhilash Jhodia! The *malis* echoed back.

Bhagaban Majhi, reflecting on the situation, said:

> It was a moment of intense pain and great loss for all of us. But we had to steel our nerves. We assessed the situation that the killing was to check the movement spreading and sent messages accordingly. And, we resolved not to cancel our Rapkana program and let their sacrifices go in vain. Once the funeral work was over, we started preparation. The day after the funeral, people of distant villages began walking with rice, *ragi*, *kandula* and other vegetables and stayed overnight in nearby villages. On 20 December, nearly 10,000 people gathered at Rapkana. People mourned and wept, sang and danced and once again resolved not to part with their land for the company.[3]

When someone near and dear dies, people observe certain rituals for the peaceful rest of the soul of the dead. The state has its own rituals too. When it shoots somebody dead, it declares some amount of money as compensation for the living dependent of the dead. It settles the account. Can this process be reversed? Can people kill someone representing the State and declare compensation for it to square the account? After the Maikanch firing, when the government declared compensation, the people of Kashipur asked this question. Perhaps, the question was too unsettling. Perhaps, they found it barbaric. But the government had no answer.

It is surely civilized of the State to kill its people.

More rituals follow. Whenever the state carries out atrocities, it is ready to set up a commission to whitewash its murderous acts. Thus, a Commission of Enquiry was set up. Retired Justice Mishra headed it. Once again people rejected it and declared their non-cooperation.

The Commission of Enquiry

The Commission went on with its enquiry for more than three years and submitted its report on 17 January 2003. It found many things ranging from manipulation of FIRs to the overzealousness of police officers to the use of gross excessive use of force. The Commission also raised doubts and questions about the action and attitude of the police. Permit us to quote only a few lines:

> There was also no justification for such a large contingent of force to enter inside the village unless, of course, the intention was to teach the protestors a lesson. The Commission further observed: The perception that police force acts under the influence of political masters or for the rich and the influential has gained ground not without justification in many parts of the State and more so, in the comparatively less developed areas. A police officer particularly at the thana level considers himself as the sovereign of all he surveys forgetting that essentially he is a public servant and his primary duty is to serve the interest of the society. (Mishra Commission Report 2003)

But while enquiring about the causes of firing, the Commission also found that the proposed alumina plant would not cause pollution. Was it supposed to assess environment impact of the project too? Heaven knows what scientific evidence led the Commission to conclude this.

Of course, it is sacrilegious to cast doubt on the motive of Justice Incarnate.

The report without punishing the culprits added to the woes of the victims by giving moral credence to the alumina project. It was an exercise in turning the entire issue of life and livelihood of people and loot of natural resources by companies into an environmental issue, albeit minus human beings who are an integral part of it. All vested interest groups used the report as a hammer to beat down people's resistance.

When the Commission was busy in its enquiry, PSSP took up the issue of the delisting of Jhodias from the Scheduled Tribe (ST) list to consolidate its base with the call that the fight for the *mati* (land) is also the fight for the *jati* (tribe). The Jhodias as a tribe were delisted by the government of Odisha in the year 1992 and put under Other Backward Caste (OBC), which debarred them from availing some facilities given to Scheduled Tribes. Though there were some murmurs of protest from the community, there was no widespread mobilization. PSSP interpreted the issue of delisting Jhodias as a ploy to smoothen the process of land alienation of adivasis for the company and land-grabbers. To press for the relisting of Jhodia, it gave a call to boycott Panchayat election (local body) to be held in 2002. Nine panchayats participated in it, and the boycott was a huge success.

Purchasing Opinion

After the release of the Commission's report, the Revenue Divisional Commissioner (RDC), South Range, was entrusted with the duty of collecting people's opinion on the project. Was there anything to know about people's opinion after 12 years of resistance and that too when three people had laid down their lives opposing the project? Had not the people given their opinion opposing the project in Gram Sabha meetings as per the constitutional provisions in the Fifth Schedule area? Does not the Samata Judgement clearly state that the tribal people cannot be alienated from their land even by the State as State is an alien entity as far as tribal land is concerned? Why are the laws of the land made to bend when the interest of corporate houses is involved?

The RDC went on collecting people's opinion sitting at the district headquarters, Rayagada. The entire district administration and company agents went on luring people who could be persuaded and intimidated into giving a favourable opinion for the project. Collection of opinion, literally, turned into purchase of opinion. The company's money bag and the district administration's authority was a deadly bait for some to refuse. Specifically, some local youths fell prey to it. Once again, the compensation money for land was increased to Rs 100,000 per acre from Rs 20,000 per acre. Even then, resistance to the project continued.

Finally, the most potential weapon, the coercive power of the State, was used.

Turning Kashipur into a Police Barrack

On 1 December 2004, the District Collector and the Superintendent of Police with ten platoons of police force came to D. Karal, a village near Kucheipadar, to set up a police outpost. By that time, 300–400 people, mostly women, had gathered on the road and shouted slogans: 'We want hospital, not outpost; we want medicine not lathi; we want irrigation not bullet.' The administration, obviously, did not consider these demands as demands for development. They were a threat to development: a threat to the setting up of a plant by Hindalco. Peoples Union for Democratic Rights (PUDR), a democratic rights organization from Delhi that visited the area, wrote that the outpost was going to be set up 'in an area that has little history of crime and there is already a police station not far away, in Tikri.

Significantly, this police post is set up on land already acquired by the company' (PUDR 2005). Indeed, a collaboration trend of Public-Private Participation in controlling people's dissent had begun to manifest and grow.

That day, protestors were lathi charged, and tear gas shells were hurled at them. Those injured were arrested and sent to jail. After this incident, the entire Kashipur area was turned into a police barrack. Paramilitary forces like Indian Reserve Battalion and CRPF were mobilized to crush the movement at all cost. Activists were picked up from haats, roads, hospitals and banks. They were sent to jails under charges of dacoity, arson and rioting. Armed paramilitary forces flag-marched through adivasi villages. Village-level meetings were attacked. The villages were under siege, and the reign of terror prevailed for nearly two years. Two villages near the plant site, that is, Ramibeda and Kendukhunti, succumbed and left their lands and villages. Guarded by the armed forces, the company began to construct the boundary wall on whatever land was acquired. It was a tactic to break the morale of the people who had refused to accept compensation. The company also used another tactic. It unleashed its money bag on people to buy their silence. Nearly 7,000–8,000 people of the affected villages were given monthly allowance, locally called *bhatta*. In the company's book keeping, it was marked as 'payment for non-work.' Local youths were given contracts of lakhs of rupees for village development. According to company officials, around 400 local contractors emerged during 2010–2012. Finally, the Company formed Village Auxiliary Force (VAF), in the year 2010, especially, to protect the plant site and the office premises. One hundred seven youths joined in it. Those who were most active against the company turned its protector and bodyguard (Dash 2015). It was perhaps to win away these youths from joining Maoists, who were trying to establish connection with the people.

Bhagaban Majhi, reflecting on the situation, said:

> Some get Rs 1,800 and many more get Rs 2,000 each month. This is really to do nothing. They are not given jobs or work. This is basically to buy their silence. Now you see how the *andolan* has weakened. The people have also become dependent on this money. But they are becoming lazy and not only that they feel hopeless too. This is because work does not mean money to us. Ours is an adivasi society. Work means confidence and contentment and a sense of purpose too. Our people are beginning to realize this. But the women—the older women—are not bought by this logic of money. They

have been able to see the negative side of this—the bad side—right from the beginning. They see it as destruction. This has certainly helped in a small way. It has helped people in not going to distant areas in search of work. But it is not a solution. It is a ploy so that we remain silent in all else that the company wants to do here for its own gain and profit.

But then do we conclude that the struggle has failed? Had it failed, we would not have been able to see through the tactics of the company. We would not have understood the game, the ploy and the tactics. We know that the government is not for the people; the government is for the company alone. We are conscious and aware because of the struggle we have waged and the way we understood our rights as people of this area. We are critical because of the same consciousness. We question. We simply question what meets the eye and what is unfolding before our own eyes with the truth that is within us. They cannot buy all of us. Those they have bought had become momentarily greedy. And therefore they are now fearful. The company has brought three things to the people: greed, fear and money. It has nothing else to offer. What more can it give to us than these three things?

The Crushing of Dreams and Birla's Rising Sun

As the greed, fear and money gripped the body and soul of people, the song—*Gaan chhadiba nahin, dangar chhadiba nahin*—that had united and moulded them into a community of *sangramis* (fighters) began to fade away. And everything went topsy-turvy. The people who were all *sangramis* (fighters) till yesterday became different today: Those who were uprooted from the villages became 'Displaced People' and those who ceded land to company, 'the Land Losers.' And each chose one's own path. Each got suspicious and saw the spectre of *dalal* (broker) in the other. Most remarkably, many people who were not used to such easy money came to see it, to handle it. It had its own exhilarating effect especially on the younger generation. But it also had its own dark side. It created fissures in the family, in the community and between villages. The deep alienation becomes palpable as Ambai Majhi describes the breakdown of community and kinship ties and clashes within the family. And finally, it crushed the dream of saving the land.

Except for salt and oil, the land gives us everything. Maybe we buy a few clothes to wear. We do not need money. We never had fights because of money.

But today there is *ashanti* (disquiet) in every house. There is *ashanti* when families have taken compensation and even for those who have not. There is violence, conflict and liquor everywhere. What we get from the land is nowhere near comparison to what we will get from money. Money disappears; land does not disappear. If you have life, you can make money. But if you have land, your children and their children are secure too. We want our land even now. It is not sufficient for me to see my children eat. I have to see my grandchildren eat too. Many children die. It is only when you see grandchildren eat too that you know life continues. If we did not think this way, we too would have sold our land for money. Men seldom think of the next generation. Why … you ask me? What do I say? Maybe because it is we who make this world and bring children to it. We bring life on this earth.

When I say "all of us" I mean not only us people. There are the pigs, cows, goats, and chicken that we look after too. Where will they go? We all need the land.

The struggle was not for me alone or for my family only. Our community is mutually dependent on each other. Any gain or benefit is a collective gain. I was part of the movement because I did not want mining for all of us—not one village or one community—but for the entire of Kashipur. We want the company to go even now.

She wonders and queries urging us too to engage in her querying:

People managed to stop the Tatas in Chilika and in Gopalpur. I hear that many companies have been defeated by people in other places. Why could we not stop this company? Who do I ask these questions? If you have come to ask me, I can also ask you some questions.

Out of the debris of the shattered dreams, the sun of Aditya Birla appears in the sky of Kashipur. As we move from Tikri towards the plant site, we see on each concrete wall the logo of Aditya Birla—A Rising Sun! In Kucheipadar, once the nerve centre of the struggle, one finds remarkable turnaround. Most of the houses are now made of concrete; the number of motorcycles has increased manifold; it is not even hard to find a few Boleros in the village. Ironically, tribal women of the villages in all their innocence use the silver-shining alumina powder taken from the Aditya Birla plant to do the *alpana* (motifs) in honour of Gods. Or, is it for the Rising Sun of Aditya Birla?

Hope of a Glowworm

As Birla's sun began to blaze, despondency started setting in. People of the older generation felt helpless and became silent. Those youths who were not yet caught by the bait of the company felt restive, desperate to do something to stop the company. At this juncture, Maoist cadres entered Kashipur and revived the hope of the anti-company struggle. They moved from place to place in the hills performing and mingling with the local people. They listened to people's woes in not having access to PDS (Public Distribution System) rice and about panchayat corruption. They discussed bauxite mining in Niyamgiri and Kashipur with them. In many villages, people fondly remember Denga (D. Srinivas) who seemed to be a pied piper attracting many young boys and girls to join the movement. Bulka Miniaka, the wise old man of Barigan, puts it succinctly in this way:

> What can be done? Nobody is listening and no other way is credible. We tried peaceful means but the government, administration and police have been successful in breaking them and discrediting them.... So young people are feeling let down, even we are feeling so. It is okay, people have found reason in Maoism. (PUDR 2011)

These starry-eyed youths, not yet 20, left their villages, their dancing and wooing in *Chaiti Parab*, their maize and *mandia* fields swaying in the air, and their flowering *alsi* fields for the Maoist camps. What did these young boys and girls think? Did they know what it meant to be part of the Maoist cadre? What it entailed to raise a war against the State? But they had a dream as only the young can dream.

And that dream was blown into pieces when on the morning of 9 January 2011 at Basangamali village, the police opened fire on the group resting in its camp near a stream. The people of Kashipur will never be able to forget that morning as they woke up to loud explosions.

They had borrowed utensils from some of the houses and camped next to a stream that was 1 kilometre down from Basangamali village. The police fired from the hilltops after throwing some grenades. Nine were killed while a few injured fled the spot. Of the nine killed, there were five young girls too.

It is hard for us to even imagine the searing pain of those villagers who carried each corpse uphill under police order. The police threatened to arrest them if they did not carry the dead bodies uphill. It was only the previous evening that they had greeted the group with hope and good cheer. Entire gloom spread across the region. It seemed as if the killings in Maikanch 11 years ago had not satiated the blood thirsty state. Bhagabat Rath in Rayagada who has written many appeals, memoranda and press releases for the movement was completely broken. He wrote this time by poignantly describing the event as 'the flowers of Kashipur have turned into corpses' (Samadrusti 2011).

Nirmala, who was killed, was hardly aware that she was bidding farewell to her mother the last time. Her mother recalls Nirmala's prophetic words:

> I might die, I might live. You do not have to worry. I will never leave the party. I might die for my land, my village, my community…How does it matter if one person dies for the land? Thousands of brothers and sisters will live—some older, some younger. (At the Crossroads 2013)

The hope of the glowworm had lit up their minds and strengthened their resolve. Some were babies and some being born when their entire community fought against bauxite mining since the early 1990s. They had entered teenage seeing their people in rallies and marches. They had grown up seeing memos and appeals being sent to the powers that be in Rayagada, Bhubaneswar and even New Delhi doing the vanishing trick! They had seen company agents offering liquor and money to their elders. They had seen their near and dear ones booked under false cases and intimidated by police and company goons. They had witnessed the sacrifices the elders made for years to protect their ancestral land in vain.

Three years had passed since Manohar Jhodia's daughter too was killed in the same 'encounter.' With his eyes not wavering for a second from her photograph, he said:

> These children were not even born when we started the movement. They grew up seeing us getting arrested or bashed up by company goons. They could not speak but were observing everything. That is why they stepped out to give their blood. If our movement had prospects of victory, this loss would not have occurred. We once had an argument why she joined the party. She asked me 'why were you beaten by the police? If you do not retaliate, who is to be blamed? The police are killing thousands of people. What is wrong if we kill them?' The next day she stopped talking and left home. And she died two months later. They killed her so that they could set up the Company.

Yes, the company has now been set up. Production has begun. Aluminium smelters vomit fumes and release toxic effluents.[4] Kashipur, once known as the land of Champakam, has found many flowers of her soil turned into corpses leaving behind profound questions for all of us, for the entire humanity, as Bulka Miniaka says:

> When peasants weep, the country weeps. Imagine adivasi peasants being killed....! The State claims this earth, this country as its own. Let it claim the Sun, let it claim the Moon! Our ancestors sacrificed blood to protect and preserve the land and forests from wild beasts. We are again giving our blood in this struggle to protect the land. (At the Crossroads 2013)

THE DEEP DISQUIET

There are many changes, albeit with disquiet. Ambai Majhi reflects on the complexities unfolding:

> Look at the state of people in Ramibeda. They have nothing to eat after having sold the land. They like a concrete house. But it is a trap to let you die in it. We adivasi people can live anywhere in the open. But we depend on the land for our sustenance. If the land will be used for houses and mining as they are doing, everything will be over. It is only a matter of time ... If the government wants to do more, it can. But it hides behind the company after taking our votes.

The UAIL plant swallowed up three villages and thousands of acres of land. The payment for non-work, that had intoxicated the youths, has stopped. Many more people are so sure today that there was no good in giving up the land. Yet, the coercion worked for some, the money worked for others in succumbing. They are usually referred to as people who sold the land and therefore different from those who still resist doing so. The latter have been blacklisted as *sangramis* unworthy of the dole! There is no clear picture why some have been compensated and some have not been compensated. Again, why some people receive the monthly *bhatta* and some do not is unclear; only the company agents would know. These are the deep divisions creeping in fast within a community that had held together against the government and administration and were ready to die for the land.

I feel I was called everywhere because people said Ambai is so strong and so sincere. If Ambai comes, other women will come too, they said. I went to many meetings, I went to Bhubaneswar and Delhi too. So many women would come with me. But the government did not once listen to us.

We want our demands from the government. We vote for the government and not the company. But the government never comes before us.

What did I get? Whoever is silent or quiet gets something. Whoever is clever gets something. Not someone who thinks for others too.

Ambai Majhi questions why the act of refraining from bribes and not succumbing to the lies of the company is today upheld as a virtue.

They tell you that Ambai is good, she remembers everything, and she did not compromise. But I was like this always, even before the *andolan* started. So, why should I bow to compensation? Is the truth not obvious to all that Baphlimali should not be destroyed for bauxite? If I did not compromise, that does not make me great. That was the beginning for us to have gone ahead to make our lives better the way we understand our pain and sorrow. But today there is money given to all, there is violence, there is alcohol, there is conflict. And then it is said Ambai is different. Will I not feel sad to hear this? No one asks me, so how can I explain that I am one of them. They are my people. If there is sadness in their minds and hearts and in their houses, I cannot be happy because I did not compromise.

'The *andolan* was for the entire of Kashipur', she said, sweeping her hand in a wide circle.

Kashipur has crossed the threshold of transition with much pain and many losses. Salu Majhi, singer and visionary, reflects:

Our ancestors nurtured this land by doing *bethi* (forced labour) for the kings. They have sacrificed blood to protect it from bears and tigers. But we could not save the same land. Our people could not maintain unity, they could not understand the language of resistance. They fell prey to the lure of money and jobs. Not even five of every hundred got jobs. What would all others do? Would the jobs go to the next generation? Whatever we had also has begun to vanish. Earlier, our houses were not locked. Our people were not used to lies, thieving and cheating. I am blind but I know houses are being locked today. This is all due to money. People who are doing duty in the company are not finding time to participate in our *parabs*, to participate even in death ceremonies. So much has changed forever. I hear that companies are still extracting bauxite from more and more *malis*. They will take more and more land. What will we adivasis do? We will simply die. Earth and life are one and the same. If the earth goes, so goes life.

Notes

1. The consortium of UAIL has changed. TISCO moved out in 1997–1998 because of the delays caused. Norsk Hydro withdrew after the Maikanch firing incident being pressurized by human rights group in its country Norway. In 2007, ALCAN moved out citing local opposition as the reason. The activist group Alcan't in Canada protested in sustained manner in Canada. Hindalco bought the shares of ALCAN. After the division of the property of Birla House, the firm is under Aditya Birla.
2. From notes taken for a PUDR report in July 2001.
3. From notes taken for a PUDR report in July 2001.
4. Each year during the rainy season, the INDAL (now part of HINDALCO of Aditya Birla) smelter at Hirakud releases massive toxic waste that destroys large areas of vegetation, mainly paddy fields. It also causes fluoride contamination in the nearby villages. People have been complaining for years in vain.

References

Brown, Dee. 1970. *Bury My Heart at Wounded Knee*. London: Vintage.

Burgos Debray, Elizabeth. 1984. *I, Rigoberta Menchu*. Translated by Ann Wright. London: Verso.

Das, Achyut. 2008. *Kashipur Diary (1980–85)*. Bhubaneswar: Shiksha Sandhan.

Dash, Minati Kumari. 2015. *Resistance and Decline: A study of an Anti-Mining Movement in Orissa*. PhD thesis, Delhi School of Economics, University of Delhi.

Debarajan. 2013. *At the Crossroads. A Documentary*. Bangalore: Pedestrian Pictures.

Mishra Commission Report, Govt of Odisha. 2003.

PUDR. 2005. *Halting the Mining Juggernaut*. New Delhi: PUDR.

———. 2011. *Loot of the Land, Livelihood and Life: A Joint Fact-Finding into Incidents of Crime Against People in Odisha*. New Delhi.

Samadrusti. February 2011. Bhubaneswar.

CHAPTER 9

Juhar Niyamraja

The earth was created by the assistance of the sun, and it should be left as it was...The country was made without lines of demarcation, and it is no man's business to divide it... The earth and myself are of one mind. The measure of the land and the measure of our bodies are the same. ... I never said the land was mine to do with it as I chose. The one who has the right to dispose of it is the one who has created it. I claim a right to live on my land, and accord you the privilege to live on yours.
Heinmot Tooyalaket (Chief Joseph) of the Nez Perces
—Dee Brown, 1970

In the severe drought of 1985 in Kalahandi district, Rama Gahir of Mahirajor village sold her four-day-old infant boy for Rs 30 and two sarees. And Phanas Punji of Amlapali village sold her thirteen-year-old sister-in-law. The Sarvodayi activist Parvati Giri shared these stories in an interview with the local daily *Hirakhand*. Prime Minister Rajiv Gandhi visited the drought-hit region and met Phanas Punji in her village. The media instantly made Rama Gahir and Phanas Punji the poster women of Kalahandi's chronic poverty.

Over thirty years passed. Yet another story hit the headlines. A man with a dead body on his shoulder walked with a young girl keeping step with him. His wife had died of tuberculosis in the Kalahandi district hospital in Bhawanipatna. It was her wish to be cremated in their village. Neither the hospital nor anyone else could arrange a vehicle to travel those

R. Padhi, N. Sadangi, *Resisting Dispossession*,
https://doi.org/10.1007/978-981-15-0717-5_9

17 kilometres. The little daughter with two small bags in her hand was the fellow traveller in this surreal journey. After walking 10 kilometres, they reached the Sagada check post. Someone saw the duo walking and informed a journalist. The image that splashed across print and electronic media on 25 August 2016 was that of Dana Majhi from Melaghar village in Kalahandi district.

Kalahandi's chronic poverty once again became a topic for discussion, a pastime.

In between, this benighted land drew attention for an altogether different set of reasons. Sterlite India Limited signed an MoU on 3 April 1997 with the Government of Odisha to set up an alumina plant at Lanjigarh by extracting bauxite from the nearby Niyamgiri hills. The narrative quickly shifted from calamities to development, from poverty to prosperity, from misery to 'mining happiness.'

Both natural calamity and development have one thing in common. The sufferings of many benefit a few. A popular saying in Kalahandi tells, '*Amar kaje akala, mahajanara kaje sakala*' (What is hard time for us, is good time for money lenders). The children of Niyamraja see development as death and destruction. They say: The fish dies when you take it out of water; we would die if you uproot us from our hills.

The Children of Niyamraja

> Listen carefully my dear friends to the story of the past
> No one else knows but I will sing for you.
> This is the story of creation, how the world was made
> First there were three people, they made seven siblings
> The seven were two sisters and five brothers
> The story is about them, none else knows but me.
> The sisters were the earth; the elder brother ruled the sky
> The next was the sun; two were village guardians
> Niyamraja was the youngest; he ruled the mountain and streams. (Video Republic 2007)[1]

Lying in the south-west of Odisha, the Niyamgiri mountain range spreads regally over 250 square kilometre straddling parts of both Rayagada and Kalahandi districts. Low hills rise up one over the other and peak up to 4,913 feet. Numerous streams emerge from the bellies of these hills and flow down, sometimes murmuring and at other times roaring. And, they form the sources of two rivers, Nagabali and Bansadhara, which empty into the Bay of Bengal at Kalingapatnam in Andhra Pradesh. Kondh settlements have grown on the head, on the lap, on the shoulder and on the foot of the Niyamgiri since ages, but nobody knows when and how. The Kondhs, who reside on the foothills of the hill range, are known as Kutia and Desia Kondh and those on the upper parts known as Dongrias. They believe that Neba Huru or Niyamraja is their King, their Father and Mother; they are the children, the subjects. Niyamraja is of them and they are of him. He looks after their well-being, and they worship him and follow his path.[2]

In 1900–1901, British geologist T.S. Walker was exploring minerals in the erstwhile Kalahandi State. In his words:

> There are two fairly distinct peoples, the Hindoos of the plains who speak Uriya and make some claim to Aryan descent, and the Khond hill men of the 3,000-foot plateau who are aborigines only very slightly influenced by the doctrines of the Hindoos who inhabit the low country. Though the Khonds are still regarded as wild tribes, they devote themselves to agriculture and to the collection of forest products, and now they have abandoned their old barbarous custom of sacrificing human lives to their gods, they seem to be little behind their Hindoo neighbours in civilisation, who are their inferiors from a physical point of view. The great moral virtue of Khond is his truthfulness, as his vice is drunkenness. The progress of civilisation among the Khonds—vis., the Hinduising and Uriyanising of these aborigines—does not seem to improve them. The light-heartedness of childhood is characteristic of Khonds of all ages. ...
>
> Their [Khondalite] distribution in Peninsula India so far as at present is known is almost subject to the same boundaries as Khondistan or the country of the Khonds. Instead of the awkward descriptive name, garnet-sillimanite-graphite schist, I propose to call these rocks Khondalite, in honour of those fine hill men the Khonds in whose mountain jungles Khondalite is better developed in any region hitherto described.... (Walker 1902)

Walker is no more. His discovery of Khondalite would prove to be a curse for his 'fine hill men.' But can any power separate the people from the soil that bears their own name? To the outside eyes—the company, politicians, bureaucrats—the Dongrias or their Niyamraja do not matter. What matters is bauxite, the 73 million tonne bauxite mountain.

THE BEAST ON THE PROWL

> Niyamraja decided where there would be fruits and grains
> Which seed would be soft and which one would be hard
> Niyamraja lives on the top of the mountain, he said to us
> Not a single tree to be cut, not a single animal to be killed here.
> No one else knows, I will sing and sing

The mountain range helps them eke out an existence. Bhima Majhi of Turiguda village said:

> What you see here (showing char seeds, *mahua* flowers, mango pulp drying on date-leaf mattresses on the entire village lane) are the gifts of Niyamgiri. These help us to survive four to five months, besides our agriculture. Once they mine out Niyamgiri, streams will die. You know, Kalahandi is drought prone and a very hot place. We do not face these here for the blessings of Niyamgiri.

Five years flew by after the MoU was signed. Local Kondh villages on the foothills of Niyamgiri were not aware that their lands had been signed away. They woke up to the imminent danger of being displaced when the Kalahandi District Collector served notice on them on 6 June 2002. Twelve villages got the summons: Belamba, Basantapada, Sindhibahali, Bandhaguda, Kapaguda, Borbhata, Kinari, Kardwar, Dengsargi, Kansari, Boringpadar and Turiguda. Villagers were informed through the notice to register their opinions on the proposed plant. And, they did it ceremoniously! Nearly 1,000 people submitted a memorandum to the chief minister demanding the cancellation of the project. One hundred ninety-nine individual petitions were also filed to that end. The Collector heard and disposed those petitions. He convened the Gram Sabha meeting on 26 June at two Gram Panchayat headquarters, Batilema and Lanjigarh, to complete the formality of seeking public opinion. People responded to the call immediately. They unanimously rejected the project by not allowing the Gram Sabha at Batilema. But the gram sabha at Lanjigarh took place. No resolution was passed. But something mysterious did happen. The report sent by the Collector to his higher-ups stated that people had expressed their opinions in favour of the project.

You can leave such happenings to the mystery of democracy where truth is not always fathomable. Or, you are at liberty to choose your own truth.

It became official truth that people had given their consent to the project. But when the survey team reached the villages, they were chased away. Police forces were pressed into action to make the official truth prevail.

Once, around March 2003, police picked up seven people from various villages and reached Turiguda. Women of Turiguda quickly sensed that the police had come for more people and that these seven people were being taken to the police station. They gheraoed the police van and released the seven from the clutches of the police. This made the Collector uneasy. He started going from village to village to cajole, to scold and to intimidate people into leaving their land for the project. He told them, 'You Kondhs are wild and unruly, know nothing of the ways of the world. You do not understand that once this plant is set up, this area would become a city like Bombay. You will transform into proper human beings.' The adivasis of this benighted land saw a Collector for the first time courtesy the Sterlite project. Indeed, they learnt from him that it was in their good to leave their own land. What a wonder a Collector can be! Popularly, the Collector Saswat Mishra was renamed Sterlite Mishra from that day onwards.

These people of the forest who are adept at chasing away many a beast from their crops did not have much experience to chase away a predator in the guise of a company that wanted to devour their lands and Niyamgiri hills. With much deliberation and pondering, they formed Niyamgiri Suraksha Samiti (NSS) and held meetings, rallies, dharnas and *padayatras* in the ways of the non-forested people who came out in their support and solidarity.

But the predator was a cunning one. It attracted the members of a Youth Club of Lanjigarh with the lure of jobs and small contracts. The bait worked well; the unemployed youths believed in what the company had to offer and enlisted themselves in Sterlite's battle against their own neighbours. The first casualty of the fratricidal battle that followed was Lingaraj Azad, Odisha State Unit President, Samajwadi Jan Parishad, who was actively supporting the struggle. The members of the youth club beat him up and handed him over to the police. Then, he was sent to jail. Very soon, around 250 people, including 150 women and children, from 7 villages headed for the police station to demand why he had been arrested. But they were attacked on the way with lathis and cricket bats by almost a 100 people from the youth club who came on motor cycles and a commander jeep. Since the people were unarmed and taken completely unaware, they escaped by running helter-skelter. And they saw the tip of the tail of the beast that would keep coming back to claim their land and lives.

They got a view of the sarkar too when on 8 June 2003, Chief Minister Naveen Patnaik landed at Lanjigarh to lay the foundation stone for the refinery project accompanied by representatives of J.P. Morgan and Barclays and many foreign executives. Police camps were set up at every nook and corner of the entire area. Once again the hired agents of the company rounded up youths from the local youth club to be stationed at each police camp and identify anti-company elements. Such devious moves at every turn gave rise to the nomenclature of being pro-company or anti-company. Protesting villages were cordoned off. People were not allowed to step out to even attend to the call of nature. Despite such tight security arrangements, some activists sneaked into the ceremony area and distributed anti-company leaflets. Dedicating the plant to the development of people of Kalahandi, the chief minister flew back. People destroyed the foundation stone, the symbol of Kalahandi's development, the next day. Police swiftly arrested Abhi Majhi and Durlabha Majhi of Kapaguda village.

These symbolic actions were like mere nettles that the behemoth shrugged off and carried on the prowl. Four villages fell prey to it and accepted the compensation. It was a bloody blow. Close neighbours got divided as pro- and anti-company. It was the beginning of the destruction of the community that people could sense too soon. Still, the remaining villages gave the chase. On 7 April 2004, under the banner of NSS, nearly 2,000 people walked in a rally from Belamba to Lanjigarh dancing, singing, beating drums and brandishing their traditional weapons. Activists from Kashipur, from Gandhamardan and other parts of Odisha joined too. While returning from the rally, some of them vented their anger by setting fire to the construction materials of the company. The police arrested thirteen activists including two women the next day near Ambadola station while they were still on the way to their villages. Most of them were from other areas. The resistance of these ordinary adivasis made headlines in the media. Groups across Odisha and outside protested against the arrests.

These arrests had a ripple effect in the district headquarters of Bhawanipatna. A group of youths, intellectuals and lawyers held a protest demonstration at the Collector's office. Subsequently, a solidarity group, Kalahandi Sachetana Nagarika Manch (Concerned Citizens Forum of Kalahandi), was formed. In the year 2005, its members made a dramatic action on the occasion of the August Revolution of the country. Satya Mahar, Nayan Dash, Trilochan Panigrahi, Giridhari Patra and Jayant Nayak went to the visitors' gallery of the Odisha Assembly. Right in the middle of the assembly session, they shouted slogans 'Long live Niyamgiri! Long live Kalahandi Sachetana Nagarika Manch!' and threw anti-Vedanta leaflets from the gallery of the Assembly before being whisked away by the security personnel. It created a furore in the Assembly and became breaking news.

Indeed, it sent out a message that everybody had not been fooled by the campaign that Vedanta is supposedly bringing development to Kalahandi.

The more the people devised newer methods to trap the predator, the more it took to violence, subterfuges and false cases. Many incidents of terror and intimidation followed that no doubt cast a pall of gloom at times. But that also strengthened the resolve of the adivasis not to let go of the struggle. And solidarity for the movement grew. The foothills of Niyamgiri reverberated with slogans:

> *Ama jami jaga amaku thau, Sterlite company hati jau*
> [Our land be with us, Sterlite go back]
>
> *Maribu pacche daribu nanhi, Niyamgiri chhadibu nahi*
> [We would rather die than fear, We will not leave Niyamgiri ever]

On the evening of 27 March 2005, Sukru Majhi, an active member of NSS, was returning to his village Kansari from a preparatory meeting in Asurapada for the celebration of the Sahid Laxman Nayak Day on 29 March. While walking down the metalled Dahikhal-Lanjigarh Road that had been newly built by the company, he was run over by a jeep. When people went to the police station, the police officer did not receive the complaint stating that he was not run over by Vedanta's vehicle but by some outside one. There was no investigation. NSS insisted that the vehicle belonged to the company because no other vehicles have been seen on that road earlier or later still. It was ominous.

In March 2006, villagers of Bandhaguda staged a protest against the acquisition of their common village lands for Sterlite's refinery. The local police arrested thirty-two villagers including a 16-year-old boy on charges of having trespassed into the refinery premises and assaulted its employees. Of those arrested, thirty-one young men were released on bail after spending three days in prison at Bhawanipatna. However, upon their release, police officers in plainclothes forcibly took them along with their families on a week-long pilgrimage to the pilgrim town of Puri, stating that their prison term had 'polluted' the adivasis. The purification of the adivasis was a ruse for a bigger trick the company had devised. When they returned, they found that the refinery had annexed the land over which they had been protesting, including burial grounds located on public land. A new boundary wall had been erected!

Also, the imposition of false and fabricated cases became a potent weapon for the company. The National Human Rights Commission (NHRC) Eastern Region Special Rapporteur records that during 2005–2010, more than 65 cases involving at least 250 persons have been filed against members of local communities. As to the main cause behind such fabricated cases, the Special Rapporteur noted that 'contrary to the claims made in the proceedings of the Gram Sabhas [elected bodies of village councils] that everyone present in the meeting loudly supported the project, the fact is that right from the beginning, the project-affected people have been protesting against the acquisition of their land without adequate compensation and provision of alternate means of livelihood. The company has chosen to suppress dissent through inducement and coercion, often with the full support of the local police. Protestors have been booked in false cases including dacoities [banditry]. The police have forced them to sign agreements with the company, undertaking to vacate their land and houses at the company's terms, under duress.'

The Many-Faced Beast 'Transforms' Kalahandi

> Niyamraja is crying today, the hill will turn into mud
> The rocks will crumble and everyone will die.
> Will there be any rivers left, if there are no streams
> Will there be any streams left, if there are no hills?

The lament by Dambu Prasaka became prescient. Within a few months of the Lanjigarh refinery beginning its production in 2007, toxic effluents were discharged into the Bansadhara river. Just as Vedanta claimed on its web portal to be the first alumina refinery in the country to be equipped with the Zero Discharge System where no effluents or discharge goes outside the refinery, the Bansadhara river angrily spewed venom on its own people. There began a spate of illnesses and deaths. Doctors reported on the spiralling increase in skin and respiratory diseases that the refinery brought about because of water and dust pollution. The ritualistic Corporate Social Responsibinity (CSR) gesture of constructing a twenty-bed hospital proved to be in vain as doctors pointed out the health hazards caused by contaminated water (Varadarajan 2009). The large red mud pond built next to the refinery cut off water from the streams to thousands of acres of land.

These issues were clearly expressed on 25 April 2009 when a public hearing was held at Belamba village. Instead of addressing their grievances, the company had plans for a six-fold expansion for which a public hearing was called. Villagers came prepared to depose their views on pollution of water and air and on illnesses and deaths. There were people from all communities—the Dongrias, the Kutia Kondhs, Dalits from the villages as well as some people from Lanjigarh town (Video Republic 2009).

It was pointed out how setting up a hospital made no sense as someone said:

> What do we do with a hospital and doctors? The poison is being put inside us.

Linga Majhi of Rengapalli village said:

> We are Kutia tribals. We thought that we would get something and therefore let go of our land. What do we do with a Red Mud Pond? Vedanta has now made our village an island in its toxic waste pond. Nine people in our village have died of illness. We want our land back.

Lada Sikaka from Lakhpadar village said:

> They want to displace us to some barren land. We won't give up Niyamgiri for any price. What can you give us in return? Niyamgiri is not a pile of money. That mountain is our life. We won't flinch if you take our flesh. But we won't tolerate Niyamgiri being dug up. We are the children of Niyamgiri. It seems the British have returned like a monster and are out to devour us. I have this axe ready for them.

The rage and anger of villagers spilled out as the Additional District Magistrate (ADM) and the Odisha State Pollution Control Board (OPCB) official sat frozen. Towards the end, the landlords and business people got provoked when they too were implicated for having entertained company officials and government officials. Chaos prevailed when they began yelling and walked up to the stage menacingly. The public hearing was disrupted.

Villagers protested against the expansion and shouted slogans: Vedanta Go Back!

However, the press promptly carried the report that the public hearing was successful and that people want the project provided Vedanta took care of them! Within three days, the Ministry of Environment and Fores (MoEF) gave Vedanta the permission for mining.

The company obtaining a clearance with the administration sending its own fabricated story to the press that publishes it within 24 hours has become the trend in eastern India.

Right in the midst of seething unrest in the villages of Niyamgiri, as people were falling ill and sick with toxic effluents, the Golden Peacock award was announced for Vedanta for excellence in environmental management! It's an old ploy for companies to get their corporate crimes greenwashed. Activists turned up at the event being held on 13 June 2009 in Palampur, Himachal Pradesh, and created a din. The award was held back.

Once the construction work was almost over, the company delayed enrolling people from the surrounding villages in the promised jobs. They were left to the whims of local contractors. The women—largely dalit—fought against all odds for the jobs that had been offered to them before the company started. When the test production took place, one man died along with some cattle too because of the river getting polluted. The collective shock gave vent to rage. In protest, people broke the pipeline coming out of the plant. And they locked up the company gate on another day. The wife of the MLA was sent to Chatrapur village to meet the women who spoke of the water pollution and the illnesses and deaths. When she tried to explain that Vedanta was not responsible, she was booed away by the villagers (Video Republic 2008). Unable to meet the situation, the administration and the company filed an FIR on ten women for stealing a few thousand tonnes of steel material! Five women were taken to Lanjigarh thana. The five who were taken to the Bhawanipatna thana had two small children who were arrested too (listed as drivers). The FIR dated 22 February 2010 accused the women of entering the refinery premises and causing random violence for over three hours and stealing a few thousand tonnes of steel material. When we met Jayanti Dakri, Nilabati Nayak, Purnami Bibhar and Tulsa Bibhar, they said:

> Kamla Bibhar passed away three months back. She was constantly worried about the fate of the court case. It has been eight years now and we continue to be branded as thieves and dacoits by outsiders. On the day we were arrested we were working in the fields and nowhere near the company. We have been punished simply because we were agitating and struggling tirelessly to ask the company for the jobs it had promised when it first came to the area. We saw before our eyes a few hundred workers being brought from other states. We want regular jobs even now. Is that not a reasonable expectation? Before the company came, we would earn from wage work in the

> fields. There's nothing left now. And the pollution is causing so much ill health and distress too. What crime have we committed? We were young then, we are still young. Out future is before us.

The villages were hounded by police and agents who would arbitrarily enter houses at any time—day or night. The terror and intimidation continued throughout 2010 and 2011. Meanwhile, the beast on prowl displayed its antics in the cities. The image of the company's conquests was flaunted on billboards in Bhubaneswar and on newspapers and magazines. Within one week of the ten women being arrested and put in jail under false charges of theft for demanding jobs, a full-page advertisement appeared in national dailies. It had an image of a Kondh woman with a wide smile, rings on nose and ears, tattoo mark on the forehead and a chubby baby girl with nose rings wrapped in a piece of white cloth tied to the mother's neck. The ad line proudly declared: 'Vedanta's 5 Million Tonne Alumina Project providing Employment & Livelihood Opportunities To Over 20,000 common people (The Indian Express, 27 February 2010)'. You might as well have a peep at Vedanta's own literature:

> One of the driving forces behind the planning of the refinery was to minimise the displacement of families and we managed to reduce this number to only 121, 76 of which had a family member to take a job in the refinery while the remainder were helped to find other sources of income as there was no eligible member for employment. A further 1,846 people were deemed to have been affected by the project and a compensation programme was set in place and detailed data is available....
>
> In social matters, the refinery employs a total of about 2,500 workers, of whom 550 are VAL employees and around half of those are graduates and professional staff. The remaining 1,950 staff work for contractors in jobs such as raw material loading, catering, maintenance, gardening, fire protection and security. (The Lanjigarh Development Story: Vedanta's perspective 2011)

The advertisement's last tag line was: Kalahandi Is On The Move—Let Us Be Part Of This Transformational Journey.

Yes, Kalahandi is being transformed. Now, you choose to be or not to be part of this 'transformational journey' of Kalahandi.

The Kondhs well understand that trees shed their leaves and barks, or snakes shed their skins in the forest. But it remained a mystery for them why the company shed its Sterlite skin and assumed the name of Vedanta.

Felix Padel and Samarendra Das in their book 'Out of this Earth' have unravelled that mystery: malpractice at Malco after acquisition, its controversial takeover of BALCO, its indictment by SEBI for illegal insider trading on the Bombay Stock Exchange, its illegal and unethical acquisition in Australia and violation of environmental laws in Zambia and Armenia. They concluded, 'It is this dubious history which Sterlite wiped away with the adoption of a brand new—and very ancient—name: Vedanta (Padel and Das 2010).' The Kondhs of Niyamgiri did not have any means to know it.

They only saw a line of houses, similar in shape and size, with the plinth area of 400 odd square feet built on 10 decimal plots and an arch at the entrance gate with the inscription: Vedanta's Rehabilitation Colony. Things became clearer when in early February 2004 Kinari, Borbhata and most of Sindhibahali and Kotduar villages were razed to the ground. Villagers, animals and materials were loaded together onto the truck and sent to the rehabilitation colony called Vedantanagar. Security guards were placed at the gate. Outsiders were denied easy access or asked to produce their identity documents and purpose of visit. Even, the near and dear ones of residents of the colony were not allowed in. Company goons roamed around the colony on bikes. It was more of a gated colony than a new settlement for people who have never lived under any scrutiny ever. Security guards stood close to overhear any conversation they had a chance to have with anyone coming to meet them. Even today the inmates of the colony feel reticent to open up. A kind of uneasiness, an undecipherable fear shadows their faces when you ask anything about their present living condition. The disquiet is palpable.

Whose Law Protects the People

The company's own transformational journey from Sterlite to Vedanta helped it to get registered at London's Stock Exchange. Transformation did happen to Anil Agarwal too. 'An ordinary man with an extraordinary story' bought a 10 million pound house in Mayfair that once belonged to Shah of Iran. And, the refinery plant at Lanjigarh began to rise towards the sky and a wide road slowly wound through the thick forest to the summit of Niyamgiri for mining.

In November 2004, Biswajit Mohanty, Secretary of the Wildlife Society of Orissa, brought the matter of Vedanta's violation of forest and environment laws to the notice of the Supreme Court of India. Prafulla Samantara, social activist and environmentalist, and R. Sreedhar, a Delhi-based geologist, filed two more petitions questioning the role of Vedanta, Odisha Mining Corporation (OMC) and Ministry of Environment and Forest (MoEF) in allowing illegal activities in Lanjigarh and Niyamgiri. The Court entrusted the task of looking into these allegations to its advisory body, the Central Empowered Committee (CEC). The Law followed its own course, and the company took the by-lanes and gullies of the Law to sneak out. However, it was proved that Vedanta had encroached and cut down a patch of forest land without legal clearance. It paid a little over Rs 11,000 as fine!

By September 2005, the CEC finalized its enquiry and submitted a report to the Supreme Court. We are quoting here its observations and recommendations at length:

> The CEC is of the considered view that the use of the forest land in an ecologically sensitive area like the Niyamgiri Hills should not be permitted. The casual approach, the lackadaisical manner and the haste with which the entire issue of forests and environmental clearance has been dealt smacks of undue favour/leniency and does not inspire confidence with regard to the willingness and resolve of both the State government and the MoEF to deal with such matters keeping in view the ultimate goal of national and public interest. In the instant case, had a proper study been conducted before embarking on a project of this nature and magnitude involving massive investment, the objections to the project from environmental/ecological/forest angles would have become known in the beginning itself and in all probability the project would have been abandoned at this site.
>
> Keeping in view all the facts and circumstances brought out in the preceding paragraphs it is recommended that this Hon'ble Court may consider revoking the environmental clearance dated 22 September 2004 granted by the MoEF for setting up of the Alumina Refinery Plant by M/s Vedanta and directing them to stop further work on the project. This project may only be considered after an alternative bauxite mine is identified.
>
> This Hon'ble Court may please consider the above report and may please pass appropriate orders in this matter. (CEC Report 2005)

The court considered the report and asked for yet another report from the Forest Advisory Committee of MoEF. Wildlife Institute of India, Dehradun, as part of the committee, sent a team and submitted a report confirming the observations of the CEC. The court also took note of the fact, 'Vedanta Resources has been banned from Norway for non-compliance of labour laws and for violation of human rights.' It went on to say, 'We cannot take the risk of handing over an important asset into the hands of the company unless we are satisfied about its credibility.' But, the court suggested creating Special Purposes Vehicle (SPV) for scheduled area development of Lanjigarh in which stakeholders shall be State of Orissa, OMC Limited and M/s SIIL. Finally, on 8 August 2008, the court was pleased to pass appropriate orders in this matter: it did not direct Vedanta to stop further work on the project. It granted clearance for mining bauxite from Niyamgiri upon the condition of the approval from MoEF. It perplexed many people; none had a clue about the ambiguity. After passing the judgement, Justice Kapadia announced in an open court that he too held shares in Sterlite!

Does this statement of the Justice leave any clue for the answer?

Going Green in Kalahandi

This long four-year legal battle that ended in a defeat for the people had its unexpected blessings too. It delayed the mining of Niyamgiri and opened breathing space for NSS to organize people against mining, especially the Dongrias living at the hilltop. Vedanta's illegalities exposed through the CEC report became a topic of discussion in small urban centres of Kalahandi. The Sachetana Nagarika Manch and NSS mobilized people's opinion of the entire district on the issue of environment and Vedanta drawing water from river Tel. Sensing the popular mood, Bhaktacharan Das, the Congress leader from the district, joined the anti-Vedanta politics by forming an organization called 'Green Kalahandi' and thundered 'Vedanta would not be allowed to take a fistful of soil from Kalahandi.' But the same Bhaktacharan Das in 1996 was almost begging in the Indian Parliament for a large alumina plant in Kalahandi for the solution of its chronic problem. Listen to him:

> The government of India and the Orissa government should take a keen interest to set up at least a large alumina plant because we have got a heavy deposit of bauxite in Niyamgiri and Sijimalli of Kalahandi district. Several discussions have been held at the state and central level. But there has not been any alumina plant. If there is an alumina plant, then a minimum of 40,000 people can be sustained out of the different kinds of earnings. From that, sir, I am suggesting some permanent measures. This is a chronic problem. (Lok Sabha 1996)

His entry into the anti-Vedanta politics gave a different turn to events. The Congress Party took an extraordinary interest in the issue of Niyamgiri. Rahul Gandhi came to Niyamgiri, dined with the Dongrias and declared:

> I am going to fight for you. I am your soldier, I am in Delhi; nobody can take away this forest from you, this mountain from you.

The Congress Party smartly played the adivasi and green card in a calculated way and reaped rich electoral harvest. When in May 2009, elections for Indian Parliament and Odisha state assembly were held, Bhaktacharan Das won from the lone Parliament seat and Congress Party won four out of five assembly constituencies of the district. In November 2009, Jairam Ramesh, the then Environment Minister, cancelled the 'in principle' approval for mining and set up two committees headed by Dr. Usha Ramnathan and Dr. N.C. Saxena to look into the issues of forest rights and community rights under the Forest Rights Act (FRA). Both these committees found gross violations of FRA and other environment laws. Finally, the MoEF withdrew the environment clearance for the mine on 11 July 2011. The government of Odisha through Odisha Mining Corporation (OMC) went to the Supreme Court challenging the order of MoEF. And, another round of legal battle followed. Niyamraja heaved another sigh of relief.

Jai Niyamraja

> He created fruits in the hills, grains in the plains
> He is the first of the Dongria Kondh
> No one knows this story, lakhs of people are unaware
> I will sing, I will sing why our land the outsiders must spare.
> After making pineapple, mango, jackfruit and grain
> Niyamraja said to us, 'live on what I have given.'

Activists like Rajkishore, Lingaraj Azad and Satya Mahar had already been mobilizing people against the Lanjigarh refinery plant. Word spread fast of Vedanta's mining plans right up to the villages atop the mountain. The Dongrias were directly confronted with the fear posed by the imminent destruction and uprooting of their habitat. Meetings began to take place. They spread the word among the villages scattered on the mountain range. Drenju, a frontline activist of NSS, said how they began fortifying themselves as they became cautious:

> One day we saw a jeep on the summit. We thought that it might be a company jeep. We realised that the danger had reached our doors. Then, some people gathered and rolled boulders from the hilltop to stop the vehicle coming. We cut trees to block the road. After that, no company vehicle came up.

Alerted to the danger of losing their Niyamraja, the Dongrias arose and the entire hill range echoed, *Moribu poche daribu nahin, Niyamgiri chaadibu nahin!* (Let us die but not fear, Let us not leave Niyamgiri). Messages of rebellion spread from mouth to mouth, from ear to ear, from hillock to hillock like fire in the jungle. On 5 October 2009, Dongrias in their traditional attires and with weapons in hand and women with wild flowers in their hair came down the hill to participate in the demonstration at Muniguda, Rayagada district. The Lok Sangram Manch, Rajurguda, and Ma Dharitri Club, Karadabandha of Muniguda block, Rayagada district, also joined in. It was a first major anti-mining demonstration.

Slogans rent the air evoking the courage and sacrifice of martyrs like Laxman Nayak, Rendo Majhi and Birsa Munda.

> *Rendo Majhi Dakara Diye; Lodhoi kori Bonchibo!*
> [Rindo Majhi beckons all; To survive is to struggle!]

The Niyamraja *Parab* became an occasion for rebellion. All the villages across Niyamgiri hill range gather at the wide, flat summit of Niyamgiri for two days. *Disharis* and *Bejunis* (priests and priestesses) of Dongrias chant mystic incantations and offer cocks, pigeons, goats and pigs to propitiate Niyamraja for good rains, good harvest and good health. Young boys and girls dance and sing, and exchange messages of love and rebellion. Village headmen discuss strategies and actions to resist Vedanta. All of them reaffirm their faith in the Niyamraja and reassure Him of protection at the cost of their lives.

> We Dongrias have so many festivals that we celebrate as a community and drink and dance. We offer meat to all. Each village used to celebrate in its own way. But now the *andolan* has become the coordinating point; it tries to bring all people together who inhabit this mountain so that we get to know each other and build out strength for what we have in common.

> Initially, very few villages participated, 3 and then 5 and then 21 and then 60. But today all 122 villages come for the festival. Our common purpose is to protect the mountain that belongs to all. (Lada Sikaka)

Since then, the resolve to protect Niyamraja has been reiterated in meetings and demonstrations, at district headquarters and state capital. And the struggle continues unabated.

The anti-Vedanta mining protests spread far and wide. People in other cities began solidarity actions. The campaign gained ground overseas too. The London-based organization FOIL Vedanta lobbied among investors for withdrawal of their shares from Vedanta and held demonstrations before the Annual General Body Meeting in London each year. FOIL Vedanta also disseminated information round the clock about the crimes committed by the company in distant shores.

Meanwhile, the newly formed government of the United Progressive Alliance headed by the Congress party initiated a range of repressive measures. On 22 June 2009, the central government banned the CPI (Maoist) party as a terrorist organization using the provisions of the amended Unlawful Activities (Prevention) Act (UAPA). What ensued were endless operations under Operation Green Hunt to basically 'de-infest' mineral-rich adivasi-dominated areas. Armed paramilitary forces were deployed in the entire area in Niyamgiri. These forces raided houses in the night, picked up local activists from villages and roads, destroyed crops and kept villages under siege for hours together. It became a routine in the hills and villages of the entire region. Lada Sikaka, one of the tallest leaders of the anti-Vedanta resistance, was abducted on 9 August 2010 when he along with a group of representatives of Dongria Kondhs were going to attend a conference in Delhi to narrate their experiences of their struggle and police repression. He was released after being kept for two days in police custody. As he recalls:

> Once, a group of our leaders were going to Delhi. Advocate Siddharth Nayak was with us. Suddenly, 15 armed police appeared and stopped us at Izrupa. Guns were in their hands but they were in plain clothes. Leaving others, they picked up me and Sana Sikaka. After a few hours, they threw out Sana Sikaka at Bijepur and I was left alone. They took me to Rayagada police station and kept me for two days. The police officers asked me about 'Mahabadi' (Maobadi is pronounced as Mahabadi by many Dongria Kondhs). I told them, 'How do I know who is a Mahabadi? Has he grown horns on his head and tail on his back.' Many people come to Niyamgiri to support our strug-

> gle. We consider them to be our friends. Then, they threatened me to put me in a Maoist uniform and kill me in the forest. I told them, 'You do whatever you want to do. We are ready to die but not leave Niyamgiri.'

Drenju Sikaka was picked up along with two other adivasi youths. He spoke to the press:

> I had gone to Rayagada by train from Muniguda. We were picked up by the police at 1 pm. They took us in a vehicle to a forest. They were talking to us in our Kui language. They took us to a police camp. We were three of us: I along with Dadhi Sikaka and Pramod Sikaka from Dangamati village. They took us to separate places for questioning. They accused us of helping Maoists to get into Niyamgiri. How have the Maoists survived for the past 3–4 years, they asked. They have survived with your feeding them, they said. They got me naked and tied me to a tree from 1 pm to 11 pm. Then they let me go.
>
> Even now the police come to our villages at least six times a month. They loot everything—money, axes, country guns and other things. They warn us not to go out to weekly haat in the Lanjigarh market. But how can we stay without going there? (KBK News 2012)

Thus, the Dongria Kondhs had to constantly resist the repression meted out by state and administration on behalf of the company. These interrogations and searches to purge the area of Maoists was the ruse to curb resistance in many other adivasi-dominated mineral-rich regions in east India.

While the repression was going on deep in the forest, the Supreme Court in the metropolis was hearing a litany of petitions on the religious and cultural rights of Dongrias on the hills of Niyamgiri under the newly enacted Forest Rights Act. On 18 April 2013, the Supreme Court delivered a judgement that the religious rights of the Dongrias over Niyamgiri hills would be decided by the gram sabha.

> The question whether STs and other Traditional Forest Dwellers (TFDs), like Dongaria Kondh, Kutia Kondh and others, have got any religious rights i.e. rights of worship over the Niyamgiri hills, known as Niyamgiri, near Hundaljali, which is the hill top known as Niyam-Raja, have to be considered by the gram sabha. Gram sabha can also examine whether the proposed mining area Niyama Dangar, 10 km away from the peak, would in any way affect the abode of Niyam-Raja. Needless to say, if the BMP, in any way, affects their religious rights, especially their right to worship their deity, known as Niyamraja, in the hills atop the Niyamgiri range of hills, that right

> has to be preserved and protected. We find that this aspect of the matter has not been placed before the gram sabha for their active consideration. (Supreme Court Order 2013)

The court verdict created unprecedented media hype on gram sabha: the fate of one of the most powerful corporate houses was now in the hands of adivasis! The government of Odisha interpreted the court verdict to hold gram sabhas only in 12 villages out of 122 villages around Niyamgiri Hills during July-August. All of a sudden these unknown and unheard villages became the centre of gravity for both pro- and anti-company groups. The company set its agents upon villagers to vote in its favour. Maoists gave a call to boycott gram sabha. NSS asserted the need to participate in it. As the day of decision making got nearer, the political chemistry of the area was sizzling hot. Lada Sikaka captures the dynamics of the situation:

> From below Trilochanpur, all villages used to be pro-company in the beginning. They repeatedly approached the Dongrias to agree to what the company was offering. They tried convincing them that mining is for their own good. But when two *dalals* (agents) from that area got killed, it silenced everybody. Nobody makes any offers anymore.

A dalit woman in Phuldumer gave another view of the uncertainties they were going through:

> We all were asked to say NO to mining. We voted against the mining. Yes, it is certainly quieter since the gram sabha meeting took place. Ours is a small village. We work hard from morning to night. How do I say whether mining is good or bad? How do I say whether it is better now or before? The company used to give us sarees and rice now and then at least. Now we get nothing. Life is the same. We are poor and will remain poor depending on these *dangars* only. If you can understand what I am saying. Yes, we cannot live without these *dangars*. Ajit Patnaik got killed because he was a *dalal*. He worked for the company. But then even we have been called *dalals* just because we are not adivasis. But then there are adivasis who are *dalals* too. We work hard but we live in fear.

The gram sabhas were held between 18 July and 19 August 2013. People asserted their religious and cultural rights over Niyamgiri in all twelve meetings. Speaker after speaker reiterated the same:

> Niyamraja is our father and mother. We have been worshipping Him since time immemorial. He gives us food, water, air and medicine to live. He is everywhere in the entire hill range. If you mine one part, it will hurt his entire body like the entire body hurts when you hurt the leg or hand. The government has not created it. How can it claim it as its own? If anybody wants to sever us from Him, there shall be blood bath. (The Referendum 2013)

An unusually long month of anxious moments came to an end when the result of the last gram sabha at Jarpa was declared. Drenched in the monsoon rains, people danced to their victory. They knew that they would win. They also know that so long as bauxite is in the belly of the mountain, companies and governments would find ways and means to prey upon it.

The Price of the Victory

> If Niyamraja will not be there, I will sing, I will sing.
> What will we do without the fruits, grains and buffaloes?
> What will we do without Niyamgiri?
> What will the animals do without the big forest?
> What will we do without its plants that save lives?

Monsoon gave way to winter in Niyamgiri hills. The three fears—*megha, bagha* and *jara* (rains, tiger and fever)—of the forest people receded. The fear of mining momentarily receded when the MoEF rejected the approval to Vedanta on 8 January 2014. Despite the victory of the gram sabha, there was no respite for them. The company sought for the expansion of the Alumina Refinery Plant from 1 million to 6 million tonnes per annum. The Odisha Pollution Control Board (OPCB) held a public hearing on 30 July 2014. The expansion of the plant continued even as the company's illegal operations became news for all across the globe. There was no notice or announcement made in any village. Yet, by word of mouth, over 1,500 Dongria Kondhs and anti-mining activists gathered. Once again, they affirmed their resolve not to give up an inch of Niyamgiri for mining and expressed their opposition to the plant. But, as mysterious as the earlier public hearings, the Collector once again sent the report that people had given their consent to the refinery expansion plan!

The Dongrias began to come down the hill to weekly haats (markets) to sell their produce and to buy pieces of new clothes for the *parab* or to simply meet a loved one. They were oblivious of another kind of danger that awaited them: the presence of police in the haat. Dillu Majhi of Sanakhemundi Padar recounted his arrest from the haat. He had spent two months in jail. The mere recall of being taken in a police vehicle and having to wear the prison attire weighs down on him still:

> I had gone to the haat to sell our fruits and vegetables. The police overpowered me and insisted I get into their vehicle. I told them 'why should I get into your vehicle? I do not want to sit there. I do not know where you will take me. What have I done? I am here to simply sell whatever I have. We work hard for our living. Why do you want to take me?' Later, I got to know that I was arrested because of that old case in 2008 when we sat on dharna outside the plant. They kept me in jail for two months and I was made to put on the striped uniform. I did not like wearing it. Vedanta or Sterilite—whatever the name maybe—should not venture to come anywhere near the Dongrias. Survival has been the struggle of our lives all along but the same old survival matters more than ever now. The daily harassment at the haat becomes unbearable and we have to protect each other. Sometimes the younger people or women get intimidated and do back out. But if they say anything while we men are around, we give it back in full measure. We have decided to do so. We have to fight back. Otherwise they will not let us come even to the haat. We know that if they ever dare to touch us or our children, we can even kill them.

When police forces prowl through the haats, CRPF and COBRA (locally called 'Cabra') battalions comb the jungles. The ominous shadow of combing operations and surveillance looms large on these villages round the year.

The documentary 'When Cuckoos Stopped Singing' shows a wedding celebration where the villagers of Lakhpadar are going to Phuldumer to bring the bride with them.

> The monsoons have arrived. It is the second day of July in 2016. On this day, Drenju is getting married to Sami. Her father is not willing to give her away for some reason; even then, the group persuades her to come to their village. The women from Lakhpadar sing to Sami: 'We have come to take you to our village with us. Come with us sister and become a family member in our village. Bring along your memories and cherish them.' Drenju is despondent. He would have liked Sami's mother and father to have been happy too. The wedding party moves up the path to Lakhpadar. As they come across a stream, the women lift up Sami and gently carry her across the

> stream. The bride should have no difficulty on the way to her new abode. These rituals are being followed since ages. Yet it is different this time. The singing comes to a stop. There are armed CRPF personnel in uniform on the way. Lada Sikaka stands vigil till the entire group has passed the CRPF men. Incidents of molestation of women and harassment of youths have become common. The wedding party moves in dead silence till the next village. The silence is deafening. (Patra 2016)

The presence of these battalions in the midst of daily routines is hard to bear. Some children have stopped going to the school at Trilochanpur. They are offered sweets or biscuits by CRPF forces on the way to school and queried whether any outsider has come to the village, meaning Maoists. The children of Tadiguda village thus stopped going to school.

The combing operations also result in CRPF personnel helping themselves with impunity to whatever the Dongrias manage to collect for their living, including small savings.

> As adivasis, we live in the forest and hills. We collect and make a bit of money from whatever we sell: ginger, turmeric, bananas, wild roots and forest fruits. We sell these to take care of our hunger and keep the money for our needs. It maybe two rupees or five paise, it maybe ten rupees or a hundred... But the CRPF enter our houses and take away the money and our traditional weapons. Does it belong to them?
>
> Twice they have pulled my hair and beaten me up. There is a constant pain in my back since then. Once they caught me in the jungle. And the other time they entered the village and took away three thousand rupees from my hut. They have carried off our *ragi*, paddy and millets too. (Sani Sikaka in The Referendum)

The daily harassment of the Dongrias seems incomprehensible to Lada Sikaka and his village people. Theirs is the legacy of a people who have protected the Niyamgiri since as long back as they remember. The gun-wielding police and paramilitary are an intrusion. He said:

> Today we are being told that the mountain and its minerals will bring development and that we Dongrias are coming in the way. Suddenly, the sarkar has begun guarding the mountain with police and CRPF. Why are they guarding the mountain today? It is we and our people who have been guarding it ever since we remember. This mountain has been with us even before

India became free of British rule. The independence from the British made little difference for us adivasis. Our lives have had nothing to do with general elections or assembly elections.

When the sarkar or company come here to promise health and education, we tell them that we do not need all that. We only want the mountain to be left untouched. We will say NO to anything that they offer us until they remove these companies not only from here but everywhere. Does Lanjigarh belong to them? Can they show us the proof? How long will a job last? Or how long will the money last? Can the children and their children live on that money? And then what do you do when the money is over? Everyone here is dependent on ***dangar*** cultivation—from the children to the elderly.

Our children and future generations will survive only if we keep the mountain forever. Anybody can tell clearly who the mountain belongs to and who has preserved it. Where does the government figure here? Where was the government all these years? Some few powerful people made the law and called themselves the sarkar. So, is sarkar God then? Why is it that the state is keen to bring education and health facilities only now when mining comes? What will school do to our children? It will send them to the same company for livelihood. Who can they choose for a job? How many jobs can they give? They do not give even one job per household. You tell me if they have done even that in any place where they have taken land. They lack honesty and they know it.

To break this resolve of the people, the random picking up of adivasi youth or throwing them into the darkness of prison became the modus operandi.

Twenty-five-year-old Dasuru Kadraka was arrested in March 2015 from the village of Gorata. He was charged with nine cases including planting of IED, killing one Shyam Kadraka, pasting Maoist posters and blockading roads. When a fact-finding team met him in May 2017 in the Bissamcuttack jail, he said:

I was arrested and taken to the Rayagada SP's office. There I was tortured with my hands tied and electric wires attached to my ears and electric shock given to me, to force me to surrender as a Maoist and to make me leave the Save Niyamgiri movement. But I refused and said, I am not a Maoist, why should I say I am? The andolan is my life and I will never stop protecting the Niyamgiri hills and forests. When I am released from jail also I will continue with the andolan. (Report of a Fact-Finding Team 2017)

He was released on bail in February 2018.

Drika Kadraka of village Dhamanpanga was picked up by the anti-Maoist squad in the third week of November 2015. Unable to bear the mental torture and pain, he managed to escape prison. And he committed suicide within a few days in his house. Niyamraja quietly absorbed the shock and trauma of the villagers.

Twenty-year-old Mando Kadraka was killed by the security forces in 2016.

Seventeen-year-old Saiba Pushika of Gorata village was arrested in February 2017. He languished in the Berhampur juvenile jail for an entire year.

The police descended on the house of twenty-year-old Kuni Sikaka on 1 May 2017 when the village had gone to sleep. They whisked her away as a Maoist. In her own words:

> I have been active in the Niyamgiri Suraksha Samiti movement for several years. I have been married to Jagli Pusika two months back. On 1 May at 1 am, a police force including 6 police women banged on the door of my in-laws' home in Gorota village. The police had cordoned off the entire area. They took me away and when villagers tried to intervene, they showed guns and threatened them. They never told any of the villagers or me what I had done to be arrested this way.
>
> I was taken to the Rayagada police station and kept till 3 May. There the SP of the Rayagada police station repeatedly told me that I must surrender as a Maoist. I said, 'I am not a Maoist, I have been a Niyamgiri Suraksha Samiti activist for several years.' But he repeatedly said that if I didn't agree to surrender as a Maoist, they would send me to jail for 12–15 years. But if I surrendered they would release me immediately. My father-in-law Dadhi Pusika who is also a leader of the movement, arrived there and so did my husband Jagli Pusika. The police then insisted that both Jagli and I surrender or else I would be jailed for several years. I am newly married and my family and in-laws thought I should avoid going to jail, which is why my husband and I signed surrender statements, under threat of jail. But neither of us accepted the Rs 2 lakh each that the police offered as the package for surrendered Maoists.
>
> I had gone to so many places in the country representing the Niyamgiri Suraksha Samiti, how could I have done that if I was running with the Maoists. (Report of a Fact-Finding Team 2017)

To brand any popular resistance as Maoist has become a potent weapon to stamp out all resistance. Thus, the Home Ministry declared Niyamgiri Suraksha Samiti to be a Maoist outfit in April 2017.

> The Maoists tried to strengthen coordination between its mass organizations and other like-minded organizations to undertake programmes against alleged state violence and for protection of democratic rights. In 2016, the issue of displacement of local communities remained the main plank of mobilization by the mass organisations. In Niyamgiri Hills area (Districts Rayagada and Kalahandi, Odisha), the outfit continued to guide the activities of the Niyamgiri Suraksha Samiti. (Annual Report of Union Home Ministry for 2016–2017)

Six years have passed since the gram sabha gave its verdict. The bauxite is still in the belly of the mountain, and the beast is still on the prowl. Arrests, incarcerations and torture of the Dongria Kondhs continue till today. The entire mountain is simmering in rebellion.

On 20 October 2018, Lada Sikaka questioned the Muniguda administration why he had to be forcibly dragged and physically tortured to the thana to discuss a demonstration for which the NSS had already obtained police permission. He had been to the Lanjigarh haat along with some youths to sell oranges. Barely had the Tata Magic vehicle started its journey back to the village, when some policemen pounced on him and dragged him by his hair into another vehicle. He was blindfolded and beaten up with hands tied to the back. The Tahsildar who was waiting for him in the Muniguda thana insisted they call off the demonstration planned for 23 October. He alleged it was a Maoist event. The demonstration was against the daily intimidation of the CRPF forces stationed around their villages and a demand to end it. It was not allowed to happen.

In a press conference in Bhubaneswar, Lada Sikaka said:

> The Tahsildar repeatedly asked me to tell him everything. Then he said that he is officially in charge of *pattas* and land titles and that we could come to him for anything. I said: If you can give titles, then give us one title. Give us a title for the entire of Niyamgiri. The Tahsildar went quiet.

When Dodi Kadraka from Gorata was picked up by the Rayagada police and tortured for four hours, the police reprimanded him for going against a government that gives them rice at Re 1 per kilo. A mountain inhabited by adivasis can be bought by charity. These welfare schemes seem to pave the way for the bauxite in the mountain.

The adivasis of Kalahandi have fought many a valiant battle as we see in recorded history. More than a century earlier, the Kondh chieftain Rendo Majhi from Urladani had fought the British for protection of both th land and cultural practices. In 1853, he was captured and taken away to jail amidst much resistance. A prolonged fight with the British ensued. Finally, he was killed on 10 December 1855 (Academy of Tribal Dialects and Culture 2007). In 1882, the Kondhs of Kandhan (Kondh land) had risen in revolt against the exploitation of the imperial and feudal forces to establish their right over their land and forest. It was violently crushed by the British forces by burning down villages, arresting people and hanging their leaders. The colonial officer in charge of suppressing the rebellion, writes historian Fanindam Deo, 'was praised for his presence of mind and courage.' The burning of villages by Berry and the flogging of Kondhs was merely seen as a loss of a few grass huts and that the men flogged were the lowest of the low, semi-savages, to whom the pain of the punishment appeals but who are not sensitive to disgrace (Deo 2009). Is post-Independent India any different?

Today, the future of the mountain and its people is at stake. In the short story *Aloda* (Unwanted) written forty years ago, Gopinath Mohanty had foreseen the Dongrias being gradually pushed out of Niyamgiri by government institutions, police stations, hospitals, farms, mining plants and factories. Finally, the deluge comes with the setting up of an atomic mineral processing plant that razed down the entire hills to dust. And the community disappeared (Mohanty 1978). Despite such a grim picture, he had later said that the only way is to hold on to one's land, confront the situation firmly and resist being uprooted (Pattnaik 1980).

The Dongrias have dared to fight; it is they who have infected us with the most powerful dream that life on earth can dare to dream. It is a fight for the mountain, its habitat and the entire humanity. Niyamgiri will continue to stand mighty with all its streams, trees, animals and birds. It is a new history in the making. A new literature too will be born.

Thoda samay chahiye dharti ko
Aur ek din mukt kar legi
Woh khud ko tumhaare niyamon se,
Bhar legi apne saare ghaav,
Ugaa legi phir se hariyaali
Bula legi phir se lupt ho chuki aadim sabhyataaon ko
Aur lupt ho chuki unki bhaashhaon ko. (Jacinta Kerkette 2018)

[The Earth needs but a little time,
And she will set herself free
From your rules and regulations.

Her wounds she shall heal,
And make the lands once more green.
She shall invoke once again the ancient civilizations sunk into oblivion,
And their languages, too, lost to extinction.]

Notes

1. Song by Dambu Praska in the film 'The Lament of Niyamraja' by Surya Shankar Dash, Video Republic. This chapter has been woven around the different stanzas of the song. The song basically narrates the creation myth of the Kondhs of Niyamgiri and laments the destruction that awaits the children of Niyamraja if the mountain is mined.
2. Gopinath Mohanty has recorded this oral tradition in his novel *Anama* (Nameless).

References

Academy of Tribal Dialects and Culture. 2007. Sardar Rendo Majhi. Bhubaneswar.

Annual Report of Union Home Ministry for 2016–2017, New Delhi.

Brown, Dee. 1970. *Bury My Heart at Wounded Knee*. London: Vintage.

Central Empowered Committee. 2005. *Report in IA No.1324 Regarding the Alumina Plant Being Set Up by M/S Vedanta Alumina Ltd at Lanjigarh in Kalahandi District, Odisha*. Delhi: GOI.

Deo, Fanindam. 2009. *Roots of Poverty, A Social History*. Bhubaneswar: Amadeus Press.

KBK News. 2012. Voice of Niyamgiri. See https://www.youtube.com/watch?v=ouPc-BoVMZM

Kerkette, Jacinta. 2018. *Jadon Ki Zameen* (Land of the Roots). New Delhi: Bharatiya Gyanpith.

Lok Sabha Debates Session III (Winter) Thursday, November 1996

Mohanty, Gopinath. 1978. *Aloda*. Samabesh: Bhubaneswar.

Padel, Felix, and Samarendra Das. 2010. *Out of This Earth*. New Delhi: Orient Blackswan.

Patra, Amitabh. 2016. *When the Cuckoos Stopped Singing*. A Documentary Film.

Pattnaik, Surasingh. 1980. *Gopi Babu nko Adivaasi Samaj O Taahoro Bhabisyata: An Interview*. Unpublished Paper.

Report of a Fact-Finding Team. 2017. https://peoplesvoice.in/2017/05/18/niyamgiri-suraksha-samiti-activists-subjected-illegal-detention/.

Samadrushti Televisions. 2013. The Referendum.

Supreme Court Judgement dated 18 April 2013 on Writ Petition (Civil) No. 180 of 2011.

The Indian Express, 27 February 2010.
The Lanjigarh Development Story-Vedanta-Perspective. 2011. http://lanjigarh-project.vedantaaluminium.com/The-Lanjigarh-Development-Story-Vedanta-Perspective.pdf
Varadarajan, Sidhartha. 2009. In Kalahandi, Battle for Livelihood Trumps War for Votes. *The Hindu*, 13 April.
Video Republic. 2007. The Lament of Niyamraja: A Documentary.
———. 2008. Niyamgiri: The Mountain of Law – 06.
———. 2009. The Real Face of Vedanta.
Walker, T.S. 1902. The Geology of Kalahandi State, Central Province, Memoirs of The Geological Survey of India, Vol. XXXIII, GSI, Calcutta.

CHAPTER 10

The Taste of Steel

It took longer to get into the forest. It seemed that the trees, feeling that they were losing the argument with human beings, walked deeper into the forest.
—Ben Okri, 1991

It was a cold and wintry day. A funeral procession had begun to slowly make its way from Champakoila. White shrouds covered the bodies on string cots and marigolds of orange and yellow were put on them along with hibiscuses. The flowers and shrouds together covered their bullet wounds. Grief-ridden hearts raised fists and shouted aloud: ***Kalinganagar ke shaheedon ko lal salaam!*** (Red salute to the martyrs of Kalinganagar). And other voices responded: ***Lal salaam, lal salaam!***

As they were marching to Ambagadia carrying their dead, it looked like as if a collective catharsis had descended upon them. When they reached the funeral site, the twelve bullet-ridden bodies were gently placed on the ground one after another. Women smeared oil and turmeric paste on them. Some of them had stumps of chopped off palms raised to the sky. The atmosphere was all sombre. Everyone was crying—men and women, old and young alike (Samrajyabadi Birodhi Mancha 2007). The hills, the trees and the skies watched mutely, as if barely able to absorb the rhythmic sobbing of people that had converged there.

As the funeral pyres were lit, the flames rose up and embers flew to the sky. With them the grief and tears gave way to a steely resolve. It was a

R. Padhi, N. Sadangi, *Resisting Dispossession*,
https://doi.org/10.1007/978-981-15-0717-5_10

moment of reckoning for those whose land was being coveted for steel production.

The telecast sent shock waves all across the nation and beyond. Many stories did rounds as people came to terms with the loss of lives and the sheer bestiality of an elected government.

Jayant Mahapatra evocatively penned down:

> It is my ardent wish
> At times
> To walk down the road
> Where,
> One after another twelve pyres were lit
> That day.
> And the earth,
> Before surrendering,
> Became speechless for a few moments,
> Witnessing the deafness of the pyre. (Mahapatra 2015)[1]

A memorial built on this spot is named Birbhumi. There are stone pillars put up in the name of each martyr:

> *Mukuta Dei Bankira*
> *Aati Jamuda*
> *Ramchandra Jamuda*
> *Deogi Tiria*
> *Sudam Barla*
> *Bhagaban Soi*
> *Landu Jarika*
> *Gobind Lagori*
> *Janga Jarika,*
> *Ramlal Mundoya,*
> *Ram Gagrai*
> *Bona Badara*

More pillars have got added since 2006 as people fell prey to the tyranny of the company and the government each year. Shyamo Gagarai, Kisan Buriuli and Bir Singh Gop of Chandia succumbed to their injuries sustained during the firing and succumbed in the following months. Amin Banara was gunned down on 1 May 2008. Laxman Jamuda fell to police bullets in May 2010. Dabar Kalundia died ill and heart broken in January 2014.

The Steel Rush

The Ho-speaking adivasis of Kalinganagar hail from the present-day Jharkhand region that shares its border with Odisha. In the aftermath of the Birsa Munda rebellion, they came to this area. The Raja of Sukinda gave them land titles and was keen they make the land cultivable. Many of them were given copper plates as land grants or titles. Over a period of a century of backbreaking labour, it became home. The present-day rulers wanted the same land to make steel and therefore sought to dispense them.

In 1990, Biju Patnaik came to power selling the dream of a second steel plant in Odisha after Rourkela. He persuaded the NRI industrialist Swaraj Paul to set up a steel plant here. To mark the occasion, each of them planted one *kadamba* sapling. However, Swaraj Paul's industry, for reasons not known to people, did not take off. Meanwhile, local people say one sapling grew into a big tree and another one died. The steel hub in the making was named Kalinganagar. The name proudly evokes the memory of ancient Odisha when people of this land were supposed to be rich and prosperous because of maritime trade and commerce. The area seemed to be an ideal choice for setting up steel production units for investors. The NH200 connects Paradip Port to this iron- and manganese-rich belt of Jajpur (particularly Sukinda) and Keonjhar districts with the Brahmani flowing serenely nearby.

By 1992–1994, the Odisha Industrial Infrastructure Development Corporation (IDCO) began acquiring land in the area to develop infrastructure for companies. Such was the euphoria created around it that most people believed in the promised El dorado and looked forward to the prosperity that industrialization would usher in. Middlemen and government lackeys did the rounds in building up dream houses and jobs in exchange of lands. Local people, mostly adivasis, agreed to leave their land for a meagre price with no resistance, hoping for jobs and improvement in their lives, once factories were set up. The saga of adivasis being thrown again and again after having made the land habitable has in this way become the predicament of modern times too.

The people got the first glimpse of the government's brute power in 1997 when they were forcibly displaced from their villages to make way for the Neelachal Nigam Industries Ltd (NNIL) steel plant. It so happened that a large contingent of police arrived in the middle of one night and asked villagers to immediately leave for the newly set up rehabilitation centre. People resisted and wanted written assurances of jobs before leaving but in vain. They left with resentment and anxieties aplenty. This incident marked the beginning of coercive displacement and resistance in Kalinganagar.

In Jajpur district, the betrayal happened at various levels and in different points of time. Chakradhar Haibru, a leading figure of the Bisthapan Birodhi Jan Manch (BBJM), said:

> We did not have record of right (ROR) over most of our land that were shown as *'anabadi'* land in the revenue records. The compensation was meaningless without giving us ROR over the land. I remember our raising this issue in one of the earliest meetings with the new ADM of Kalinganagar. In fact, he had expressed surprise that there had been no land settlement in the area since 1928. He promised to look into the matter. Nothing happened.

Rabindra Jarika once explained:

> Around 1992, local leaders and middlemen were successful in making people of Gobarghati and Chandia agree to leave and accept compensation money. They argued that we adivasis knew nothing and said that industry was good for us and that if we did not agree the government would in any case acquire our land and dismantle our settlements using bulldozers. That we would not only lose land but also get nothing in return. This subtle threat worked. People then thought that it was prudent to get something rather than nothing at all. They were paid at the rate of Rs 35,000 per acre. It created fissures among people. After acquisition, some land was levelled and thus rendered uncultivable while some was left as it were. Whose land became unfit for cultivation began to live by the compensation money and went to nearby towns to do wage work. But whose land was still cultivable they continued to grow crops on it. Some years went by like this. The money they had received got exhausted. Yet, the promised employment was nowhere near sight.[2]

Thus, doubts and mistrust had begun to creep in. People were enraged when they learnt that IDCO was selling the same land to companies at much higher rates. Once the illusion of the sarkar as *maibaap* (protector) began to crumble into pieces, the shock and anger they felt turned into collective resentment, and it soon manifested in organized resistance.

In 2004, Maharashtra Seamless Company began *bhoomi pooja* near Gadpur-Khurunti without even consulting the legitimate owners of the land. People got suspicious since they had been in this land for hundreds of years. How could the company begin work without talking to even those who had *pattas*? They gathered at the spot and did not allow the *bhoomi pooja* to take place. When the police and the administration intervened on behalf of the company, the people still remained steadfast. As a result, the Additional District Magistrate (ADM) of Kalinganagar had to rush to the spot.

The ADM did not engage in any discussion. He not only ordered lathi charge but also came charging at the protestors pushing down some of the women to the ground. The police began chasing and beating up the people. Women were kicked around and pulled by their hair. People resorted to stone pelting in self-defence. They set the ADM's vehicle on fire and thrashed him badly. When the inspector-in-charge of Kalinganagar PS came to his rescue, he too was beaten up (PUCL Report 2006). The situation went out of control, and the police had no option but to retreat.

Fearing retaliation, most men hid in the surrounding hillocks. As expected, the police returned the same day with reinforcements. This time the women and children bore the brunt of the brutal violence. Some twenty-five women who were arrested from Chandia village remained in jail for a full one month. There was no one left in the village to take care of the sick and infants and elderly. As a result, two infants died; an old man who had sustained grievous injuries also died a few days later.

This is the collateral damage wreaked in the war of development.

Meanwhile, TISCO and others also acquired land from IDCO. Despite the repression, people were persistent in their demand for fair compensation. By now they had understood that it was futile to expect from the companies or the government that they would protect their interests. The incident had taught them they had to now fight their own battles.

Thus, they formed the Bisthapan Birodhi Jan Manch (BBJM). It had several adivasi leaders representing the affected villages. The Manch began to discuss the high rates at which the land was being sold to the companies. It entered into negotiations with the administration as an organized representative body of the many villages. One of their first demands was a second round of compensation for those whose lands had already been acquired by IDCO. Towards the end of 2005, when the word spread that TISCO was going to begin its construction work, the Manch decided to call for an immediate meeting. A delegation was formed to speak to the Collector when they come for the levelling of land the next day.

2 January 2006

On this second day of the New Year in 2006, TISCO brought bulldozers to level the fields. People of Champakoila sent messages to other villages that the company has come with bulldozers. As soon as the nearby villages received the message, they left whatever work they were doing and rushed to the spot, carrying their bows, arrows, sickles and other traditional weapons. Women and children also ran all the way. When over 400 people from 15 villages reached the spot, they were bewildered to see the massive police deployment and presence of high-profile government officials. They remained on an adjacent field to the site, close to Champakoila village.

Daylight robbery of the people needs massive deployment of police. The entire area was cordoned off with ropes. Armed policemen were placed all around it. The corporations are always assured support in this grand looting; the Superintendent of Police and the District Magistrate stood in protection of the company and its officials. There were twelve platoons of police with them.

The people understood that the battle lines were clearly drawn and the administration had come prepared for an all-out combat. Otherwise, on whose behalf do an elected government and its administrative machinery work? Why does the government need to send an SP and a DM to stand guard in protection of a private company and its officials?

The platoons started taking positions, equally divided on all three sides of the fence that was erected using long ropes; one platoon was kept aside meant to give protection to the top brass present if the situation went out of control (PUCL Report 2006). Perhaps, the thrashing of the ADM seven months back was haunting them!

The engines of bulldozers and earth movers were making whirring sound. The huge metallic monster began moving around to level the uneven field under its colossal wheels. As the villagers became more and more animated, the commotion increased. The delegation of four that was supposed to meet the Collector stepped forward. But the police refused to budge. People pressed against the rope cordon. Manhandling by the police further infuriated them.

Just as both sides were busy jostling with each other, an explosion took place. No one was sure what caused the explosion. Some say it was a land mine; others testify having seen the police pull a rope that set off the explosion. Whatever it was, all hell broke loose after that. Police started firing upon fleeing people. Stun and tear gas shells as well as rubber pellets were showering on them from all sides. As people were running in all directions to save their lives, some policemen tripped and fell. They turned back to get at them. An unarmed havildar named Gopabandhu Mohanty was mauled up by the people. The police went on rampage and continued firing with no holds barred. People stumbled and fell on the ground as they were fired on the back. They were given a chase as firing continued.

The area cleared up. There was smoke and dust. At the end of it, the battlefield was strewn around with a mass of people: some lay dead, some injured. It was all dead quiet.

Villagers ran screaming all the way:

> *Aamo ku maaribaaku aasichonti re; aamoku maaribaaku aasichonti!!*
> *Tata aamoku maaribaaku aasichi; Tata aamoku maaribaaku aasichi!!*
> [They have come to kill us; they have come to kill us!!
> Tata has come to kill us, Tata has come to kill us!!]

Sini Soi, whose son Bhagaban Soi also fell to the bullets that day, recalls:

> People came running from that side yelling that our people have died. The boy next door ran up to me and said he saw Bhagaban falling down but he could not help him as the firing was going on. My children clung to me and cried out 'our brother is dead, our brother is dead.' My head began reeling and my mouth went dry. There were no tears in my eyes. Can a mother cry when her children are clinging to her seeking consolation? I started walking in that direction. I wanted to see him. But the police had removed the bodies. I watched from a distance. A vehicle was taking them all. My son was still alive at that time. One of the girls was alive too. Their hands were moving. People asked me to go back since we might be killed.

As the police went after the people and shot randomly, many more were hit. Hearing shouts, Deogi Tiria, a woman from Champakoila village, stepped out of her hut to see what was happening. She fell prey to a random bullet and died. People calmed down each other. Some were given traditional medicines at village squares. Many had sustained grievous injuries. The collective trauma and shock was overpowering.

Who can they turn to when their own administration was on the offensive? People feared taking the injured to the nearest Danagadi Hospital. So they carried them on shoulders, bicycles and string cots. They brought them to the main road through the thickets to reach hospitals in Cuttack or Jajpur.

The site got cordoned off with only the police and some bodies, dead or injured. The police carried the dead and the injured to Jajpur. Later when they returned the bodies to the families, it was discovered that five of them had their palms chopped off. Their names were Ram Gagrai, Aati Jamuda, Landu Jarika, Bhagaban Soi and Mukta Bankira. Soon the word spread about physical torture and mutilation of genitals.

Sini Soi recalled:

> They must have tortured and killed them on the way. We would not have got the bodies had we not blocked the road and refused to move till the bodies were returned. But still they did not return the palms. They gave us six bodies, including my son's. There was a garland on him. What will garlands do? My son's palm was severed from his body. Later they asked us to come to claim the palms. I fainted on the way.

The doctors claimed that the palms were chopped off for fingerprints to identify the bodies. However, it could have happened only under police instruction. As the news covered the national media, the doctors responsible were suspended. The State Human Rights Commission ordered the hospital to return the palms. The families insisted that a DNA test be done to make sure that the palms belonged to their kin. But the administration has not conducted any DNA test even after passing of 13 years. The palms are still lying preserved in a box kept at a local youth club in Ambagadia near Birbhumi.

The spot on the Daitari-Paradeep National Highway where this protest first began saw a long resistance called by the Bisthapan Birodhi Jan Manch. A blockade was organized that stopped heavy vehicles carrying goods and raw material between Paradeep and Sukinda. This nonstop sit-in lasted for more than a year. The united political action with solidarity pouring in from across the country was inspiring. Of course, the trucks and vehicles found a way out and silently plied their way on the road from Duburi to Danagadi with the same goods and raw material.

The Persecution Intensifies

The killing of thirteen adivasis and a policeman finally brought into force the new Orissa Resettlement and Rehabilitation Policy, 2006. At that time, Tata Steel Rural Development Society (TSRDS) began to make inroads into the villages with much ingenuity. Chakradhar Haibru recalled:

> After the firing incident, the administration could not enter the area anymore. On the other hand, we also did not go out for the fear of arrest. Mr. B.N. Lal from Jamshedpur began visiting villages in the ruse of providing services. He told people that the government might have killed their people but that he had come to offer support. His team distributed medicines, rice, lentils and even small amounts of money. At the same time, he

persuaded people to leave their villages for the Rehabilitation Camps as they would get jobs and many other benefits and facilities. Sadly, our movement did not take any step to curb the activities of TSRDS.

Many families began accepting compensation in the months that followed the police firing. Perhaps the amended terms in the R&R policy seemed tempting; perhaps the fear of continuing to live in the face of state violence and company hooliganism seemed daunting; or perhaps their own need to get on with life seemed more pressing. They started moving to the new tenements that came up at Sansailo, Trijanga and Gobarghati DP colonies.

Soon sections of these people were mobilized to aid the company and administration in favour of industrialization. The pro-company lobby often came in traditional attire to attack those sitting in the blockade.

The sacrifices must have made the people of Kalinganagar tired. They might have rested to heal their wounds. Some might have withdrawn from the fight. It is human to do so. But the Company is unlike human beings. It does not experience fatigue. It uses a repertoire of tricks and games: bribery, coercion, murder, repression and fratricidal war; and sells all dreams: job, good life and prosperity.

The rehabilitation measures taken up by the Company reeked of pious platitudes. NGOs and consultants were hired to cloak the coercion with titbits. But those who did not give in to their coercion were persecuted relentlessly.

Leaders and active members of BBJM were persistently hounded by the company goons and administration. Dabar Kalundia survived three murderous attempts on his life. One such attempt was made on his life on 1 May 2008 when Arvind Singh, an employee of the company, along with a group of assailants, fired at him in front of Rohit Ferro Tech. The bullet hit Ameen Banara, and he died on the spot. The assailants got away scot free.

Earlier on 13 March, Jogendra Jamuda was also targeted in a similar fashion when he was riding past the Kalinganagar police station on his motorbike with his wife and mother on the pillion. A bullet came flying from an unknown direction. He survived.

In terrorizing people, the administration was not leaving any stone unturned. A leader named Anna Reddy was picked up from Kalinga Hospital in Bhubaneswar while undergoing treatment. In another incident, a teacher and researcher in solidarity with people's struggles against displacement, David Pugh, was stopped by Odisha police and interrogated for several hours when he was returning from Kalinganagar on 12 August.

The two activists accompanying him, Pratima and Pradeep, were also arrested under charges of sedition. Pugh was deported out of the country, while Pratima and Pradeep languished in prison for a long time before they were acquitted of all the charges by the court.

In this way, state power and corporate muscle worked hand in glove to deluge leaders with countless fabricated cases.

The murder of an ASI and one constable on 29 July 2009 at the Bramhanipal police outpost in the neighbouring district created a panic about Maoist presence in the area. Mainstream media fuelled the hysteria. As a result, over seventy cases were registered at Jajpur Road and Kalinganagar PS naming almost twenty-five people. The police swiftly took into custody two prominent leaders of BBJM—Chakradhara Haibru (Junior) and Nanika Jamuda.

On the eve of the fourth anniversary of the Kalinganagar firing in 2010, the entire village of Gadapur was in deep slumber when the police force comprising 200 personnel led by a DSP came and arrested two leaders—Kunja Gagarai and Budansingh Jamuda—as a preemptive measure.

Trolley puller Rasananda Patra's body was found near Gadapur two days later, when he protested the razing down of his hamlet Bandragadia on 21 April 2010. Medical negligence killed some. Mechcha Hanaka, who was admitted in a hospital in Cuttack in clandestine manner, died of TB and renal failure on 18 May. Yet another villager named Madan who had got bail in fourteen cases with two cases pending had pleaded the judge for immediate medical assistance. The plea was rejected, and he died three months later on 3 August. Twelve-year-old Janga had gone missing from Baligotha on 30 March. On the midnight of 31 December, she was killed by the police in Tomaka forest near Kalinganagar in an encounter. Laxman Jamuda was killed in Chandia on 12 May, as we shall see later.

The hue and cry created for Sini Soi made her leave the village and the community she was trying to save from the company. The police announced an award of Rs 10 lakh to aid her arrest. Relations within the same community were rapidly deteriorating as bribes did their work. Some villagers thought it was an enticing reward for turning her in. She was forced to flee to her uncle's house in Jharkhand from where she was finally arrested under charges of sedition in May 2012.

The Common Corridor

By the end of 2009, almost 800 of the 1,300 families had shifted. Some villages were still continuing with their resistance. Meanwhile, the administration announced the construction of a common corridor[3] as a ruse to uproot the remaining villages. It took many platoons of police and a fierce fight to raze down Chandia, Bamiagotha, Kalamatia and Baiduburi.

Baligotha held out the longest. It was only on 28 March 2010 that a core committee had been formed to negotiate with the police and administration. The DC, the ADM, the Sub-Collector and the District Welfare Officer (DWO) present in this meeting discussed what was required from the villagers, especially the shifting of household belongings of those who had already shifted from the village four years ago. However, when heavy police deployment began the next day, the people were taken aback by the betrayal. The meeting was a hoax.

Hundreds of people gathered on 30 March to protest against the construction of the common corridor. The police went berserk. They razed down a school and a community hall built by the adivasis, the Birbhumi memorial was desecrated, houses were set ablaze after pillaging valuables, livestock was either taken away or shot dead, television and radio sets were broken and grain bags were destroyed. The police also shot at a BBJM activist from close range on his chest and legs, houses of Dabar Kalundia and Rajendra Kalundia were especially targeted, media was not allowed inside and three journalists were beaten up and their cameras were confiscated.

Armed police were deployed along with anti-Maoists Special Operation Group. No doubt, it was a brutal invasion in the name of road construction. For the next many weeks, Baligotha was kept in utter isolation. Policemen and hired goons of TISCO guarded all entry points. Many people who could not reach hospital on time died in this period. On 5 April, a man from Gobarghati village died of cerebral malaria as he could not get treatment. One of the BBJM leaders Ghanshyam Kalundia also died. No one got to know the reason of his death. Sikandar Kalundia and Balema Goipai died within a week of falling ill because of lack of access to medical care.

The police started doing the rounds of Chandia in May on the pretext of helping a few families from the rehabilitation colony retrieve personal belongings from their old houses. The number of such rounds increased, as also the policemen who were now accompanied by bulldozers. On 12 May, the police began to pull down houses of those whose occupants had not yet agreed to shift. When villagers from Baligotha and Gobarghati rushed to help them, they were stopped midway. Men were kept at least 200 metres away from the village. Only women and children were allowed to stay. When some women protested, they were beaten up. Tear gas and lathi charge were used to disperse them and pellet guns were shot at men who tried entering the village. Many were injured by these pellets.

Laxman Jamuda was hit by pellets as he tried rescuing his granddaughter Mukta. His nephew Lalmohan went to inform his elder brother. When he came back to help his uncle, he was beaten up and then taken to the Kalinganagar police station. Laxman Jamuda's body was brought dead to the Danagadi Hospital around 11 am.

Media reported that he died of sunstroke while the police alleged that his death happened due to stampede. The doctor who conducted the post mortem said that multiple penetrating injuries and foreign particles were recovered from his body. The cause of death in his report was due to neurogenic and haemorrhagic shock.[4]

The torture of Lalmohan continued in the police station. The same evening, he was taken to Danagadi where he was told of his uncle's demise and was made to sign several blank papers. He was taken to an unknown place in the night and again brought back to Danagadi the next morning. He somehow managed to call his brother Chandramohan and told him about his uncle's death and the police's plan to take his body to Puri for cremation.

Lalmohan managed to escape and reached his village the next day. The family had no clue of the whereabouts of the body or when they would get it back. The police had already cremated the body at Swargdwar, 150 kilometre away, that same night. The clandestine cremation was performed according to the rituals of caste Odias. Was it their way to sanctify their crime?

In all, twenty-five people were injured that day. Jema Hanka, who was bedridden for some time, narrates the incident:

> A policeman grabbed my neck but I broke free. But immediately a policewoman came charging and hit me on my chest with a baton while another policeman kicked me all over.
>
> Our only fault was in agreeing to let them demolish the houses whose occupants had already left. The Collector had also agreed and had assured us that they would demolish only the empty houses and would not bother us. We had allowed them into the village on this condition.
>
> But once inside, their attitude dramatically changed and a hefty policeman ordered to break all the houses. He asked, 'Why are you staying here? Go away!'
>
> We said, 'We have everything here. Our home and hearth; our farms and gardens. Everything...where would we go?'

> He taunted us saying we were beggars and that he would break all our houses and we could do nothing.
>
> To which we said, 'Kill us first.'
>
> He was furious and screamed, 'How dare you raise your voice.' He then ordered his men to beat us all and opened fire. Some pellets hit my hips, abdomen and shoulder.
>
> I am still not able to sleep. I am rendered useless. But we will not leave our homes even if they come again. Where would we go? (Samadrusti Televisions 2010)

The people of Chandia and Baligotha resisted till the last. With the death of Laxman Jamuda and the fresh phase of resistance and negative publicity for Tatas, the company and the government decided to leave out Chandia and Baligotha and instead targeted smaller villages like Bamiagotha and Baiduburi. Kalamatia was left with only two houses. All other houses had already been demolished in different phases. Those left behind dreaded the Tata goons the most. Some of the goons who came along with the police were familiar faces from the same village. The use of state terror combined with divisive tactics resulted in shrinking of their collective strength. As a result, many were forced to accept compensation and leave.

Dabar Kalundia lived in the village of Baligotha. The police dreaded him; they dreaded the magic influence he had on his people even more. But when we met him in 2010, on two occasions, he seemed broken though resolute still:

> We can fight the sarkar. We know how to fight the companies too. But how do we fight our own people? Our own people who had once lived in this village came from the rehabilitation colony armed with tangias, bows and arrows. They have been enlisted by the company to do its work. And they accompanied the police here.

Dabar Kalundia's health deteriorated sharply after the events of 2010, even though he had survived three murderous attempts on him. He was a broken man when he finally died of kidney failure. Who can tell what killed him actually? Was it the rapidly advancing boundary wall around the steel plant or the shrinking of ancestral land and the drying up of streams and water bodies right before his eyes? Was it the severing of ties with the past and its traditions? The years following 2010 to 2014 were bewildering for the villagers left behind in the five villages that continued the resistance. Solidarity for the struggle from outside petered out gradually. Baijanti's struggles multiplied after her husband Ramlal Mundoya was killed in the police firing of 2006. She said:

> When we were at the peak of resistance, people and activists from all walks of life came to stand by us and our struggle and we got a lot of courage and motivation. But now confrontation with the police is replaced by daily struggles for survival and resistance. No one comes to know in what condition the people are living and how they are keeping their resistance alive because even our five villages have not given the land to the government.[5]

Baijanti received Rs 10 lakh from the government and Rs 1 lakh from the local unit of the Congress party as compensation. She is still anxious of the future. The money in the bank on whose interest she lives is earmarked for many things: children's education, buying of a patch of land and building a house. She gets Rs 3,000 monthly interest in which she manages her household expenses. However, the last two years' drought has yielded little from her land. Being a mother of two, she cannot even go out of Kalinganagar on wage labour. It is unthinkable for women like her to seek work in any of the industrial projects. In her words:

> How can I work for these companies or give up my land for them? They have built their factories on our chest and their lands are witness to the murder of our men.

Many women and girls in Kalinganagar had false cases and were branded as Maoists. The stigma of being in resistance ostracizes women even more. When they go to work or for getting medical treatment, the shopkeepers, the doctors and local people shun them upon knowing that they are from either Baligotha, Chandia or any nearby village, which is still resisting the Tatas. As a young girl asked:

> If we are called Maoists then who are those who fired at us in broad daylight and murdered our men in cold blood? We do not have guns, the police have!

Sini Soi in Prison

Pelagueya Nilovna asked, 'Why should I lie idle when my son gives up his life for the sake of truth?' in Maxim Gorky's celebrated novel *Mother*, when her revolutionary son gets arrested defying the Czarist authority.

The mother's heart leads her to do whatever she can for the cause that claimed her son. Finally, she too meets the fate of her son. Sini Soi might not have heard of Nilovna, and she might not have ever read Gorky. But she is still a mother. Bhagaban Soi's death enraged and propelled her into struggle.

Soon, she found herself in prison charged under sedition. The bewilderment and pain felt at being treated like a criminal when fighting for one's land stays even after emerging from the darkness of prison life. She recalls slowly:

> I was arrested on 1 May 2012 near Mayurbhanj-Chaibasa border. I was staying with my uncle's son in Chaibasa. They took me to Jashipur police station and interrogated me for hours. They brought me to Baripada and informed my son. I was finally taken to Panikoili. My son landed up at Panikoili police station looking for me. They asked me what I wanted: House, money or jobs for my sons. I said I did not want any of that. They told me I was a Maoist. I said, 'Yes, if you think I am then I am a Maoist as my denial would not change your view.' The interrogation went on for four days. They asked me to surrender. I said, 'You have already arrested me, then why should I surrender? Either you send me to jail or kill me if you wish to.' They said they would take me to the jungle and kill me there. I said, 'You have every power to kill me here also.' Finally, they threatened to kill my son before my eyes. I said, 'You have already killed one son before my eyes and now you would do it for the second time.' I asked them to kill me. All these four days, I did not take any of the food that they offered. My health deteriorated sharply and I fell unconscious.

The sad tales of the mechanisms of confinement and intense mental torture to succumb to pressure and admit affiliation to communists are the same in every society.

Many continents away, Domitila[6] was being interrogated and tortured by the Bolivian prison authorities. She had just lost a son due to their callousness. Not being able to withstand the brutal torture anymore, she pleaded with the authorities to kill her too. She warned them that if she was left alive she might become a communist. She said that she might actually become a communist also because of the deeper hatred she had developed for their making her suffer so much.

> In deep anguish and pain, Domitila passes out. She sees herself falling from a high cliff. She sees herself falling in pieces of flesh and brains that fall on

> the black crags. She reaches the bottom. Dressed in a white gown, she gets up to collect her flesh piece by piece with great difficulty. She claws at the crags and as she finds a drop of blood she cleans it with the corner of her gown. In this way, she rises higher and higher. She keeps telling herself that when she reaches the light at the top she will be safe. She keeps cleaning the blood on the pieces of flesh. When she finally wakes up, she is in a clinic with the faces of a doctor and some nurses looking at her. (Chungara and Viezzer 1978)

Sini Soi wakes up to find herself in a hospital ward:

> They had not even admitted me in my own name. I was in the Jajpur Road Hospital as Basanti Munda. I shouted out in the ward 'I am Sini Soi of Kalinganagar. My son was killed in the Kalinganagar firing incident.' Shouting out my name drew the attention of a journalist present there. This is how the news broke and people got to know about my arrest. This is how all of you got to know too. They wanted me to be admitted as a 'mental case'. The doctor gave me three pictures and asked me to draw them. I drew the three pictures for him. I was lucky that he reprimanded the police. 'She is fine. Do you want me to lose my job by admitting such people who are absolutely fine?' I had also refused to take saline or any medicine. I insisted, 'I am fine. I do not need anything from your hospital. I would rather want you to kill me instead of finishing me as being mentally ill.'

From the hospital, she was sent to Choudwar jail where she remained confined for 21 months.

Picking up the Fragments

It took 21 long months for Sini Soi to be acquitted of charges of sedition. Meanwhile, the organized resistance had become weak. The company achieved its aims by getting some thrown in prison and luring others with money.

Her disillusionment with her own leaders grew:

> Gradually, our leaders began to talk less about the movement and more in favour of the steel plant and development. During my days in the prison, none of the leaders came to meet me. Nor did they come when I was released. I do not think this is because of any fear that I have been charged with Maoist link. This is rather because they cannot face me eye to eye. When all of them have been sold out to company or have benefitted, this

> way or that, by the company, I have languished in the prison. I feel people are on the right track. It is our leaders who betrayed them.

Sini Soi's house was razed down as a compound wall built by the company swallowed up the last few remaining houses of Gobarghati. For the Ho community, the loss of house is seen as the severing of ties with the dead who are also believed to inhabit the same dwelling. When anyone dies from among the clan, a stone is laid near the settlement in his or her memory and honour. They believe that the stone pillars watch over the rest of the clan. For them, they are sacrosanct and living. When any new settlement is built, they too need to be brought to the place. Sini Soi moved the stone pillars from the ruins of the old house to the new one. She invited all her relatives from Jharkhand for a feast for *Diri Dili Sunum* (offering oil to the dead)—a sacred ritual of the Ho community.

In 2016, the bulldozers were back again for the second phase of land acquisition with the company wanting to expand the production capacity from 4 MTPA to 8 MTPA. More lands, more forests, more villages needed to be razed and levelled. The injustice continues to torment some still. Four adivasis proceeded to file a petition at National Green Tribunal against tree felling and levelling of land in forest land area.

The National Green Tribunal (NGT) of the Eastern Zone is situated in Mother's Wax Museum in New Town, Kolkata. Ram Jarika, one of the four petitioners, said:

> We had not appealed to the courts till now. So we thought we should now take the legal route as the last resort. We filed RTIs that revealed that the acquired land was still in the name of IDCO. Who has given it the authority to transfer the land to the company? Is it the central government? The RTI opened our eyes. The way the company was going on cutting trees without any forest clearance was illegal. We went to Kolkata to file a stay on these activities but they vacated the stay in two days' time!

The company did not stop there. Agents of the company, mostly locals and ex-leaders of the movement, began luring people to agree to level their own land and fell the trees for cash. It is made to seem voluntary. Videos and photographs are taken by the police while they are made to do this. What goes on in the hearts and minds of these people who have held on to their land long after most people were coerced to leave can only be imagined.

On 5 April 2017, some people of Gobarghati found the door of the Birbhumi club ajar. The box in which the palms of the dead had been kept preserved had been tampered with. They were lying strewn on the floor. There was deep disquiet. Mutual suspicion spread once again that it was someone from within the community behind this. Was it done to scare the people further? The insistence by Sini Soi and others to file an FIR was scuttled by the erstwhile leaders-turned-contractors of BBJM.

However, Mathura Honaga is one of the few whose thoughts and reflections on the Kalinganagar saga hold hope even today just as Sini Soi continues to dream a way out of all the destruction and dispossession. Mathura was one of the most active members of the Bisthapan Birodhi Jan Manch from the beginning. His life was no different from that of countless others who followed a dream, a dream for their people. Dealing with the numerous cases foisted on him, he continued to live in Baligotha. Company agents did the rounds offering lucrative compensation and at the same time issuing veiled threats. Often, he had to pacify the growing fears of his wife and in-laws.

Making one's way to Baligotha is like a snapshot view of all that has been destroyed in the great steel rush. You also get to see the tenacity with which some survivors live. The bike snaked through the bumpy, *kachha* road of Chandia, Bamiagotha and Baligotha. Chandia was the most recent to be swallowed up. Once the main centres of resistance, they no longer exist. Every physical construction has been razed to the ground, trees cut down and the land levelled. But it is not easy to forget that till now people had lived here and fought, had dreamt and resisted. A lively rhythm reaches your ears. A portable hauler is hauling paddy in Baligotha. Mathura Honaga greets us. We were keen to know how he looked back at the movement. He pondered over each point that came to him:

> Let me put it this way. My role in the *andolan* was akin to a driver of a vehicle. I was simply following the orders to drive it. I cannot create a vehicle, that is the work of the engineer. Our leaders were like the engineers. When the road blockade was on, some of us were sent outside of Kalinganagar to garner support for the movement. But the leaders who were here were not able to sustain the struggle. Hundreds of families left for the transit camp and rehabilitation colony during the blockade. There was so much pressure on each family to accept compensation. Who could they look up to? Even by 2008, some leaders had mobiles in their hands and Boleros at their doorsteps. Our BBJM was organizing football matches for the youth with support from the company. Slowly the 2 January programme became a

> ritual. Our leaders accepted financial assistance for even that programme. People grew suspicious and began to lose faith in the leadership. They found ways for themselves. The company and its goons went to every house with the lure of job and compensation. Many people felt it was sensible to eventually move out with at least some money and the promise of a job in the factory. The same happened during the construction of the common corridor. People had to choose between rehabilitation and compensation or facing daily harassment from police and company agents with no leaders to turn to.

Mathura Honaga tells you how he thinks of ways to rekindle hope in his people even today. He says, 'If we have gone to the courts now, we must believe something will come out of it. The police cases tie me down. Otherwise, I could do so much more.'

What Kalinganagar Portends

> *Lohe ka swaad lohaar se mat poocho*
> *Us ghode se poocho, jiske moonh mein lagaam hai.* (Dhumil 1977)
> [Do not ask the smith about the taste of the steel
> Ask the horse in whose mouth is the bit.]

The P K Mohanty Commission submitted its report in the Odisha Assembly on December 14, 2017. It took over 11 long years to conclude that the 'quantum' of force used by the police on that fateful day was justified to face a thousand adivasis with axes, bows and arrows and other 'deadly' weapons. The 10 platoons of police deployed with modern arms and ammunitions had to resort to 'self-defense'. The Commission acknowledged the discontent brewing among the villagers about compensation rates; yet, no level of authority – district or state – had made any attempt to enter into negotiations with the villagers.

In 2016, the central government approved the establishment of a National Investment and Manufacturing Zone (NIMZ) in Kalinganagar. The Rs 4,241 crore project is envisaged to provide employment to 1.5 lakh people. A huge industrial township will be built over 163 square kilometres equipped with modern facilities. The creation of NIMZs is part of the National Manufacturing Policy. Kalinganagar is projected as an affluent township in the making with over a few lakh population.

It is true that land acquisition has been happening since two and a half decades now. All resistance to the steel industry has been clamped down with the formidable combination of state and corporate power; any entity—individual or organization—who dares to question such development gets added as a statistic to the list of Maoists to be arrested, killed or made to surrender; and industrial workers throng the plants and go speeding by with yellow helmets on bikes or bundled into overcrowded auto rickshaws.

But what is happening in the lives of people who live here? What is happening to babies being born? What is happening to the mountains and forests and streams of Jajpur district?

Sukinda valley in Jajpur district, which has 96 per cent of chromite reserves of the country, is situated only 60 kilometres away from Kalinganagar. The contiguous zone stretching from Sukinda to Kalinganagar has turned into a series of ecological nightmares. The Blacksmith Institute in 2007 declared Sukinda to be one of the ten worst polluted places in the world. It is being dug up by more than fourteen mining companies for years. The Damsala Nala, which is a tributary of the River Brahmani, was once known as the lifeline of the villages along its banks. Today, it carries death and destruction as it flows sluggishly to empty into the river. Effluent discharge comes directly from mines, from monsoons when rains flow down from the overburden dumps, and from dumps collapsing directly into the water. The release of chromium hexavalent into water sources is going unchecked despite ETPs being there. Villages have paddy fields buried under nickel deposits since six or seven years. Meanwhile, cyberspace is rife with accolades being paid to companies for their environmental concerns.

Statistics available with two PHCs at Jakhapura and Rabana through RTI reveals that more than 25,000 people have diseases resulting from contaminated water. More than a hundred people have died. If the data from PHCs of Danagadi, Sukinda and Kaliapani are added, the number of affected persons will cross 1 lakh (*Odisha Post*, 24 April 2017). It is in this way that adivasis, dalits and economically marginalized communities are being exterminated through man-made diseases caused by the great steel rush.

The glittering lights and the massive structures of steel giants that dominate the landscape hide another stark reality. Within a few kilometres lies Nagada of Chingudipala panchayat of Sukinda block. Little children, consumed by poverty and chronic malnutrition, rushed to death one after another in the summer of 2016. Ironically, they were taken to the hospital made by Tata Steel at the Kaliapani mining complex. Twenty-one children died within three months. These are children of the Juang community that believes it is born of the earth at the mouth of the Baitarani River. Today, their fate is tied up with the Ho community that is being thrown out of the same land. One community has been uprooted while the other is dying. Dispossessed.

> How much money are people in towns and cities earning? How much more can they earn? What will happen to all that money they are going on amassing? Can they eat money to live? Can they chew it? Or do they not need rice and wheat and vegetables to survive? However much they earn, people have to eat food at the end of the day. They cannot eat money. We are cultivators. We grow food for our people and for others. What is this land for, if not to grow food? Does society need steel or paddy? (Dabar Kalundia)

Notes

1. This is a translated version of the poem. It was first published in *Jhankara* on April 2006 under the title *Bulibar Ichha*. A revised and larger version of the poem titled *Chinda Kuhudira Padare Bule Jebe Mun* was published in *Nabapatra*, September–October 2015.
2. Interview with a team from Women against Sexual Violence and State Repression (WSS), 8 November 2011.
3. The proposed common corridor was supposed to be a four-lane 8-kilometre-long road stretching from Rabana to Neelachal Ispat Nigam. It became the plea to escalate the process of land acquisition after the incident of police firing in 2006.
4. Notes of an unpublished report by PUCL, Bhubaneswar. 2010.
5. Interview with WSS team, 8 November 2011.
6. *Let Me Speak!* is a first person account of a courageous woman named Domitila whose husband was a tin miner in Bolivia fighting for their rights in extremely exploitative circumstances.

References

Chungara, Domitila Barrios de, and Moema Viezzer. 1978. *Let Me Speak!* New York: Monthly Review Press.

Dhumil. 1977. *Kal Sunana Mujhe*. Varanasi: Yugbodh Prakashan.

Kalinga Nagar: Chandia Police Firing – 3 A Documentary Published by Samadrusti Televisions, May 16, 2010.

Mahapatra, Jayant. 2015, September–October. *Chinda kuhudira padare bule jebe mun, Nabaputra*, Rourkela.

Odisha Post, 24 April 2017.
Okri, Ben. 1991. *The Famished Road*. New York: Doubleday.
PUCL, 2006. *Police Firing at Kalinganagar*. Bhubaneswar.
Samrajyavadi Birodhi Mancha (Odisha). 2007. *Kalinganagar ro Ganahatya: Luteraa nko Prakrut Swaroop*.

CHAPTER 11

The Betel Smiles

When the last tree is cut, the last fish is caught, and the last river is polluted; when to breathe the air is sickening, you will realize, too late, that wealth is not in bank accounts and that you can't eat money.
—Alanis Obomsawin, 1972

The most ordinary people—betel vine growers, fisherfolk and subsistence peasants—with the most extraordinary courage have sent the giant steel corporation POSCO packing. There were the children and the elderly, the women and the youth, the landed and the landless who fought valiantly to the end. The saga of dispossession in this region has its echoes even before independence when the British had put up the kingdom of Kujanga for auction in the Cuttack courts. It had been ruled by the Sendha dynasty for 200 years from 1661 to 1868. When the last few kings plunged into indebtedness and losses due to destruction caused by cyclones, Kujanga was sold to the zamindar of Burdwan of Bengal for Rs 5.5 lakh in 1868 (Panda 2006). He remained its sole custodian until 1951 when the rule of zamindars ended with the passing of the Orissa Estate Abolition Act.

Fifty-five years later, the elected representatives of a democracy put up the same land and resources for auction to corporations and foreign investors. Ironically, an elected government aided the process of land acquisition with military-like operations. Indeed, the signing of an MoU has become akin to a declaration of war against people.

R. Padhi, N. Sadangi, *Resisting Dispossession*,
https://doi.org/10.1007/978-981-15-0717-5_11

The Memorandum of Misunderstanding

The Government of Odisha signed an MoU with the South Korea-based Pohang Iron and Steel Company (POSCO) on 22 June 2005 for setting up a 12 million tonne per annum integrated steel plant in Jagatsinghpur district with an investment of Rs 52,000 crore. The project planned to have a captive port at the mouth of river Jatadhari and to source iron ore from the Khandadhar mountains straddling over the two adjoining districts of Sundergarh and Keonjhar.

The MoU was hailed as the biggest FDI made in the country. Mainstream media was going gaga about the giant leap the state government had taken in its pursuit of development. The National Council for Applied Economic Research (NCAER) quickly made predictions that this venture would create 8.7 lakh jobs in the next thirty years.

However, this multicrore dream turned out to be a nightmare for nearly 22,000 residents of Dhinkia, Gadakujanga and Nuagaon panchayats, in the Ersama block of the Kujanga tehsil. The land requirement of the project was 4,004 acres, of which over 3,000 acres was classified as forest land. This vast tract of forest land is integral to the economic life of the local populace. Besides, the river Jatadhari and its mouth sustained the livelihood of nearly 20,000 to 25,000 fisherfolk of neighbouring villages.

The villagers left no stone unturned. They wrote appeals, ran signature campaigns, issued press statements and organized dharnas, satyagrahas and *padayatras* in which women, children and elderly participated. In their desperation, they even requested the chief minister to visit their villages and talk to people, but he never came to listen to their grievances.

Resistance Sparks Off

The first notice for land acquisition came in November 2005. The entry of so-called agents unnerved the people initially, who came to speak sometimes on behalf of the company and at other times the administration. People were shaken, irrespective of their party leanings, especially those who had shifted their loyalty to Biju Janata Dal (BJD) more recently. Babaji Samantra, one of the leading activists in Dhinkia, shared:

> I was in the CPI for several years. Being a poor party, we never had resources for people, though, we very much wanted to work for the welfare of the village and people. In 2000, when the BJD initiated schemes and welfare measures, an entire lot from our village joined it. But the mask came off

after a few years. The local BJD MLA Damodar Rout had once called some of us for a meeting. As we were leaving, he announced that a company would come and bring prosperity to all. He said we had to give up our land. That night we returned to our village shaken and angry. We wondered if this was the party for which we left CPI. After all, we had brought BJD to power and now they wanted our land, uproot us for the sake of a foreign company. It was bizarre to imagine how they could betray us.

The initial shock slowly paved way for a resolve to fight the government that claimed their land. They organized themselves and blocked all entry points and guarded the area day and night. The wave of rebellion spread across the three panchayats. The unity built in the initial phase to resist POSCO was overwhelming. The presence of Nava Nirman Samiti and Rashtriya Yuva Sangathan led to active mobilizing. The POSCO Pratirodh Sangram Samiti (PPSS) came into being on 11 July 2005 to plan strategies and lead action against land acquisition. It was a joint front bringing into its fold people across party affiliations. Dhinkia became the stronghold of the movement. Leaders like Abhay Sahu, Sisir Mahapatra and Manorama Khatua from the Communist Party of India (CPI) were at the helm, giving direction and garnering support. The collective resistance that emerged was vibrant and dynamic.

The government soon swung into action and retaliated. Babaji Samantra had been working as the postmaster in Dhinkia for the last twenty-eight years. When he stood up against the injustice of the government, his services were suspended in December 2007 without any prior notice. He remained unfazed and continued working in the post office. He challenged the illegality of the suspension order and demanded back wages and pension. Despite a favourable court order, the payment remained pending. He was not alone. Kailash Biswas was similarly victimized. He was working in a government school of Dhinkia and lost his job of twenty years as punishment for resisting the company. He did not even have the means to go to the court. Then one fine day, the postal bags stopped coming to Dhinkia. With the post office operations suspended, correspondence for admissions by young villagers to colleges or universities and aspiring job applicants went for a toss. It became clear that moves of the administration were in the company's interests. People's appeals for dialogue went unheeded. Organized protests were dealt with a heavy hand throughout. However, the government underestimated the people's affinity to land and their dependence on betel cultivation.

DHAAN, MINA AND PAAN

Just as in the Baliapal region in Balasore district, betel vine growers in this region too are a happy lot. The natural habitat is the ideal ground for all that betel cultivation needs. The geography and topography become a unique combination, providing a recipe-like set of ingredients for betel vines to grow and flourish. The *paan* cultivators mix the sand from the nearby coast with other organic wastes like mustard husk and layer the betel vine plot carefully. This sand is very special, as it comes from the adjacent forest land. This mix of sand and forest, along with the sweet water, gives a perfect blend for betel vine production. It's an entire economy at work that gives villagers sufficient returns and some autonomy. No wonder that the imminent loss of land became the biggest challenge.

For betel cultivators of the area, *paan* is a divine gift. When we wanted to know about its origins and whether it came from Bengal or Benares, Debendra Patra from Gobindpur gave the most mystical smile for a long time. Then, he narrated:

> One day, Lord Shiva reaches his abode from Lord Indra's Rangasabha. Upon seeing him, Parvati asks: 'Why are your lips so red?' Shiva smiles and says: 'I have chewed a leaf known as *paan* in the heavenly garden of Nandan Kanan that turns the lips red, if chewed.'
>
> Parvati becomes curious to see the leaf and decides to visit the heavenly garden herself. When she reaches, the gardener allows her in but with one condition. She is forbidden to pluck anything from there. Parvati readily agrees. As she is taking the round, her gaze falls on the *paan* leaf and she quickly recognises it from the description her husband had given. Mesmerized, she forgets the gardener's instructions and plucks it. But she immediately realizes her mistake. Embarrassed, she hides the leaf in her saree folds and leaves. The gardener was so familiar with the garden and its vegetation that nothing could miss his eye. When a little later he surveys it, he discovers that a leaf was missing. He decides to report this to Lord Bishnu, who gets so furious that he commands the plant to be uprooted and sent to earth.

That piece of earth might well be Benares, Balasore or Jagatsinghpur, where the affinity to the legendary *paan* is expressed with such delight. It is also believed that the secrecy attached to the *paan's* arrival on earth remains with it throughout its entire lifecycle:

When the betel vines are grown, they are covered in such a way that the leaves remain hidden from the world's gaze under the thick foliage of casuarinas. And when leaves are plucked (*nodiba*), they are kept aside in a big bamboo basket away from all prying eyes. Also, when they are sorted (*nachha*), it is done within the confines of the four walls of a house. Finally, they are carried in baskets covered with leaves and cloth. Even while chewing, it remains hidden in the mouth before dissolving and leaving a red mark on the lips of the chewer!

When the story was being narrated to us, those listening were eager to take us around the vineyards. They explained how it takes some amount of investment and immense care to yield the relatively high returns. They say it with pride that the leisure and autonomy that betel cultivation gives in return is so much more compared to the servitude of jobs elsewhere. No wonder that they assert their autonomy as a community and decry the government that has given them nothing till now. Latika Parida from Dhinkia furiously contends:

What benefits can the government give us? We are happy to be left alone with our betel vines intact. The government is playing with our money; it gives rice at Re 1 per kilo to sell us onions at 50 rupees per kilo!

Sanjukta Mantri from the same village went along with her, saying:

We have never asked the government for even five paisa worth of dole. Not once have we asked for a loan or anything. We live on our own earnings. Why does the government want to dislodge us from our land? Is the government there for the people or are people there for the government? Why is the government going against the interest of the people? (Mahapatra 2013)

Even for the landless, subsistence farming is the primary mode of production and consumption here. Apart from betel, cashew is also grown a cash crop. Paddy cultivation ensures feeding of entire families. People als grow a variety of vegetables and fruits like papaya, drumsticks, pumpkins ladies' finger, bananas, *kunduri* (ivy gourds) and *saag* and collect fores produce like firewood and mushrooms throughout the year. Many o them raise livestock. The nurturing and selling of goats is quite commo Women in fishing communities sort, dry and salt the fish after the cat comes in. They also work on betel vine plots; those living close to Kujan and other small mofussil towns work as vendors, hawkers and cooks. Given the threat to such a land that provides inhabitants their *dhaan*, *mina* and *paan* (paddy, fish and betel), it was but natural for them to rise against the company and the government.

Barricades Against POSCO

When the ragtag army of a few thousand people stood up against the company, the government showed its true colours. The deployment of armed police, flag marches, cordoning off the area, lathi charge, indiscriminate spraying of rubber pellets, foisting of false cases and arbitrary arrests became the government's and administration's modus operandi. Yes, it was a war; the battle lines were drawn. Manorama Khatua lives in Dhinkia. She worked as a teacher in a government school and became fully involved in the resistance movement. She recalls the initial phase:

> Initially, there were repeated attempts to enter the area. We blockaded the entry points at Balitutha and guarded it day and night. Everyone was involved, including the women. In the beginning, there was tremendous unity among us. We marched to the Vidhan Sabha in Bhubaneswar in October 2005. All political parties were with us except the ruling BJP and the BJD. In November we mobilised the entire Kujanga tehsil for a *padayatra* in which thousands participated and resistance kept building up. For ensuring our rights and implementation of laws of the land, PPSS knocked at the doors of all those in power who mattered. But there was no encouraging response. Our eyes opened wider when the Odisha police killed 13 adivasis in Kalinganagar in the neighbouring Jajpur district. We realised that the company and the police could go to any extent once they got entry. To condemn the police firing, we organised a protest five days later on January 7 where over 6,000 gathered in which we vowed not to let POSCO enter our areas. To stop the entry of BJD's Damodar Rout one day, thousands gathered at the Balitutha barricade, he has tried entering through Nuagaon many times before. Then on 11 April, he was detained along with the Zillah Parishad President Sabita Mahapatra for five hours. The day ended with charge of attempt to murder put on 52 people. That was the beginning. Since then, they have regularly used the tactics of foisting criminal cases on almost everyone in the movement. Even after POSCO's withdrawal, we are still fighting those cases. Protecting one's land is worth all the criminal charges and police cases! Isn't it?

Notifications issued under the Forest Rights Act, 2006 (FRA) in January 2008 legally empowered forest dwellers to opine and decide on the use of forest land for non-forestry projects. The Act was a big boost to the struggling people of this region. The gram sabha of Dhinkia lost no time in passing a resolution and inviting claims under the Act.

Meanwhile, the ruling party made quick inroads into every village by luring people with money and promise of jobs. The formation of the United Action Committee in the area, which included a large section of the BJD, was created by the MLA Damodar Rout. Hired supporters were given a mandate to act solely on behalf of the company and the administration. PSSP worked overtime to check the advance of POSCO as well as counter the pro-company lobby. It spread the message of resistance across the country and garnered support and solidarity. However, the real test for such unity is seen at election time. Though it was a joint front cutting across political affiliations, internal differences reared head when the panchayat elections were announced.

The Panchayat Elections

When the panchayat elections were held in the three affected gram panchayats in 2007, the two pro-movement winners were both affiliated to Congress—Bhaskar Swain and Nakul Sahu in Nuagaon and Gadakujanga. In Dhinkia, CPI's Sisir Mahapatra was projected as the anti-POSCO candidate for the post of sarpanch by the leadership. But a controversy broke out when some Congress supporters, also part of anti-POSCO movement of the village Patana, sought to put up Salila Nayak, wife of deceased former sarpanch Basant Nayak. Congress supporters were threatened, if they did not support Sisir Mahapatra. The election to Dhinkia Panchayat was countermanded due to alleged rigging. The atmosphere became hostile. Some Congress supporters sought the help of the administration, which, in turn, grabbed the opportunity to deepen the divide within the people. Almost 52 families left Patana village for what came to be known as the Transit Camp.

When the elections were held in 2009 again, Sisir Mahapatra won the post of sarpanch; while Prakash Jena, a leading figure of the movement who was languishing in jail, became a samiti sabhya. The elections did not bring out the best in the movement's leadership. The manner in which the 2007 dispute was handled by PPSS remains mired in controversies Reflecting on these events after almost ten years, Tuna Baral, a PPSS activist from Gobindpur village, said:

> It's a fact that villagers of Patana had gone to the administration to put some pressure on the leadership for some sort of relief. Unfortunately, the movement could not take any pro-active role to sort it out, nor could anybody foresee the extent of damage that would happen. Perhaps, we should have reached out to them and assured them that the movement is with them and they should not leave their homes.

THE TRANSIT CAMP

The transit camp came into existence as a result of the movement's rift with Congress supporters in Patana village providing an opportunity for the administration to move swiftly to deepen this divide by projecting them as company supporters. The administration immediately made arrangements for those who left the village to stay in the premises of a government women's college from 26 June 2007 till almost February 2008.

An elderly man, sitting near the road to the camp, greets a team:

> Please come and see the camp daughter. There is nothing to be hesitant about. We want you to see and know the hell we live in and how our lives have become a torment. We lost everything. No one is happy here. You all go inside and talk and come and tell me if you find a single happy person. We only want to go back to where we come from but they will not let us do that now. We never left the village of our own accord. We were forced to leave and now we are being forced to stay here. Only after you visit each house and return this way, you will tell me that this old man is speaking the stark truth.[1]

There was no livelihood as they had lost everything, and when they approached banks for loans, they were refused. Even their demand for a piece of land to do share cropping for sustenance got no response from either POSCO or the administration. Soon a barbed wire fence came up around the camp as the company feared that people would begin occupying the surrounding fertile agricultural land for their own survival needs. The company also closed down the school that was being run in the community centre after some time. There was no primary health centre or hospital nearby, and people had to go up to Kujanga for their medical needs.

Over time the small tin sheds became even smaller as families grew in size. Soon the Rs 4,000 that they got each day for the community kitchen fell short as the prices of food grain increased and the number of feeding mouths grew. A few young people managed wage work in a factory nearby, but they wondered how long it would continue.

They laughed dismissively when asked whether they were in favour of the steel plant. A woman said:

> We did not want either the company or the compensation. Living in the village were the best years of our lives. Even if we get out of this hell hole, life will never be the same. We have made several appeals to the administration to let us return to our village. We want to return even though we know our status will never be the same again. We may have to remain dependent on the mercy of those who stayed back there for our safety and security. But we still want to return. Where is the company they wanted to make? Where are the jobs? I really wish the company succeeds and it gets what it so badly wants. Our lives have remained suspended for too long now. Let them be over with it once and for all so that we too live freely after that. This uncertainty gives us sleepless nights.

Despite being branded as company supporters, they were not spared from police harassment. They would often get arbitrarily detained and intimidated only to be released the next day. A young twenty-five-year-old resident said:

> It's just like a jail. Even those who oppose the company live in a jail unable to step outside their villages as they have cases on them. There is no difference in the two situations. We have all been imprisoned. We were also anti-POSCO. Even now we are. We can see through what the company and the administration have done to us and our families.

They reiterated that there was no sarkar that existed for them with the district administration keen in guarding only the company's interests.

True to its name, the camp remained transitory in nature because the company was not sure of its own future. Its inhabitants remained in suspended anticipation for nearly a decade. The children grew amidst many doubts and uncertainties as they saw the elders in deep despair. Shunned by the movement, forgotten by the administration and kept endlessly waiting by the steel giant, theirs was indeed a unique plight.

However, those in their teens who had arrived to the camp as small children continue to meet their old friends from the village often taking risks:

> We cannot leave our friends and so we continue to meet them on the sly behind a temple or in the woods, behind the idols on festive occasions like during Ganesh puja or Saraswati puja because nobody goes behind the gods! We don't usually tell our families about these meetings because they fear for our safety. There is no need for them to know. How can we stop seeing friends with whom we laughed and played as we grew up together … is that possible? We meet secretly even if our folks are divided as pro or anti-POSCO.

The Death of Tarun Mandal

Even as the movement kept the company and the administration at bay, rifts among its ranks and leadership were manipulated. The pro-company lobby became the biggest terror. Propped up by sections of the media, the sole objective of United Action Committee was to counter the demands as well as malign the movement. It threatened people to make them agree to accept compensation and even made physical attacks on PPSS activists.

Like most of the landless from Gobindpur, Tarun or Dula Mandal was active in the Samiti right from the beginning. His death was one of the most tragic events. Subhas Sahani was with him in the ambulance to the Cuttack hospital. He recalls:

> It was 21 April 2008. More than a thousand of us from the entire panchayat were participating in the *shramdaan* activity organised by PPSS. The dredging of the mouth of the Jatadhari river had to be done as the water logging in our paddy fields was causing much difficulty. This spot is only 3.5 kilometres from the village. We had barely been working for two or three hours when news came that pro-company supporters were issuing threats and warnings in our village. The news made us tense and some people returned but still there were 600 or 700 of us left behind. We decided to finish the work we had come for, even though, our minds were disturbed. While returning we gathered in a field nearby and had a small meeting. It was decided that the best way to deal with the situation was to keep peace and restrain from getting into any scuffle.
>
> As we reached the village, we saw them in the school building; some of them had gathered on the roof. They were perhaps 70 or 80. We were more. They lobbed country-made bombs at us that fell on the ground and burst. This provoked some of us who started hurling stones and bricks at them. Those on the rooftop aimed their bombs at us. All hell broke loose. I felt a searing pain in my thigh and fell down. I could not get up and I saw Dula a

> few feet behind me on the ground crying in pain: *'Mamu, moon mori goli, mamu moon mori goli'* (Uncle, I am dying, I am dying).
>
> I tried hoisting him up but since I was on my knees myself I could not drag him. I had a two-inches deep wound on my thigh. I asked another person for help to be carried. We were then made to lie down on a veranda. That was 3.30 pm. Our people made frantic calls for an ambulance and kept waiting for hours. No one came. Private vehicles also refused to enter the area. Prakash Jena's father Kalindi Jena was also badly hurt. Finally, a cousin of Dula came in a vehicle and drove all three of us. Dula kept saying: 'I do not think I will survive. You must look after my family. It is your responsibility now.' He was most worried about them. At times he was also calm. But when we reached the hospital in Paradeep, the doctors gave us some first aid and suggested we go to the big hospital in Cuttack.
>
> The ride to Cuttack was long and arduous as we had to avoid certain routes. We could not take the risk of running into more company supporters. Just a few minutes before we reached the hospital, Dula went silent and listless. When we were taken inside, the doctor declared him dead.

Hundreds of people gathered at Gobindpur when the news arrived that Dula Mandal was no more. People across the panchayat mourned deeply. It was the first life that the movement had claimed. From that time on they began to see through the divisive tactics of the ruling dispensation and the means it could employ. As the collective anger mounted, it got directed at the attackers who had been locked up in the school. But the local leaders of PPSS did not allow people to retaliate. Instead, the attackers were held hostage for two days and then handed over to the police unhurt. Over twenty of them have criminal cases on them till today.

Dula Mandal's family slowly came to terms with the loss of a family member, unaware of yet another tragedy that awaited them. Subhas Sahani who was badly injured did not know that worse would follow. Meanwhile, resistance kept growing with a momentum of its own. People remained undeterred.

The FRA Ceases to Exist

The year 2010 was marked by a dramatic set of events around the non-implementation of the FRA. The Supreme Court had issued an 'in-principle' clearance for the diversion of forest land in 2008. When the UPA-II formed the government at the centre in 2009, the new Environment Minister Jairam Ramesh made it mandatory on 3 August for certificates from the gram sabha for any diversion of forest land. The struggle was at its peak. The PPSS leader Abhay Sahu was arrested on 12 October 2012. He was actually chained to his hospital bed in the government hospital in Cuttack as the most dreaded criminal. Images in media evoked both horror and rage. He spent ten months in jail.

Meanwhile, the company announced the construction of a 10-kilometre-long road from Dhinkia to Paradeep as part of CSR work of the POSCO Foundation for charitable work. The doling out of a pittance to make a road or set up a health care centre was a ruse to enter the area, a mask of sorts not to let go off the bigger pie. Nobody took notice that Dhinkia had been without electricity till then.

On 29 November 2009, a huge *padayatra* commenced from Dhinkia to Beldal in Puri, demanding the scrapping of the project and condemning the heavy losses incurred by the inhabitants. Many organizations and movements from other parts of the country also joined the *padayatra*. This pushed the government at the centre to ask POSCO to obtain a fresh license for its project on 15 December.

The company had actually not shown its required 4,004 acres of land on paper to the government, which is mandatory to acquire an SEZ status for a project. Two extensions had lapsed meanwhile. Even then, both the centre and the state were desperate not to let go of POSCO. The confusion that prevailed between the two governments was costly. Barely within ten days of the district administration beginning the process of seeking gram sabha approvals, the environment minister went back on his own recommendation made on 3 August and gave a final clearance for diversion of forest land. The FRA stood suspended. The minister would be repeating this yet again.

The district administration was adamant working out the details of the compensation package. When POSCO officials entered Patana in the second week of January 2010 to conduct a household survey so as to include villagers in the company's CSR programme, they were nabbed by villagers and held hostage for a day. They were released unharmed and warned not to enter the area again.

Hectic preparations were on in the capital city as Republic Day drew closer. On 26 January, villagers were back at the dharna site at Balitutha and refused to give access to either company officials or the district administration that seemed determined to enter the area. That very morning, President Lee Myung Bak of South Korea was regally felicitated as the nation's guest of honour at the Republic Day celebrations in New Delhi.

Hundreds of kilometres away, people were guarding their own strategic interests against the South Korean steel giant.

Around the time the centre was asking POSCO for its new license, the DC of Jagatsinghpur asked the Block Development Officer (BDO) of Ersama to obtain the approval of the gram sabhas for the diversion of forest land, which was welcomed by the people who had been waiting for this. Gram sabha meetings in Nuagaon, Dhinkia and Gobindpur held between 4 and 6 February passed resolutions outrightly rejecting the diversion of forest land to POSCO and asserting people's rights as provided in the FRA. The PPSS proceeded to burn copies of the rehabilitation package offered by the company. Yet, from February 2010 onwards, the administration actually began clamouring that there were no traditional forest dwellers in the area!

The DC sent a letter to the authorities in Bhubaneswar that the processes required under the FRA had been completed. PPSS objected the government's audacity for reaching such a conclusion without implementing any of those processes. People were aghast as to how Dhinkia could even be mentioned in this context when government officials had not entered the area for the last five years.

However by mid-March, the state government conveyed to the central ministry of environment and forest that all processes required were completed. It took a month for the MoEF to make a request for translated copies of the gram sabha resolution in Odia.

While New Delhi continued to posture eagerness for translated copies, the police and the administration were ready to strike down on the area with their shining paraphernalia. The orchestrated chaos displayed between the centre and the state was not the routine confusion. It simply portended worse to come. The FRA ceased to exist.

On 11 May 2010, twenty-five battalions of police, five ambulances and two fire engines moved into the area. People came out in hundreds and gathered at the Balitutha site. They erected their tents and refused to budge. On 14 May, a CPI MP and a Congress legislator were arrested on the way to the dharna spot. No one was to be spared. In physical terms, people's demonstration is the barrier to the coveted land. And coercion was the only means to enter.

On May 15, around 2 pm after repeated announcements asking people to leave the area, the police triggered the violence. And one of the most brutal and bloody assaults took place. Over 200 people were injured in lathi charge, as also by rubber pellets and tear gas shells. The police went on a rampage and burnt the makeshift tent that was used by the protestors and burnt and destroyed small shops and huts near the area. The police brutality uncannily resonates with events in the same area eighty years ago in the 1930s when hundreds of women had participated in the Salt Satyagraha under the leadership of Malati Choudhury and Bhagyabati Mahapatadei, the former queen of Kujanga. The police had similarly broken their earthen vessels used for making salt.

The cold-blooded violence was as chilling as the double speak from Bhubaneswar. On that very morning, the CM had said to the press that the administration was trying to negotiate and that 'our government believes in peaceful industrialization.' The Odisha police fired hundreds of rubber pellets that have typically been used in other countries in the past—like in South Africa—to disperse the crowd. With the exits from the villages sealed by the police, no one could go for medicine or treatment as threats of arrests loomed large on all of them.

Tikki Bardhan, whose foot was fractured after being hit by a rubber bullet, was not able to walk for days. Her husband, Bharat Bardhan, was hit by a rubber bullet and a shotgun pellet on his face. He barely missed losing his right eye, but the bullet broke a tooth and a blood vessel in his nose because of which he profusely bled. The shot gun pellet remained embedded in his left cheek (*Sanhati* 2010). People helped each other in conducting small surgeries to remove pellets, which were stuck under their skin for days and weeks. Some removed the pellets at their own risk. Fractures, ligament tears and deep wounds were shown to anyone who visited the area afterwards for months. Some still have the pellets in them. Some lamented that the *bada* (big) hospital in Cuttack was no more for them. Bachani Biswal was arrested on the way to a doctor near Kujanga in October 2010. She laughed as she narrated her experience:

> The asthma was unbearable. I had not slept for nights on end. Of course, I knew I could be arrested. But even then I was testing whether I would be lucky to get the medicine and return quickly. Four policemen pounced on me and held me by my hands and legs. I kicked them with all my might. This was the pent up anger of many days. One leg came free, and then the other. I continued kicking. I knew they would not let go of me, so why not hit them back. They hit me with a stick repeatedly. It was not easy to break from their grip. What a beating I got! My body hurts till now. I spent seven days inside and then got bail. But I had so much fun in the jail. Some of us inmates would make fun of the food every day. I also managed to get my own *paan* and tea from outside. You know the women guards get a daily

> wage of Rs 100 only. What a shame to do so much work and earn so little. Not even Rs 3,000 a month! Who would like to do that kind of work, if not for money?[2]

People largely remained confined to their houses and villages. It was nothing short of a mass house arrest drive of the state. Cornered in a war unleashed by the state and administration, villagers were pushed to the edges of the sea with no means to venture out. It was a virtual siege. Isn't confinement illegal when people's right to work or medical care or education is affected? While the administration was guilty of violating the right to life, people continued to demand their constitutionally guaranteed rights over land, livelihood, habitat and resources.

Not surprisingly, the United Action Committtee (UAC) also began to doubt the intentions of the government. On 19 June, it put forth a twenty-nine-point charter of demands in a meeting with the chief minister. The UAC also asked for a fresh survey of the project as the MoU was expected to expire by 22 June. In the months that followed, the N.C. Saxena Committee set up by the MoEF and ministry of tribal affairs submitted its report. It held the Odisha government guilty of non-implementation of the FRA. The sub-committee set up under Meena Gupta to investigate into the violations also recommended the immediate suspension of clearances given to POSCO. Even then, there was no closure.

Time does not halt in the midst of such uncertainty. Each year had its own saga of tales; and there were many parallel narratives. An entire generation of children grew up in the midst of this war-like situation.

Children of a Lesser God

> Standing in front of the blackboard, the teacher asks the children to repeat these words aloud.
>
> We are going to learn the words 'Hands Up.' When you say 'Hands Up' he must raise up his hands because we need to find out if he has any more weapons. 'Still' means Stop. If he doesn't stop, he is dead. If he resists, we react too. If he obeys calmly, that's OK. If not, we have to react immediately. Always let him walk ahead of you. We need to learn these words when we might capture pilots or commando infiltrators.
>
> In yet another scene, they are playing. The children have caught a captive. They yell, 'Hands Up Drop your weapons!' One child bends down to search the pockets of the captive. Then he is led by five children at gun point. The biggest one always plays the American. It's not only a game: it's also training for the People's War.

The 17th Parallel: People's War in Vietnam, a film made by Joris Ivens in 1968, depicted the lives of ordinary North Vietnamese peasants confronting continuous American bombardments. By building shelters underground, tending to the sick and injured, running schools and hospitals, filling in the bomb craters to grow paddy on it again and most of all boosting up each other's morale as a community—the entire peasantry was up against a powerful enemy. The war for steel in our times too made the children of Jagatsinghpur district a part of the ragtag army that fought a pitched battle.

When the environment minister ordered the land acquisition process to resume in May 2011 after it was stopped in August the previous year, platoons of police entered the area to acquire the land along with revenue officials. Women, men and children lay down on the burning sands for hours to physically halt their advance. These images were extensively played out in the media. When solidarity messages poured in from across the country and abroad, everyone from the government to media houses decried how children were being used as human shields by the movement. It was absurd how the government that took no interest in the future of the children, raiding their lands for mining and steel production, was crying foul over the violation of child rights. When other arsenals ran out, it ordered the ministry of women and child development to conduct an enquiry for the fall in school attendance. Aren't thousands of children in villages across the state getting dispossessed of an entire future by the same government?

The National Commission for Protection of Child Rights rushed to the spot to urge families to send children to school. But it ended up urging the government to first withdraw the platoons of police who had occupied the schools. Those shedding crocodile tears for child rights never bothered to enquire what compelled the children to confront the gun-wielding policemen. Or, what compelled their parents to bring their children with them. Haven't children, the world over, forsaken education and surrendered the innocence of childhood in the face of a bigger enemy?

They are the children of a lesser god grown up in the midst of a pitched battle to protect the land from a behemoth. Many were infants who learnt to utter POSCO much before they could mumble other words. Many were even looked after by their distant aunts coming from other villages to lend a helping hand to their parents participating in dharnas and *padayatras*. The fodder of their imagination was fed by reality itself. Just as it was shown in Joris Evans' film, children's games like hide-and-seek had the Odisha police as characters while fighting a 'fake war' had POSCO as an 'enemy.' Whoever took the role of the rogue got a good beating by other kids.

On 3 March 2007, over a thousand children took out a protest march in the three panchayats. This *banarsena* rally, in which children between five and ten years old participated, was named after a legendary young fighter. These children drew their inspiration from neighbouring Dhenkanal's 12-year-old Baji Rout. As a boat boy and volunteer of Prajamandal's *banarsena* during the freedom struggle, Baji Rout had refused to ferry British soldiers across Brahmani River on the night of 11 October 1938 when they were chasing fleeing rebels. Enraged soldiers then shot him and four others. He became the youngest martyr of the Indian freedom struggle. His funeral procession impassioned people across the state. Sachi Routray was much inspired that day and wrote:

> *Nuhen Bandhu, Nuhen Eha Chita,*
> *E Desha Timira Tale E Alibha Mukati Salita.* (Routray 2001)
> [It is not a pyre, O Friends!
> When the country is in dark despair, it is the light of our liberty
> It is our freedom-fire]

Just like their own folks, Baji Rout's mother was a wage earner in the 1930s husking paddy for zamindars (Patnayak 2005). Both mother and son became part of the Praja andolan that rebelled against the princely rule and fought the British troops in 1938 that had come in support of the desperate royalty. It is small wonder then that the children talk of Baji Rout and ask why they too cannot lie down in protest against the platoons of police sent by the administration.[3] They are in a pitched battle against the police and administration that were assiduously assisting the Korean steel company in the same manner the British did for the zamindars and the rajas.

Like you too, they had learned to mug up the various five-year plans and other achievements of the nation in school. But being children of a lesser god, they got tossed in a ferocious tumult caused by the worldwide turn the economy took. Their little villages became the vortex of a storm raging across thousands of villages in this country in the saga of dispossession. Their mothers, undeterred, continued to dream of securing a future for them.

MAGICAL HANDS

Let us again go back to the day when hundreds of people lay on the burning sand in protest. There were rows of children and women followed by men. The villagers actually dared the government to resume the land acquisition process upon their bodies.

Jemma Katakia expresses the trauma that haunts her[4] every now and then:

> Lying on the hot sand was not easy at all. We covered our eyes and faces from the blazing sun with our *gamchas*. It was painful. Although we had *pakhaal bhaat* [fermented rice] and *saag* before coming for the protest, we began feeling hungry and weak just by lying under the sun. Our backs ached and our empty stomachs burnt on the hot sand. If we moved a toe or a foot or bent the ankle, the sand tore into us like a burning ember, as it touched a new spot. We shrieked in pain and laughed at the same time. We were constantly encouraging each other, who else would have come to pep us up in that heat?
>
> If the government can use tear gas and pellets, they can kill us too. We tried to tell them in many ways: kill us and the land is all yours. It was to show our willingness to be killed. We were telling the government and the POSCO to take the land by all means but only by walking over our dead bodies.

The protests were hailed as most heroic as images flashed across the world. A powerful letter of solidarity came all the way from South Korea. Sung-Hee Choi, an activist languishing in a prison there, wrote to the people of Jagatsinghpur:

> *The situation of the Gangjeong village, Jeju Island, when I, along with many others, wanted to prevent a naval base, is very much like yours. The Gangjeong villagers who have fought for four years to save their village are keeping vigil day and night against sudden crackdown by the navy and construction companies (Samsung and Daerim etc.). ...If trucks come, they block them with their bodies and if ships come, they resist them by swimming to them.*
>
> *... I could but feel great sadness and anger over the fact that a big South Korean conglomerate is to rob of and destroy your lands. POSCO is one of the big, infamous corporations, along with Samsung, which has oppressed its workers with its no-labour union policy.*
>
> *... Wholeheartedly supporting your struggle to save your hometown and your rights to live from reckless developmentalism and imperialism's hands. I pray for the success of your struggle.* (New Socialist Initiative 2011)

Jemma Katakia said how they worked hard to remain organized:

> Nuagaon people do not come anymore. They have accepted compensation. Some people from Gobindpur have also taken money. But what do we do? We do not need any compensation. So we have to stay here till POSCO leaves or we die. Now we do vigil in rounds. Patana is in charge of one day a week. Gobindpur and Dhinkia people go twice a week. This has become

> easier. We mark attendance at the dharna spot. If anyone is absent, they are fined 200 rupees. We cannot leave the dharna site. We celebrated even *Raja* here.

Raja is a major cultural festival of Cuttack and surrounding districts when the earth is believed to be menstruating. Women and girls abstain from work on these four festive days. The festival heralds the sowing season. They wear new clothes and tie swings on trees. It is time for reunions and community togetherness. Despite the war-like situation and the endless spate of protests, they did not sacrifice the joy of *Raja*. It was celebrated at the dharna site along with all the rituals and laughter and merry making! Jemma Katakia asserts that political resistance is sheer hard work that will fetch them results just as their labour yields them betel, paddy and fish:

> As long as we can eat ***pakhaal bhaat*** and ***saag***, we can continue fighting. Betel vines bring us the money. No one is without work. Even the landless get to eat. If the government has made this area a jail, we are happy in this jail. At least our tummies are full. But if the government brings in POSCO, we will starve and die. Therefore, we have been on our toes twenty four hours. We have guarded the villages from the police and the company. We sat there without feeding our children. All families come to the dharna spot. This is hard work. Not everyone can do it. Just wait and see. Whatever we set out to do, we see its results. These are not ordinary hands, they do magic. Where nothing could ever grow, we grew paddy and vegetables. Anything that we touch bears fruit. Our hard work will pay. POSCO will have to go from here.

Indeed, her prophecy did come true within a few years! By their simple questioning and tenacity, these women make the most sparkling debates on development irrelevant. They quietly ask one single question: 'How can steel production ever benefit us?'

Each long narrative has many hidden stories; and each household has its own share of conflicts in prolonged periods of struggle. A young woman tried persuading her husband to apply for a factory job in Chennai. She felt he could send money home. The husband was in a dilemma to leave his parents, who were in the forefront of the struggle. There came a tragic end when the woman committed suicide. But the FIR written by the police held the father-in-law Bharat Bardhan and the PPSS leader Abhay Sahu culpable of abetting suicide coupled with charges of dowry harassment. It's a normal practice for those in authority to don the mantle of the rescuer and shamelessly use the laws made for women to serve their own interests.

Another young woman in Patana shared her ordeal:

> My parents got me married blindly. I faced daily violence inside the house. There was no one to turn to. When I became pregnant, I was both sad and scared about the future. I left the village for my parents' house and stayed there for two years. I went to the women's commission in Bhubaneswar and put a complaint. I agreed to return with my child only after notice had been served and my husband came to the commission and promised good behaviour. I was unaware of the struggle outside and could not put my mind to it. I was fighting my own battle. But if the company is hell bent on taking this land, who knows what the future will be like?

Women whose men folk were in the forefront of resistance suffered differently. In Gobindpur, Prakash Jena's *kewda* distillery was shut down since production came to a halt. His father sustained a bad injury when Dula Mandal died. He is unable to walk properly till today. Prakash Jena was also once thrashed with rods and chains near Paradeep by hired goons of POSCO. He served prison sentence on trumped up charges because of which his sister went into a long spell of depression. Anxious and exhausted to see the entire family seeming to fight a losing battle, the mother put an end to her life. She was too frail and anxious to wait till the end to see POSCO finally leave. Soon after her death, Prakash Jena's younger brother Manas Jena got killed in a mysterious bomb blast.

The Blast

The entire village was in slumber that afternoon when a deafening sound shattered the quietness. The earth seemed to tremble for a few seconds. The rumblings were heard even 3 kilometres away. Was it a thunderbolt? But there were no clouds in the sky. Gradually, words spread that it was a bomb blast at Patana village. The explosion had created a deep crater in the ground near the house of Suresh Das of PPSS. Three people died on the spot. In the mayhem that followed, people's patience began to slowly dissipate. And Gobindpur plunged into silence. Fear and intimidation marred their deep grief at the loss of three active members of PPSS from their village: Narahari Sahu, Manas Jena and Nabin Mandal. Laxman Pramanik was rushed to Cuttack as he was grievously injured. All suspicions centred around a person who had recently fallen out of the organization and was seen in the vicinity just before the incident occurred. Narahari Sahu's daughter recalled her father receiving a bag from him. Some wondered whether the tiffin carrier he was carrying had explosives. Manas Jena was at home boiling paddy for rice processing when he got a phone call and left for the spot. He never returned.

A huge contingent of police force that had camped nearby kept sitting. The local police did not visit the spot that day. Instead, the SP announced on TV that three people were killed when an explosion took place while they were making bombs! Before beginning to even pretend making inquiries, the police knocked on the doors of the deceased that midnight to make family members sign a paper that the deceased died while making bombs. No one complied. Almost 16 hours after the incident, the police reached the spot for preliminary inquiries.

Narahari Sahu's sister-in-law and Laxman Pramanik's daughter were rebuked and sent back by the police when they went with a group of women to file an FIR. But the pro-POSCO proponent Ranjan Bardhan was allowed to file an FIR against the three deceased, Abhay Sahu and five others.

No enquiry was conducted into the incident. The mystery never got resolved.

Nabin Mandal had been beaten up mercilessly in a protest demonstration by the Land Acquisition Officer from IDCO. He was being forced by the administration to withdraw the case he had registered. Its hearing was expected within a few days. He was the brother of Dula Mandal who had been killed by pro-POSCO goons while returning from dredging the Jatadhari River. The ageing father is yet to come to terms with his loss of two sons:

> Within five years, I have lost two sons. Who do we turn to? If we go to any government official or administration, we will only be harassed further. It is sixty years since independence. But we are still fighting for our land. I tell myself that Subhash Chandra Bose and Khudiram Bose died fighting against the colonial rule of the British. My sons too fought and died opposing the military forces and the company sent by the Indian state. They too have become martyrs. (Fact Finding Report 2013)

Both brothers belong to the large dalit landless section that has sustained the movement from its inception.

We Are the Original People

It was getting dark as the two Boleros were returning via Gobindpur and Nuagaon. The team had spent the day in the area.[5] Their vehicles were intercepted by two youths. They said visitors usually leave without meeting and therefore they had been waiting to stop them. A large group, waiting behind a lane, was keen to ask some pressing questions. What about their status—the dalit landless—where do they stand?

> We are the fisher people and landless. We have been in the struggle since the very beginning both in body and spirit. Compensation for land means nothing to us. Those who migrated here from West Bengal and other places bought land and became settlers. But we are the original people of this land even if we do not have *pattas*. Our dependence on this land has been as long back as the elders only can recall. Today we are filled with anxiety. As company agents make daily visits and the pro-company trend is becoming strong, we are torn with doubts. Where is the movement that will stand up for us too? Our stakes to save the land are so high but we see villagers finally falling prey to compensation. We see neighbours parting ways. They are in terror of police and private goondas and maybe they want to put an end to their ordeal. Leading organisers are also retreating. But what will happen to us? We have no land to get compensation. Who are our allies? Will you write about us too?[6]

They are the Kaibartas and the Gokhas who have lived in the area since so many years that they call themselves the original people. They were skilled in sea voyages when the region was known for its rich maritime history from the seventh up to the nineteenth century. In fact, they had earned the sobriquet of Kalinga Serpents. The Solabhai (sixteen brothers) organization that has existed since hundreds of years is still the decision-making body of these people. In the struggle against land acquisition, it is these fisherfolk who formed the bulk of resistance. But in the movement, the losses borne by fisherfolk and other landless dalit families remained overlooked.

Almost 20,000 people, from many other panchayats too, would have lost their livelihood by the proposed captive port. They do fishing around the mouth of the Jatadhari River and the adjoining bay area. Those from Gobindpur were filled with searing doubts and anxieties, especially when people (with *pattas*) who had been resisting POSCO began taking compensation. Some furtively ventured into creating betel vine plots in order to claim compensation.

The fisherfolk and agricultural labourers formed the Khyatigrasta Panachasi o Sramik Sangathan and held a demonstration on 22 December 2014 at the office of the Revenue Divisional Commissioner in Cuttack. They demanded the return of acquired land to betel vine farmers; compensation for acquisition to farmers; payment of the promised labour *bhatta* to agricultural workers who have lost livelihood due to acquisition and withdrawal of all false cases against villagers of Gobindpur, Dhinkia and Nuagaon. There was growing anxiety that they will be left nowhere at the final end that seemed to be coming soon.

Gobindpur Matters

The fate of the company remained uncertain for a long time.

In late 2012, POSCO shut down its camp office at Kujanga. The entire office furniture was seen being loaded in a truck. People assumed that POSCO was finally leaving the area. Prakash Jena said:

> I had been to Bhubaneswar. I made a phone call to D.N. Singh, the MD of POSCO. I had once told him that I would meet him only when POSCO withdrew. But when I met Singh he soon began speaking about land acquisition at Gobindpur. I was left shocked. I realized that the closure of the office at Kujanga was only a ruse to fool people.

The administration made the last desperate attempt to enter Dhinkia in January 2013, although PPSS had already sent the gram sabha resolution of Dhinkia opposing diversion of forest land. Three thousand villagers sat in a protest demonstration. Meanwhile, the company scaled down the production capacity from 12 MTPA to 8 MTPA. Similarly, the land requirement was cut down to 2,700 acres.

The administration tactically left Dhinkia out of the acquisition process and targeted Gobindpur. In early February 2013, twelve platoons of police descended upon Gobindpur and went around cutting down betel vines.

On 6 March, the PPSS announced to press that 'if the police forces are not withdrawn, women will protest naked in front of the police.' A mass demonstration was called on 7 March 2013.

It became an awkward moment for many supporters in Bhubaneswar. They pleaded to the leadership to withdraw the decision as it would be a great 'shame' for the 'mothers and sisters' of Dhinkia and Gobindpur. In the confusion that prevailed in the name of shame, the silence of women's voices was deafening. The leadership claimed it had called off the plan and maybe the message did not reach all. Three women bared themselves that day. What followed was a heavy lathi charge, and many were badly injured. Women's bodies have always been the battlefield.

A young dalit woman whose hands and shoulders were still red and swollen said:

> Is this the only reply they can give? How much can we tolerate? How much more beating can we take, you tell us. We are landless. But we depend on our work here for our livelihood. Each time we protest against POSCO, the government only uses the lathi. My mind is not working anymore...what can I say? I can only show the marks on my body since you all have come to meet us. (Fact Finding Report 2013)

The administration foisted charges under the Indecent Representation (Prohibition) of Women Act on the three women who bared themselves in the March demonstration. The police acted upon the complaint filed by a pro-POSCO villager and booked Abhay Sahu under it too. There is a method in which the laws of the land made for women are used by the law makers. In both Kalinganagar and Jagatsinghpur, many senior male activists have been charged with sexual assault too.

On 11 May, Abhay Sahu was arrested in Bhubaneswar airport while boarding a flight to Coimbatore. This time round, sections of the movement were sceptical of the conditions under which the arrest took place.

Police presence intensified in Gobindpur. On 26 June early morning, twelve platoons of armed police led by the SP and Collector arrived in Gobindpur to demolish betel vines. Some 200 youths were hired to oversee the operation. In Orwellian style of doublespeak, the administration called it 'voluntary and peaceful.'

In the documentary *War for Steel*, a young man appears broken and can barely hold up his head:

> Ranjan Parida and his wife and mother have been in tears since they lost their vineyard. Ranjan had agreed to the demolition of his betel vine as he was afraid and intimidated by the presence of a large number of police. Weeping copiously, he tells the camera: 'I had been to my vineyard. They suddenly asked me if I was interested in demolishing the vine. I was so afraid that I couldn't deny. And said yes. Then they demolished my vine and pushed a cheque in my hand. My head reeled. I couldn't think of anything.' (Mahapatra 2013)

The village has over 500 houses. With a police camp set up right in the middle of the village, there would be flag marches at day time and midnight raids to arrest activists at night. Twenty-six platoons of police remained there round the clock. Tuna Baral quietly tells us:

> Each day, the TV showed people receiving cheques from the district official for voluntarily dismantling their own betel vines with their own hands. If the process was so voluntary, why did it take them seven long months to acquire seven hundred acres? We were resisting it every bit of the way. But their cameras were used to concoct lies for the world. We had no leaders to turn to. It was the darkest period. Our ties with the people of Dhinkia got broken. Where were they?

Remember Debendra Patra's story. Was the *paan* being banished from their corner of the earth this time just as it had been banished from the heavens? The land is sacred and so also the story of the betel.

Fragmentation of Ties

The blast that claimed the lives of three people from Gobindpur became an eye opener. Many pro-POSCO people of the village wept and asked for forgiveness from the seniors. Perhaps it hit them hard that they were but pawns in a game that was far more powerful and vicious than their transient partisan loyalties. Perhaps, they feared it was the beginning of the end where there is nothing in store for the people but more deaths and more destruction. Frayed nerves feel fatigue too.

As news of POSCO's withdrawal had begun to trickle in since 2015, those from the Transit Camp began returning to Patana. They began to resume betel cultivation. The reader might be left wondering about their hardships and trauma of ten long years. Who will pay for the disruptions in their lives and that of their children? There are no answers.

The pro-POSCO lobby led by Tamil Pradhan from Nuagaon and others remained bewildered. Even before POSCO withdrew, their eyes had opened up to the situation unfolding before them. The United Action Committee was running out of steam too. People who had taken compensation or were still in two minds were left to their own devices. Nobody seemed to be pro-company when the company itself was on its way out.

No doubt, the divide between pro-POSCO and anti-POSCO lobbies will take time to bridge. But the rifts among those opposed to the company are there still. Sitting late into the night, Prakash Jena, Tuna Baral, Bhramarbar Das and Debendra Mohanty pieced some stories:

> Narahari Sahu and Dhruba Sahani along with a few others played a leading role in bringing the people of Gobindpur into the anti-POSCO struggle. It was tough to break out of the hold of the dominant pro-POSCO lobby in the village. They showed us the courage to stand up for our land. People joined gradually and Gobindpur put its entire stakes into the movement.
>
> In 2008, Dhruba Sahani took objection to PPSS leaders receiving funds from Dharitri Construction. He persistently questioned how the movement can fight against POSCO by taking funds from another company. He stopped going for meetings when his question was not addressed by the leadership. There was fear his absence might affect the unity of the village. One morning he was forcibly dragged from his house and taken to a meeting. His humiliation in that meeting was the last straw. The very next day he left the village. His betel vine plot was taken over by a section of PPSS. A cow and calf also got picked up from his house. His family witnessed all that was happening.
>
> In 2009, his mother passed away heartbroken. He could not return to the village for her cremation. He was in fear of PPSS activists. But Abhay Sahu made a call to the same villagers and persuaded them to allow the two brothers to take the body to Puri for cremation.
>
> After staying with his sister for a long period, Dhruba Sahani had moved on to the Transit Camp. Where else could he go? Sometime in 2011, he came to the village with a group of almost 30 others in the dead of night. Ostensibly, they had come back to claim their place in the village and begin betel cultivation. But they also badly beat up some PPSS members. They fled. The very next morning, a section of PPSS members raided his house.

His wife, Sabita Sahani, recalls the trauma of that terrible day when their house was raided by PPSS:

> They had come armed with sticks. I was in the house with my sister-in-law. They entered and began breaking everything. When this went on for some time, my sister-law-law told me quickly to pretend fainting. I did that. She put my head on her lap and cried: 'See what you have done. You either take her to the hospital. Or give me the money to take her to the hospital.' They were so petrified that they left. Her husband was in the betel vine plot at that time. Prakash Jena who lives next door was in jail. There was no one for us. That evening her husband too had to leave the village for his own safety. The hostility against us was too much.

> Everything changed for me. My children are upset till today about the turn of events. My husband has stopped speaking completely. Our belongings are still lying in the cyclone shelter. I have to get the trunk back. It has the horoscope of my son. How can I arrange his marriage without it?
>
> It's such a long story. This house used to be the centre of all meetings and so many people from outside like you have stayed with us too. But who do we turn to? We have been attacked by pro-POSCO lobby in the initial years and by the anti-POSCO movement in later years.

These reflections on the recent past are cathartic. Prakash Jena shares what he thinks was missing:

> We never aired our differences as the struggle to win was of paramount importance. The events of 2013 opened our eyes. It is only now that we can discuss these matters openly. Even after the attack on Dhruba Sahni's house we remained united. Our common enemy was POSCO. But the use of force and intimidation on those who questioned had become a norm within the movement. Who do we turn to? While our villages were under a siege with no contact with the outside world, there was also a terrible dearth of mechanisms and tools within the movement to tide through inner conflicts and differences.

By 2010, Nuagaon had already fallen out of the struggle getting labelled as pro-POSCO. The people of Dhinkia for the first time perhaps did not rise up against the severe repression leaving Gobindpur completely isolated during Operation Bhanga Baraja of 2013. The unity of the movement that was openly fractured still has some scars to heal as we were told by people from both Dhinkia and Gobindpur. Keeping all these differences at bay, the candidate Debendra Swain who won the Dhinkia gram panchayat seat in early 2017 in a sweeping majority was from the anti-POSCO movement itself. People have since begun looking forward to a phase of rebuilding their lives and communities.

The battle for over more than a decade led to economic ruination, shattering of community ties, incarcerations and litigations, physical brutalities by the state and hired goons, and, above all, loss of lives of their fellow fighters. When POSCO officially declared to withdraw from the project, the victory trumpet seemed to be muted in the local areas. It was a pyrrhic victory.

POSCO Exits

Hiuen Tsang, the Chinese traveller, visited India during the reign of Harshavardhana in the seventh century. Before he embarked on his journey to this region, he was warned to avoid travelling to the Kujanga area for fear of falling prey to the 'Kalinga Serpents' who were known for their militancy and ferocious nature (Panda 2006). If corporations were inclined to read history, POSCO should have known that it is the same people of the same Kujanga tehsil whose land it had greedily eyed.

However, POSCO waited twelve long years to make entry into the region. The amendment to the Mine and Minerals Development and Regulation Act (MMDRA) in 2015 was perhaps the proverbial last straw. The act made it mandatory for the company to join the auction along with other bidders for iron ore in the Khandadhar mountains, thereby forfeiting easy access to the captive iron ore reserves as assured by the Odisha government till then. Speculation ran rife for a long time about the fate of the company. On 18 March 2017, the Minister of Industry announced the exit of POSCO in a press conference at Bhubaneswar. But the threat of corporate entry is not yet over. The Odisha government has started building a boundary wall to put the land that has already been acquired in its land bank. It is paving the way for Jindal Steel Works this time.

People's resistance has been the formidable barrier that has saved the land till today. These ordinary people, who assiduously nurture the balance between nature and humans to simply get two square meals in return, averted a vast ecological disaster in this region. Indeed, if the eastern coast of Odisha is not yet dotted by a mega steel plant, if the coffers of global capital are a wee bit impoverished, and most significantly, if the people continue to remain in the land they belong to, it is solely due to people's sustained resistance.

Notes

1. Notes from the WSS team that visited the area on 7 November 2011.
2. Notes from the WSS team that visited the area on 7 November 2011.
3. Unpublished document prepared by Sandeep Patnaik and Jyotiprakash Das, July 2011.
4. Notes from the WSS team that visited Patana village on 7 November 2011.
5. A twelve-member fact finding team that visited the area on 9 March 2013 was returning in two vehicles.
6. Taken from notes made during the visit on 9 March 2013.

References

Heightened Tensions in POSCO Project Area, New Delhi: April, 2013 Fact Finding Report on the Situation in the Wake of Bomb Blast in Jagatsinghpur District, Odisha.

Ivens, Joris. *The 17th Parallel: People's War in Vietnam*, Vietnam.

Mahapatra, Basudev. 2013. *War for Steel*. A Documentary.

New Socialist Initiative. 2011. Solidarity Letter to Anti-POSCO Movement from a Korean Prison, July. See http://nsi-delhi.blogspot.com/2011/07/solidarity-letter-to-anti-posco.html.

Obomsawin, Alanis. 1972. "Who Is the Chairman of This Meeting?" Chapter "Conversations with North American Indians", by Ted Poole. Also: https://www.azquotes.com/quote/820997.

Panda, Satyananda. 2006. *Paradip in Past and Present*. Paradip: Rashmi Rekha Panda.

Patnayak, Subhas Chandra. 2005. *Baji Rout: The Youngest Martyr of India*. See https://orissamatters.com/2005/10/06/baji-raut-the-youngest-martyr-of-india/. Accessed 15 October 2017.

Routray, Sachi. 2001. *Collected Works, 2001*. Bhubaneswar: Odisha Sahitya Academy.

Sanhati. 2010. Orissa: A Brief Report by Partho Sarathi Ray, May 19, 2010. See http://sanhati.com/articles/2372/. Accessed 15 October 2017.

Epilogue

These narratives have no happy endings, nor are they closed chapters. Wherever we went, people shared their prevailing hardships and turmoil. Just like the Bhakra Dam oustees have been waiting more than fifty years for their due, the oustees of the Hirakud and Rengali dam projects are still waiting to claim their rights to homestead land. Nostalgia of the old village is the emotional crutch to tide over the hardships of daily life. Western Odisha is reeling under an ongoing agrarian crisis since years; there have been many peasant suicides. And security forces hover around the Gandhamardan region making daily life hell for people. The Dongria Kondhs of the Niyamgiri mountain are subject to routine harassment by security forces that are ostensibly curbing Maoist presence. Without losing its grip over Niyamgiri, Vedanta preys upon the adjoining hills of Kodingamali and Khandualamali for bauxite reserves. A reign of terror and intimidation has been let loose against protesting villagers to pave the way for the company. In Kashipur, the menacing lights from the UAIL plant have hidden the star-studded sky forever. The monthly dole given to hundreds of people to quell resistance has come to an end. Although POSCO retreated in Jagatsinghpur district, people are up against yet another steel giant. The land acquired by the government is going to the Jindals. Steel production is so cheap in this land. When prices of steel plummeted around 2016 the world over, Tata increased its production capacity at the Kalinganagar plant and encroached forest land. Sini Soi fervently hopes that at least the Kiajhor hill across Gobarghati and the

R. Padhi, N. Sadangi, *Resisting Dispossession*,
https://doi.org/10.1007/978-981-15-0717-5

Badasuli hill of Chandia panchayat are spared. The people of Sukinda Valley in Jajpur district long to be saved from increasing morbidity. Extensive chromite mining by more than a dozen mining plants has poisoned the water they drink and the air they breathe. This is dispossession of a unique kind, a living habitat turning into a death trap.

Coastal Odisha has its own inventory of sorrows. The plight of dalit fisherfolk in Baliapal, Jagatsinghpur, Chilika and Gopalpur is becoming more terrifying every few years. While people in forests and mountains are being uprooted for mineral extraction, ports are being constructed along the 480 km coastline of Odisha from the Bahuda mouth in Ganjam district to the Subarnarekha in Balasore district to export those minerals and to import materials for those industries. Of these fifteen ports in the offing, the construction of Subarnarekha Port threatens to displace Chaumukh village; people in Baliapal are sceptical whether the rousing unity of the 1980s that had withstood the entry of the missile test range can be built again. The livelihood of fisherfolk is compelled today to compete against the exigencies of environmental protection. The Chilika is finally being cleared of the illegal prawn cultivation *gherries* that had choked it for thirty years. Yet, hundreds of young men migrate to fish in the waters of Kerala and Goa as the community is losing access to the traditional fishery sources. There is dispossession through death and disease. In its search for non-carbon nuclear fuel, there is stockpiling of thorium for India's third stage of the nuclear programme on the shores of Odisha. This is playing havoc on the lives of the people of Gopalpur and Chatrapur villages. The Indian Rare Earths Limited's monazite mining operations are speculated as the reason behind an epidemic of chronic kidney disease and deaths. Odisha is part of the Asian Development Bank-funded East Coast Economic Corridor, which is hailed as the country's first coastal economic corridor. The fragile ecosystem of the entire eastern coast is in deep peril.

There remain so many other stories that we have not been able to weave into this book, accounts from other parts of Odisha where people are rising in rebellion to protect their *malis*, streams, rivers, lands and forests. Not just Odisha, people's resistance rages across India. Adivasi communities of the neighbouring mineral-rich states of Chhattisgarh and Jharkhand bravely hold on to their subsistence economy against capitalist assault that hollows out their land and forests.

Resisting dispossession has emerged as the biggest struggle of our times across continents: the people of Zambia have sued a copper mining giant for poisoning their water; the Sapara and Kichwa communities of Ecuador have fought against oil drilling that threatens to raze down their rainforests; the Dayaks of Borneo island are up against mining and oil corporations as they protect one of the oldest rainforests of the world; the Vietnamese are opposing special economic zones that will swallow up their land; and, the people of Papua New Guinea struggle as their tropical rainforests and ancestral lands are being upended by mining and oil corporations. In 2016, indigenous groups protested against the Dakota Pipeline in North America that would cross beneath the Mississippi and Missouri rivers. The Standing Rock Sioux Tribe is continuing to fight in the courts. The pipeline threatens to contaminate the drinking water besides upturning burial grounds and other sacred sites. Also, the biggest forests of the world—the tropical rainforests of the Amazon—have been in flames since months, blackening the skies of faraway Sao Paulo city.

Ecology and people are inseparable; therefore, natural resources and the human lives that preserve and conserve these resources are deeply intertwined. Nurturing their dreams for future generations, people are resisting corporate greed with courage and tenacity. Their dreams are no ordinary dreams; they hearken a better tomorrow even if the road is uphill today. And lest we forget, it is the same planet that we all inhabit as home.

Sirf hungaama khada karna mera maqsad nahin,
Meri koshish hai ki, yeh soorat badalni chahiye
Mere seene mein nahin, to tere seene mein sahi
Ho kahin bhi aag lekin, aag jalni chahiye. (Dushyant Kumar)

[Merely causing a ruckus was never my goal,
My attempt has been solely to transform the whole.
If not deep in mine then, perchance, in your heart,
Where fire be kindled, let fire be sparked.]

Annexure A: Interview Dateline

Chapter	*Name of Interviewee*	*Village/Town*	*Date of Interview*
2. The Disease of Gigantism	Sukhdeb Kisan	Chhuipali	9 December 2014
	Lakhpati Pradhan	Mura Camp	8 December 2014
	Durga Prasad Nayak	Sambalpur	25 January, 2015
	Group discussion	Mura Camp	8 December 2014
	Karunakar Bhoi	Mura Camp	8 December 2014
	Kunjabihari Pradhan	Duanmunda	10 December 2014
	Barun Kumra	Banharipali	9 December 2014
	Gopinath Majhi	Lakhanpur	9 December 2014
	Group discussion	Barangmal	10 December 2014
3. What the King Gave Happily	Ranjan Sahu	Deogarh	13 December 2014
	Kishore Patra	Barakote	11 December 2014
	Group Discussion	Barakote	11 December 2014
	Bhagirathi Penthei	Kadamdarh	11 December 2014
	Gagan Penthei	Kadamdarh	11 December 2014
	Laxman Kumar Penthei	Kadamdarh	11 December 2014
	Narendra Sahu	Mahal Marua	12 December 2014
	Kaushalya	Srinivaspur	12 December 2014
	Dukhabandhu Nayak	Srinivaspur	12 December 2014
	Bholanath Nayak	Srinivaspur	12 December 2014

(*continued*)

R. Padhi, N. Sadangi, *Resisting Dispossession*,
https://doi.org/10.1007/978-981-15-0717-5

(continued)

Chapter	Name of Interviewee	Village/Town	Date of Interview
4. Jai Gandhamardan	Lingaraj Pradhan	Bargarh	16 March 2013
	Diamond Bhue	Laudmal	2 November 2018
	Renu Mohar	Lohasingha	18 December 2013
	Prasanna Kumar Sahu	Godbhaga	12 December 2017
	Pankajini Rout		17 December 2013
	Arttabandhu Mishra	Burla	13 February 2018
	Anuradha Purohit	Sambalpur	15 February 2018
	Nirupama Borpanda	Sambalpur	15 February 2018
	Muktokontho	Sambalpur	15 February 2018
	Jambabati Bijira	Mithapalli	17 March 2013 17 December 2013
	Gangadhar Sahu	Paikmal	1 November 2018
	Lallo Vivar	Bikram Nagar	17 December 2013
	Subodh Panda	Paikmal	2 November 2018
	Rajkishore Seth	Paikmal	16 December 2013
	Young woman	Paikmal	17 March 2013
	Sushant Samal	Paikmal	16–17 March 2013
	Meena Barik		17 March 2013
	Group discussion with women		
	Ghanshyam Sahu	Baidapalli	2 November 2018
5. The Conch and the Missile	Bhubana Patra	Dagara	2 April 2013
	Bhabani Bhuyan	Puri	6 April 2012
	Gauri	Puri	6 April 2012
	Kunja Upadhyaya	Puri	6 April 2012
	Kusadhwaja Jena	Dagara-Ambchua	2 April 2013
	Nabaghana Jena	Manik-Simulia	
	Sarada Giri	Panchupali	2 April 2013
	Minati Jena	Jamatkula	3 April 2013
	Amulya Behera	Nuagan	3 April 2013
	Puroshottam Behera	Jambhirai	25–26 March 2016
	Basanti Pila	Pratappur	
	Gananath Patra	Rourkela	20 December 2013
	Gaurang Raut	Bhubaneswar	13 October 2019
	Chhabi Mohanty, SUCI	Bhubaneswar	16 October 2019

(continued)

(continued)

Chapter	Name of Interviewee	Village/Town	Date of Interview
6. Chilika Teere	Anadi Behera	Balugaon	13 December 2017
	Hadibandhu Ghadei	Banpur	13 June 2018
	Gobinda Behera	Gopinathpur	20 March 2018 15 April 2018
	Braja Ghadei	Baulabandha	13 June 2018
	Pramila Ghadei	Baulabandha	13 June 2018
	Magi Behera	Sorana	13 June 2018
	Mahadev Behera	Sorana	13 June 2018
	Bansidhar Behera	Gopinathpur	20 March 2018 15 April 2018
	Adikanda Behera	Gola	29 May 2016 20 March 2018 15 April 2018
	Bhagaban Behera	Gola	29 May 2016 20 March 2018 15 April 2018
	Agadhu Behera	Arakhakuda	20 March 2018 15 April 2018
	Manika Behera	Arakhakuda	20 March 2018
	Tuni Behera	Gopinathpur	29 May 2016 20 March 2018 15 April 2018
7. The Kia in Rage	D. Kamraj Borma	P. Laxmipur	15 October 2015 22 March 2017 14 August 2017
	Gurudeb Behera	Badaputti	15 October 2015 22 March 2017 14 August 2017
	Narayan Reddy	Bhubaneswar Chatrapur	22 April 2017 15 August 2017
	Nageshwar Reddy	Tata Rehabilitation Colony	22 March 2017 27 March 2017
	Prafulla Samantra	Bhubaneswar	12 November 2017
	Kashinath Nayak	Tata Rehabilitation Colony	15 August 2017
	Landless peasant	Tata Rehabilitation Colony	15 August 2017
	Woman	Tata Rehabilitation Colony	15 August 2017
	Damburu Reddy	Jagannathpur	27 March 2017

(continued)

(continued)

Chapter	Name of Interviewee	Village/Town	Date of Interview
8. The Song of the Mali	Bhagaban Majhi	Kucheipadar	17 May 2014 21 November 2012 9, 10 and 11 November 2019
	Bidyadhar Majhi	Kucheipadar	10 and 11 November 2019
	Maharaj Majhi	Kucheipadar	11 November 2019
	Salu Majhi	Kucheipadar	11 November 2019
	Ambai Majhi	Kucheipadar	20 November 2012 22 November 2012
	Gangaram Majhi	Kucheipadar	18 May 2014
	Mukundi Saunta	Kucheipadar	17 May 2014 21 November 2012
	Mukta Jhodia	Siriguda	21 November 2012
	Biswanath Sahu	Siriguda	21 November 2012
	Manohar Jhodia	Siriguda	21 November 2012 18 May 2014
9. Juhar Niyamraja	Lada Sikaka	Lakhpadar	6–7 July 2014
	Drenju Sikaka	Lakhpadar	6–7 July 2014 22 February 2015
	Lingaraj Azad		5 July 2017
	Dillu Majhi	Sana Khemundi Padar	6 July 2014
	Woman	Phuldamer	6 July 2014
	Group discussion with women	Trilochanpur	6 July 2014
	Bhima Majhi	Turiguda	22 February 2015
	Jayanti Dakri	Chatrapur	16 December 2018
	Nilabati Nayak	Chatrapur	16 December 2018
	Purnami Bibhar	Chatrapur	16 December 2018
	Tulsa Bibhar	Chatrapur	16 December 2018
	Surya Dash	Bhubaneswar	1 December 2018
10. The Taste of Steel	Sini Soi	Gobarghati	13 July 2014 24 November 2014 16 January 2017 17 August 2017
	Mathura Honaga	Baligotho	24 November 2014 16 January 2017 24 January 2017 17 August 2017
	Ramrai Jarika	Gobarghati	17 August 2017
	Dabur Kalundia	Baligotho	2010
	Chakradhar Haibru	Ambagadia	1 February 2020

(*continued*)

(continued)

Chapter	Name of Interviewee	Village/Town	Date of Interview
11. The Betel Smiles	Sujata Sahani	Gobindpur	15–16 May 2016
			18 February 2017
	Babaji Samantara	Dhinkia	19 February 2017
	Sabita Sahani	Gobindpur	19 February 2017
	Bhramarbar Das	Gobindpur	22 December 2014
			20 February 2017
	Tuna Baral	Gobindpur	20 February 2017
			28 October 2018
	Prakash Jena	Gobindpur	18 February 2017
			20 February 2017
	Debendra Mohanty	Gobindpur	20 February 2017
	Manorama Khatua	Dhinkia	7 October 2015
			26 January 2017
			10 March 2017
			26 June 2018
	Subhas Sahani	Gobindpur	18 August 2018
	Prashant Paikrai	Bhubaneswar	26 January 2017
	Debendra Patra	Gobindpur	19 February 2017
	Debendra Swain	Dhinkia	19 February 2017

Annexure B: Glossary of Odia Words

Alsi: flax seeds
Andolan: movement
Asura: monster
Baraja: betel vines
Bhatta: dole
Bhatti: distillery
Bheda: division
Bheetamati: habitat
Bhoomi pooja: rituals performed on land before any construction activity
Budianchala: submerged areas
Budianchalia: displaced people from submerged areas
Chasi-mulia sarkar: peasant-worker government
Chaiti Parab: spring festival
Chowki: police outpost
Dalal: broker or agent
Dana: gift
Danda: punishment
Dangar: hillocks
Dhaan: paddy
Dharna: sit-in protest
Dhenki: wooden paddy husker
Dhobi: washerman
Dishari: tribal priest

R. Padhi, N. Sadangi, *Resisting Dispossession*,
https://doi.org/10.1007/978-981-15-0717-5

Fadi: collection centre
Gaan: village
Gaan maati: village soil
Gamcha: cloth towel
Garhjat: princely states
Gherries: enclosures
Gountias: village headman owning huge amount of land
Guntha: 4.5 decimals (a measure of land)
Haat: marketplace
Kadamba: a flowering tree
Kandula: a type of lentil
Katta: pond
Kalyug: the age of vices as per Hindu scriptures
Lal salaam: red salute
Laxman Rekha: line of caution; derives its origin from the mythological text Ramayana
Maati: earth
Mahapuru: God
Mahajan: moneylender
Mahua/Mohuli: a plant with edible flowers and oil-rich seeds
Malis: mountains
Mandia: finger millet
Mina: fish
Mudi: puffed rice
Mugalbandi: revenue-generating areas under British control
Paan: betel
Paika: peasant militia
Pakhaal bhaat: fermented rice
Parab: festival
Patta: record of right
Phullo: flower
Poda macho: roasted fish
Praja: subjects or those who are ruled
Ragi: finger millet
Rayat: rent-paying peasant
Saag: a leaf-based nutritious dish
Sama: mercy
Tendu: a leaf used for rolling bidis; also known as kendu

Annexure C: Project Profiles

R. Padhi, N. Sadangi, *Resisting Dispossession*,
https://doi.org/10.1007/978-981-15-0717-5

Chapter	*Project name*	*Area of operation*	*Date of commissioning*	*Government(s) in office and duration of office*	*Chief minister (and other ministers involved)*	*Nature of investment*	*Villages affected*	*Communities in the area*	*Names of organization involved in the struggle*
2. The Disease of Gigantism	Multipurpose development of Mahanadi Valley: Hirakud Dam Project	Undivided Sambalpur district	13 January 1957	Indian National Congress Party	Harekrushna Mahatab (1946–1950 and 1956–1961) Nabakrushna Choudhury (1951–1955)	Public (initially the estimated expenditure was Rs 76.5 crore and revised to Rs 93 crore)	249 villages of Odisha and 36 villages of Madhya Pradesh (now Chhattisgarh)	Tribes: Sahara, Gond, Binjhal Dalits: Dom, Ganda, Ghasia Others: Kulta, Kansari, Goud, Teli, Brahmin	Bandha Virodhi Committee
3. What the King Gave Happily	Multipurpose Rengali Dam Project	Located at Rengali village in Kaniha block of Talcher sub-division in undivided Dhenkanal district (now Angul district). But the submerged area belongs to present Deogarh and Angul district	March 1991	Indian National Congress (INC) Janata Dal	Nandini Satpathy (June 1972 to March 1973 and March 1974 to December 1976) Nilamani Routray (June 1977 to February 1980)	Public (initially the estimated expenditure was Rs 41.92 crore and escalated to Rs 297.945 crore as on 1991)	263 villages	Tribes: Kharia, Gond, Kisan Dalits: Jhara, Pana, Dom, Ganda, Dom Others: Chasa, Khandayat, Paika, Bhulia, Gouda	Initially, Rengali Bandha Pratikriya Samiti. Then it got divided into Bandha Nirodh Committee and Rengali Thaithan O Punarbasati Samiti

4. Jai Gandhamardan	Gandhamardan Bauxite Project	Padampur sub-division of Sambalpur district (now Bargarh district) and Patnagarh sub-division of Balangir district and Nuapada block of Nuapada district (earlier Kalahandi district)	The project was officially scrapped on 15 September 1989 due to people's resistance	Indian National Congress Party Janata Dal	Janaki Ballabh Patnaik (June 1980 to December 1989) Biju Patnaik (1990–1995)	Public sector (Bharat Aluminium Company, BALCO) Rs 58 crore	103 villages	Tribes: Binjhal, Kandha Dalits: Gana, Ghasi, Kulis Others: Kulta, Teli	Gandhamardan Surakshya Yuva Parishad
5. The Conch and the Missile	National Test Range (for testing and launching of missiles)	Baliapal and Bhograi blocks of Balasore district	The project was stopped due to people's resistance	Indian National Congress Party	Janaki Ballabh Patnaik (June 1980 to December 1989)	Public (an investment of Rs. 3,000 crore)	130 villages; scaled down to 55 villages	Tribes: Santal Dalits: Ujia, Jali, Kandara Others: Raju, Khandayat, Gola, Teli	Uttara Balasore Kshepanasatra Ghati Pratirodh Committee
6. Chilika Teere	Chilika Aquatic Farms Limited	Brahmagiri block of Puri district	The project was scrapped in 1992 due to people's resistance	Indian National Congress Party Janata Dal	Janaki Ballabh Patnaik (June 1980 to December 1989) Biju Patnaik (1990–1995)	Joint venture of Tata and Government of Odisha Rs 20 crores	135 villages	Dalits: Fishing communities like Keut, Kandara, Tiara, Kartia	Chilika Matsyajibi Mahasangha, Chilika Bachao Andolan, Meet the Students—a student group of Utkal University

(*continued*)

(continued)

Chapter	*Project name*	*Area of operation*	*Date of commissioning*	*Government(s) in office and duration of office*	*Chief minister (and other ministers involved)*	*Nature of investment*	*Villages affected*	*Communities in the area*	*Names of organization involved in the struggle*
7. The Kia in Rage	TISCO Steel Plant at Gopalpur	Chatrapur and Berhampur blocks of Ganjam district		Indian National Congress Party Biju Janata Dal	Janaki Ballabh Patnaik (March 1995 to February 1999)	Private Sector Rs 9,300 crore	11 villages (25 hamlets as estimated by villagers)	Oriya-speaking Pradhan, Behera and Das Telugu-speaking Reddy	Gana Sangram Samiti actively supported by the CPI
8. The Song of the *Mali*	Utkal Alumina International Limited (UAIL) A Refinery Plant and Mining Bauxite from Baphlimali	Plant: Near Tikri, Kashipur block, Rayagada district Mining: Kashipur block, Rayagada and Thumul Rampur block, Kalahandi	Not available	Janata Dal Indian National Congress Party Biju Janata Dal	Biju Patnaik (1990–1995) Janaki Ballabh Patnaik (March 1995–February 1999) Naveen Patnaik (March 2000–continuing)	Private Sector (initially Joint Venture of Tata, Norsk Hydro and Indal); now under the control of Hindalco of Aditya Birla Rs 4,500 crore	24 villages for plant and 42 villages for mining	Tribes: Kandha, Jhodia, Paraja, Pengo Paraja Dalits: Dom, Pana Other: Gauda, Paika, Sundhi	Prakrutika Sampad Surakshya Parishad
9. Juhar Niyamraja	Vedanta Resources Limited (A Refinery Plant at Lanjigarh and Mining Bauxite from Niyamgiri Hills)	Refinery plant: Lanjigarh of Biswanathpur block, Kalahandi district Mining: Muniguda block, Rayagada district and Biswanathpur block, Kalahandi	Year 2008	Biju Janata Dal	Naveen Patnaik (March 2000–continuing)	Private Sector (UK-based Vedanta Resources Rs 4,000 crore)	12 villages for plant and 102 villages for mining	Tribes: Kutia Kandha, Dongria Kondh Dalits: Pana Other: Gauda	Niyamgiri Surakshya Parishad

10.	The Taste of Steel	Tata Iron and Steel Company in the Kalinganagar Industrial Complex	Danagadi and Sukinda block of Jajpur district	18 November 2015	Biju Janata Dal	Naveen Patnaik (March 2000–continuing)	Private Sector Rs 22,000 crore	Not available	Tribes: Ho, Munda	Bisthapan Birodhi Jan Manch
11.	The Betel Smiles	Pohang Iron and Steel Company	Ersama block of Jagatsinghpur district	POSCO withdrew from the project in March 2017	Biju Janata Dal (BJD)	Naveen Patnaik (March 2000–continuing)	Private Sector Rs 52,000 crore—FDI	9+30 villages for plant and 32 villages in Keonjhar and 84 villages in Sundergarh for mining from Khandadhar	Dalits: Kaibartas, Gokhas Other: OBCs	POSCO Pratirodh Sangram Samiti Nava Nirman Samiti Rashtriya Yuva Sangathan

About the Authors

Ranjana Padhi is a feminist activist and writer currently based in Bhubaneswar, Odisha, India. She has authored *Those Who Did Not Die: Impact of the Agrarian Crisis on Women in Punjab* (2012). Her contributions in writing have also appeared in the *Economic and Political Weekly*, *The Wire*, *Monthly Review* and *Countercurrents*. Padhi has been part of the autonomous women's movement in India and volunteered in other autonomous, non-funded collectives. She has actively worked in many joint coalitions and campaigns around issues of democratic rights and civil liberties, state repression, workers' rights, forcible evictions caused by corporate land acquisition, sexuality and communal violence.

Nigamananda Sadangi is an activist, writer and translator based in Bhubaneswar, Odisha, India. He is currently part of the Anwesha collective—a socio-political journal in Odia that is focused on issues related to social movements as well as caste, tribal and gender concerns. He has participated in fact-finding efforts and investigations in Odisha to highlight the violation of civil liberties and democratic rights of people. He has contributed articles to Odia journals like *Samadrushti*, *Nisaan* and *Vikalpa Vichaar* and also to *Economic and Political Weekly* and *Countercurrents*. He has translated works of many leading writers and intellectuals into Odia.

R. Padhi, N. Sadangi, *Resisting Dispossession*,
https://doi.org/10.1007/978-981-15-0717-5